EVE TEASING - A SOCIAL EPIDEMIC

Eve Teasing - A Social Epidemic

Deepa Awasthi

KALPAZ

ISBN: 978-93-5128-142-9

Price: ₹ 690

First Published, 2015

Published by

Kalpaz Publications
C-30, Satyawati Nagar,
Delhi-110052
Ph. : 9212142040
E-mail: kalpaz@hotmail.com

Cataloging in Publication Data—DK
Courtesy: D.K. Agencies (P) Ltd. <docinfo@dkagencies.com>

Eve teasing : a social epidemic / Deepa Awasthi.
pages cm
Contributed articles.
Includes bibliographical references.
ISBN 9789351281290

1. Sexual harassment of women—India. 2. Sexual harassment of women—South Asia. I. Awasthi, Deepa, editor.

DDC 331.41330954 23

Dedicated to

This edited book is dedicated to all women on this earth
who dare to fight against the crime of eve teasing
with determination, instead of encouraging the eve teasers
to repeat the act by avoiding or neglecting them.

Contents

Acknowledgements

It is my immense pleasure to acknowledge the learned authors from all over the country who have contributed their valuable articles and research papers written by them with utmost pain, efforts and investment of time. Without their sincere and devoted thinking towards the serious issue of "eve teasing" it would have been almost impossible to come up with desired result.

I am also obliged to the distinguished panel of reviewers who invested their precious time and hard work in evaluating the contributions from various authors and further guiding them to make their writings focused, clear and appropriate for this book. I am also thankful to all my friends, teachers from University of Lucknow and family members who encouraged me from time to time to remain stick to the mission of publishing a book on all time burning issue of eve teasing.

Last but not the least, I thank to God and all who helped me directly or indirectly at every step and provided me emotional support to compile this edited book.

Deepa Awasthi
(Editor)

Author's Biography

Introduction

Deepa Awasthi (Editor)

Ph D.- Education, University of Lucknow

Editor is freelance researcher and social activist, associated with number of NGOs working in the field of women and child welfare as a volunteer. She is Doctorate in Education, recently submitted her thesis focused on cooperative learning and personality types. She has participated and presented her research paper in 25 national and international seminar. Her publication work involves 03 chapters in Edited books, 3 research papers in form of conference and seminar proceedings. She has also published 13 research paper and articles in various journals of national and international repute.

1. History and Tradition of Eve Teasing

Dr Mehnaz Najmi

Programme Chair cum HOD, Political Science Department at School of Humanities and Social Sciences, Galgotias University, Grater Noida, UP

Author is a Programme Chair cum HOD of Political Science Department at School of Humanities and Social Sciences, Galgotias University, Grater Noida, UP. She is PhD. in Political Science from Jamia Millia Islamia, New Delhi, M.A. in Political Science, Jawaharlal Nehru University, New Delhi, B.A. (Hon) Political Science, Daulat Ram College, Delhi University, Delhi. She has more than six years of experience in research and teaching. She has participated and presented papers in various national International seminars and conferences. Her special areas of interest are Indian politics, poverty, slum studies, women in political process, minority affairs and other women issues.

2. Eve Teasing: Hurdle for Women's Upgradation

Dr Chhaya Soni

Assistant Professor, Department of Education, Banaras Hindu University, Varanasi, U.P.

Author is Assistant Professor in Faculty of Education (K), BHU, Varanasi. She is UGC-NET qualified and completed her Doctorate from University of Lucknow. 04 research papers and 7 articles written by her have been published in reputed journals. She has participated in 5 international and 25 national seminars and conferences. She has also participated in one international and five national workshop.

3. Eve Teasing: an Extensive Social evil in India

Dr Nalini Misra

Assistant Professor, Department of B.Ed., Khwaja Moinuddin Chishti Urdu, Arabi-Farsi University, Lucknow

Dr Nalini Misra is Assistant Professor in Department of B.Ed., Khwaja Moinuddin Chishti Urdu, Arabi-Farsi University, Lucknow. Her qualifications are B.Sc., M.Sc. (Chemistry), B.Ed., M.Ed., UGC-NET (Education), Ph.D. Her areas of specialisation are Higher Education, Environmental Education and Guidance and Counselling. She has published articles in various national and international journals of repute. She has attended and participated in various national/ international seminars and workshops.

4. Eve Teasing and Patriarchy: A menace of Indian Society

Parvin Sultana

Assistant Professor, Department of Political Science, Goalpara College, Assam

The author is an Assistant Professor in the Department of Political Science in Goalpara College in Assam. She did her masters in Political Science from JNU. She did her M phil. on North Eastern Council and its role in the development of the region of Northeast. She has been awarded JRF in Political Science. She has presented papers in Three national and 1 international seminars. She writes regularly editorials for newspapers. Around eight research papers and articles written by her have been published in journals as well as chapters in edited books. Her interest area comprises of gender, political economy, Northeast and Muslim politics in India.

5. Role of Media in Solving the Problem of Eve Teasing

Sadhana Srivastawa

Assistant professor, Rama University, Kanpur, U.P.

Author is Assistant professor at Rama University, Kanpur, having more than 10 year experience of teaching graduate and post graduate student of Journalism and Mass Communication. She is associated with number of Newspapers and Magazines and written about 50 articles for them. She is also working with Radio for more than 12 years and broadcasted 12 short stories for AIR Varanasi and AIR Lucknow. She has also broadcasted 4 plays for Gyanvani, Kanpur Author has participated in 15 national and 5 International seminars. She has already contributed 4 chapters for edited books on various issues.

6. Eve Teasing: A Glance on Social Epidemic

Praveen Hoogar

Research Scholar, Department of Studies in Anthropology, Karnataka University, Dharwad, Karnataka,

Author received Masters Degree in MA/Msc Anthropology from Department of Studies in Anthropology, Karnatak University, Dharwad in 2012. He has Cleared UGC-NET in June 2014. Served as Field Investigators in Karnataka State Tribal Research Institute, Mysore, Government of Karnataka. He has published one article in International Journal and Two chapters in an edited book. He has been attended more than six national seminars and presented papers in three. Presently author is pursuing Ph.D from Department of Studies in Anthropology, Karnatak University, Dharwad.

Ashwini Pujar

Research Scholar, Department of Studies in Anthropology, Karnataka University, Dharwad, Karnataka,

Author received Masters Degree in MA/Msc Anthropology from Department of Studies in Anthropology, Karnatak University, Dharwad in 2012. She has cleared UGC- NET in June 2014 Served as Field Investigators in Karnataka State Tribal Research Institute, Mysore, Government of Karnataka. She has published one article in International Journal and Two chapters in an edited book. She has been attended more than six national seminars and presented papers in three. Presently author is pursuing Ph.D from Department of Studies in Anthropology, Karnatak University, Dharwad.

Dr T. T. Basavanagouda

Director, Karnataka State Tribal Research Institute, Mysore, Karnataka

Author is a Professor, Department of Studies in Anthropology, Karnatak University, Dharwad. Presently he is serving as Director, Karnataka State Tribal Research Institute, Mysore, Government of Karnataka, Karnataka State. He has published many research papers in reputed national and international journals. He has attended and presented many papers in national and international conferences, seminars and symposiums. He has successfully guided three Ph.Ds and presently two scholars are registered for Ph.D under his guidance. Author has been Studied and submitted more than five Ethnographic reports on different communities to the Government of Karnataka

7. Eve Teasing: A Social Problem

Ruchi Dhyani

Senior Research Scholar, Punjabi University, Patiala, Punjab

Ruchi Dhyani is a Research Scholar in Department of Education and community service of Punjabi university. She is post graduate in Education, Commerce and Economics and has PGDCA. She has been awarded UGC-JRF in Education. She also worked as lecturer in Education in Punjab College of Education. She has participated and presented the papers in 12 National International seminars and conferences. Three research papers written by her have been published in reputed international journals.

8. History Tradition and effects of Eve Teasing

Manglika Tripathi

Post Graduate student, Department of Women Studies, University of Lucknow

Author is Post graduate student in Department of Women Studies, University of Lucknow. She has also done Post Graduate Diploma in Health and Hospital Management and has an experience of more than four years in the field of Public Health. She has worked under projects like National Rural Health Mission, HIV/AIDS Prevention programme and

Rain Water Harvesting. She has given trainings on Health and Sanitation, Family planning counselling and communication skills. She has attended various National seminars and conferences. Her special areas of interest are Public Health, gender issues and Women empowerment.

9. Why do they do it

Amit Kumar Dutta

Assistant Professor, Indian Institute of Legal Studies (IILS), Siliguri, West Bengal

Author is an Assistant Professor of Management at Indian Institute of Legal Studies (IILS), Siliguri. He is post graduate in Commerce and Management, has a diploma in International Business Operations and has qualified UGC NET in Management. He is an honours graduate in Commerce from Ramjas College, Delhi. He has participated and presented papers in five national seminars besides participating in workshops. Till now he has one paper published as seminar proceedings in a national journal and some are in the process of being published. He has a special interest in education, gender and development issues.

10. Eve-teasing- Psychology of a sick mind

Dr Vishakha Shukla

Assistant professor, Department of Education, Sampurnanand Sanskrit University, Varanasi.

Dr Vishakha Shukla is working as assistant professor in department of education, Sampurnanand Sanskrit University, Varanasi. She is post doctorate on the subject relevance of Gandhian Economics in the era of globalisation and its educational implication. She is post graduate in Chemistry, Education and Sociology and has been awarded UGC-JRF in Education She has participated and presented the papers in 22 national/ International seminars and conferences. More than 15 research papers and articles written by her on various issues have been published in reputed national/International journals. Till now she has contributed one chapter for edited book. Her special areas of interest are guidance and counselling, gender issues and teacher education.

11. Eve Teasing: A Psychoanalytic Explication

Dr Zeba Aqil

Associate Professor (Psychology), Integral University, Lucknow.

The author is presently working as Associate Prof. (Psychology) in the Faculty of Education at Integral University, Lucknow. She has done her M.A. (in 1st Division with first Position in order of Merit) and Ph.D. in Psychology from Lucknow University. She has also qualified U.G.C. NET Examination. She has more than nine years of teaching experience at graduate and post graduate level. She has published nine research papers in National and Internationals Journals. She has also attended many National and International Conferences.

12. India Strict Against Eve Teasing and Sexual Harassment at Work Place

Saurabh Mishra

Sr. Manager - HR Mumbai, Maharashtra

Author is Management Postgraduate and at present working as Sr. Manager - HR at manufacturing plant of a multinational company. He has more than ten year experience of dealing with labour related issues at various construction sites and manufacturing and processing plants.

Deepti Mishra

Deputy Manager - Learning and Development, HDFC Life Insurance Company Ltd. Lucknow

Author is Post graduate in Management and Law graduate, at present employed with HDFC Life Insurance Company Ltd. As Deputy Manager - Learning and Development. She has more than eight years of experience in the field of Counselling and Guidance and dealing with Insurance personnel of all the ages and various backgrounds.

13. Critical Evaluation of Criminal Law Amendment Act-2013 with Special Reference to Eve-Teasing in the NCT of Delhi

Sandesh Yadav

Research Scholar, Department of Geography, Jamia Millia Islamia, Delhi

Sandesh Yadav is a Research Scholar in Department of Geography,

Jamia Millia Islamia, Delhi. He is doing his research on impact of land use and land cover change on urban environment. He is post-graduate in Geography, University of Lucknow and has been awarded UGC-NET in Geography. He is also annual member of National Association of Geographer, India (NAGI). During his school days in St. Anthony's College, Barabanki, he was awarded Silver Medal by the "Help Age India Organisation" for his monetary contribution to help the aged people of India. Further, he has participated and presented the papers in four national/international seminars and conferences. His special areas of interest are ecological and environmental issues, gender issues and issues pertaining to current problems.

Aayushi Chaudhary

Law Student, Gujarat National Law University, Gandhi Nagar, Gujrat

Aayushi Chaudhary is a Law Student (B.Sc+LLB Course) of 3rd year in Gujarat National Law University, Gandhinagar, Gujarat. She has done her schooling from Dr Virendra Swaroop Memorial School, Lucknow, Uttar Pradesh. So far she has worked as an intern under the supervision of reputed advocates of Supreme Court of India, Delhi and the High Court, Lucknow Bench, Uttar Pradesh. Her special area of interest is "Crime against Women".

14. Eve Teasing, Crime Against Women: Human Rights Perspective

Baij Nath

Research Scholar, Department of Human Rights, School for Legal Studies, Babasaheb Bhimrao Ambedkar University (A Central University), Lucknow

Author is a research Scholar in the Department of Human Rights, School for Legal Studies, Babasaheb Bhimrao Ambedkar University (A Central University), Lucknow. He is working on the topic titled "Rehabilitation of the Internally Displaced Persons: A Socio-Legal Study with special reference to Kashmiri Displaced Persons". He is B. Sc., L. L. B., LL M (with specialisation in Human Rights). He is Gold Medallist in LL M and UGC-NET (in Law). He has participated and presented papers in almost 15 national and international seminars. He has participated in Two Legal Aid, Legal Literacy and Lok Adalat Camps and also participated in a workshop on Human Rights. Four Research papers written by him have been published in the reputed International Referred Journals. His areas of interest are Human Rights Law with special focus on internally displaced persons, refugees, women rights, child rights, human rights education, etc.

15. Women Must Protest Against Eve Teasing

Dr Shravan Kumar

Associate professor, Department of Education, University of Lucknow

Author is an Associate professor in Department of Education, University of Lucknow. He has been awarded PhD in education from Lucknow University and also awarded UGC-JRF in Education. He has participated and presented the papers in 35 national/ International seminars and conferences. More than Ten research papers and articles written by him on various issues have been published as seminar/conference proceedings and in reputed national/international journals. Till now He has communicated Two chapters for edited books. One chapter has been published in a reputed book. His special areas of interest are value education, gender issues and teacher education.

Ankita Singh

Postgraduate in Journalism -Mass communication and M.Ed from University of Lucknow.

Author has been awarded postgraduate degree in Journalism -Mass communication and M.Ed from University of Lucknow. She has participated in seminars and workshops of Mass Media at University and state level. She has written poetry on various issues in which some are been published in reputed magazines. Recently she has communicated two research papers on topics of educational psychology in reputed journals which have been accepted for publication. Her areas of interest are special education, Educational psychology, and role of media in education.

16 Time to Introspect

Vidyavati

Lecturer in Directorate of Education, NCT, Delhi

Author is a lecturer in Directorate of Education, NCT of Delhi. For her performance in the field of teaching, she has been honored with Indira Award and State Teacher Award by Delhi Government, and received a couple of other honours from NGOs and local politicians. She has participated in a number of seminars organised by SCERT and NCERT. Her review of a book was published in NCERT journal. She has participated in two international conferences and presented her papers and got prize of best speaker/presenter in group. She takes great interest in issues related to women, environment and language teaching. Before joining the Directorate she worked in Ministry of Commerce, Goverment of India. She was selected in Rajasthan Administrative Services also.

17. End Eve Teasing: Voice through Words

Dr Manvi Yadav

Assistant Professor (Ad-hoc) Lady Irwin College, University of Delhi.

Author is M.Sc (Botany), M.Ed from University of Lucknow. She qualified UGC NET in June 2006. She was awarded NCERT Doctoral Fellowship for her Ph.D work. The topic of her research was "Influence of Education in Empowerment of Dalit Women"

She has almost eight years of teaching experience, throughout these years she was majorly involved in the teaching of Biological sciences and Educational psychology and technology. She has participated in various national and international seminars. She has also served as a convener in one of the international conference. She has been in the editorial committee of the international conference. Her research areas mainly involve Dalit pedagogy and their social inclusion.

Dr Neetu Yadav

Ph D.- Education, University of Lucknow

Author is doctorate in education from university of Lucknow. She has served as UGC-SRF for a period of almost four years in university of Lucknow. The topic of research of author's doctoral thesis is "Development of Value inculcation package on the basis of reflection of values in elementary level classroom transactions". She is M.Sc (Chemistry), M.Ed. She qualified prestigious NET- JRF in education. She has participated in various national and international seminars. She has also served as a convener in one of the international conference. She has six paper published in national and international journals and three communicated. Her interest areas are social and educational issues and currently she is involved with the education of weaker section of the society.

Dr Preetu Srivastava

Ph. D.- Education, University of Lucknow

Author is doctorate in education from university of Lucknow. She has served as UGC-SRF for a period of almost five years in university of

Lucknow. The topic of research of author's doctoral thesis is "Role of education in changing the concept of marriage". She is B.sc, M.Ed, M.A (English). She qualified NET- JRF in education. She has participated in various national and international seminars. She has also served as a convener in one of the international conference. She has two papers published in international journals and one is accepted in national journal.

18. Eve Teasing of the Marginalised Women: Experiences from Cachar (Assam)

Ruman Sutradhar

Research Scholar, Department of Political science, Assam University, Silchar, Assam

Author is a Research Scholar (M.Phil) in the Department of Political science, Assam University, Silchar. She is working on the marginalised women of India, with special reference to Dalit women. She is post graduate in Political Science and has been awarded Gold Medal (2013) in the same subject. She has participated and presented papers in Two national/ International seminars; Three research papers and articles written by her have been published in reputed national/international journals, while many others are under process. Her special areas of interest are issues of the marginalised groups (Dalits, immigrants, Adivasis, women in tea plantations), gender issues and politics.

19. Eve Teasing: Outraging the Modesty of Women

Deepa Awasthi

Ph D. - Education, University of Lucknow

Author is freelance researcher and social activist, associated with number of NGOs working in the field of women and child welfare as a volunteer. She is Doctorate in Education, recently submitted her thesis focused on cooperative learning and personality types. She has participated and presented her research paper in 25 national and international seminar. Her publication work involves Three chapters in Edited books, Three research papers in form of conference and seninar proceedings. She has also published 13 research paper and articles in various journals of national and international repute.

20. Eve Teasing: Eradication Measures

Goldy Gupta

Assistant Professor at K. L. College of Education, Dohki (Rewari), Haryana

Author is working as an Assistant Professor at K. L. College of Education, Dohki (Rewari). She has completed post graduation in Mathematics and Education. She has also completed M.Phil. in Education. Her topic of research in M.Phil. was related to personal values of secondary teachers. She also qualified UGC-NET in Education. She has been teaching at College of Education for more than eight years. She has participated in various seminars and workshops related to education. She also organised In-service Training Camps for Mathematics Secondary Teachers as an In charge. Her special areas of interest are gender issues and Mathematics teaching.

21. Eve Teasing: How Much is Too Much?

Fatima Rizvi

Junior Research Fellow, Department of Social Work, University of Lucknow, Lucknow, U.P.

Author is a research scholar in Department of social work, University of Lucknow, at present pursuing her PhD. focussing on Impacts of women's work on their families. She is Post graduate in Social Work and awarded UGC - JRF. She has participated and presented her papers in more than 12 national and international seminar and conferences. Her interest area for research are gender issues, police education and work life balance.

22. Eve Teasing in India and Bangladesh- A Conceptual Survey

Dr Rukmini U. Jamdar

Assistant Professor, Seva Sadan's College of Education, Maharashtra

Author is Doctorate in Education, at present working as Assistant Professor in Seva Sadan's College of Education for Ten years. She is Post Graduate in Commerce and Education. She has participated in more than 25 National/International seminar and conferences. She has contributed more than 12 papers and articles for edited books and seminar/conference proceedings. Her special areas of interest are guidance and counselling, Philosophy of Education, English and Higher Education.

23. Condition of Women: A Literary Perspective

Rupali Mirza

Assistant Professor, Department of English. Integral University. Lucknow.

Ms Rupali Mirza is an Assistant Professor in the Department of English at Integral University, Lucknow. She is also Director, European Centre for Languages, Lucknow. Presently she is pursuing Ph.D in English and her field of specialisation is American Literature. She is a staunch feminist, her feminist roots coming from Lady Shri Ram College for Women (LSR), Delhi University, her alma-mater, where she was an active member of WDC, Women's Development Committee. She has three publications in national and international journals. She has attended several national and international seminars/conferences. Her key areas of interest are American Literature, Literary Theory and women empowerment.

24. Women Power Line - 1090: An Initiative Against Eve Teasing

Dr Meenakshi Dwivedi

Post-doc Research Scholar in Department of Education, University of Lucknow

Author is currently a Post-doc Research Scholar in Department of Education, University of Lucknow, working on the Project for the Education of students suffering from Autistic Syndrome Disorder. She has completed her doctoral thesis on Pains and Gains of Visually Impaired Students Studying in Mainstream Higher Education. She is post graduate in Education, Mathematics and Physics. She has also worked as Assistant Professor (B.Ed) for approx seven years. She has participated and presented the papers in 12 national International seminars and conferences including 102nd Indian Science Congress. More than nine research papers and articles written by her on various issues have been published in reputed national/international journals. She has also contributed one chapter for an edited book. The teaching and research work of the author is focussed on Special Education, Psychology and Mathematics.

25. Street Harassment: The all Pervasive Gender Discrimination Problem

Dr Kaneez Mehdi Zaidi

Ph.D - Education, University of Lucknow

Author is M.Ed., Ph.D in Education and post graduate in English and Political Science. She is qualified UGC-NET (JRF) and UP-SLET. She has participated and presented papers in 12 national/international seminars and conference. She has also published Seven research papers and articles in renowned journals. Her special areas of interest are women education, measurement and evaluation in education, and education of backward classes.

26. Eve Teasing, Tears of Girls: A Study of Patiala

Palwinder Kaur

Junior Research, Scholar, Punjabi University, Patiala, Punjab

Author is a senior research fellow in department of education, Punjabi university, Patiala. She is Post graduate in Education, Political Science and has been awarded UGC- JRF in Education and UGC-NET in Political science. She did Master of Philosophy (M.PHIL) in Political science. She has participated and presented the papers in 11 national, international seminar and conferences. Three articles written by her on various issues have been published as seminar/conference proceedings and in national international journal. Till now, she has contributed one chapter in distance education departmental notes, Punjabi university, Patiala. She had also worked as field investigator in state of nation survey 2008, 2009 conducted by Lokniti and sponsored by CNN-IBN and The Indian Express.

27. Name Calling - A Misanthropic Crude Form of Eve Teasing

Puneet Kaur Dhillon

Assistant Professor, DAV College, Amritsar, Punjab

She has completed her Masters of Arts in Journalism and Mass Communication from Punjabi University, Patiala. She has attended and presented papers in many National and International Seminar/Conferences. She is pursuing her PhD from the Center of Advanced Media Studies under the research title " Impact of Women -Centric Films in Triggering

Social Change : Special focus on Sensitising and Creating Awareness among Women" under the guidance of Dr Gurmeet Singh Maan, Director, Center for Advanced Media Studies, Punjabi University, Patiala. She has also authored a book "Mass Communication Abridged (2014)", Unistar Publishers, Chandigarh.

Ritika Goenka

Assistant Professor, DAV College, Amritsar, Punjab

She has completed her Masters in Mass Communication from Kurukshetra University. She has also done her Masters in Multimedia from Punjab Technical University. She has participated and presented papers in eight national/international seminars and conferences. She has participated in four workshops and film-festivals. Her areas of interest are parallel cinema, public relations and technology.

Introduction

Deepa Awasthi

In recent years Eve teasing has emerged one of the most burning topics yet unresolved. Every girl or women is facing it in her day today life. Civilised society finds itself unsuccessful in resolving this issue. The most special thing about this crime is that it is committed to particular individual but affects to large section of society. It not only affects the victim but her parents, her other family members also. You can imagine a family in which younger sister is put to restrictions because her elder sister has met with an incidence of eve teasing. She has to live with the fear of chance of being targeted by eve teasers very similar to her sister. Although this crime is generally committed in daylight at public places but unfortunately witness of the crime prefer to remain silent without answering the question who will save their girls, sisters, and friends from the teasers committing the same acts with different faces?

This book is prepared with the intention of providing precise information regarding eve teasing which is expanding its wings in all the direction and all the fields of life. We can easily compare it like an epidemic. I hope book will provide a platform to academician, researchers to find full information in context to crime of eve teasing at one place. This book will be also useful for students of various subjects to use as reference book.

This edited book entitled Eve Teasing: A Social Epidemic includes total 27 chapters written by eminent scholars is divided in four sections :

(A) Understanding Eve Teasing

(B) Psycho - Legal aspects,
(C) Experiences and eradication strategies
(D) Miscellaneous

In the first chapter of the book titled **"History and Tradition of Eve Teasing"** author *Mehnaz Najmi* finds the problem of eve teasing deep rooted in India's cultural and historical background. Through small scale survey conducted on the girl students and professors of Galgotia University, she expresses the intensity of crime. She further held that how religion, media, bollywood, family and society are responsible for the eve teasing? She especially criticises the bollywood and television for objectification and commoditisation of women by exposing her body or sexual capabilities ignoring her other attributes. She points out the need to censor the cinema and media which promotes vulgarity and sexuality in society.

Author *Chhaya Soni* in her chapter entitled **"Eve teasing: Hurdle for Women Upgradation"** has exposed various hurdles in way of upliftment of women in country. She also discusses the factors responsible and consequences for eve teasing and other violence against women. She has also suggested few necessary initiatives which can really make the difference to curb the problem of eve teasing.

In the third chapter entitled **"Eve teasing: an extensive social evil in India"** author *Nalini Mishra* has outlined the difference between eve teasing and sexual harassment. She discusses the need of appropriate education to curb the evil of eve teasing. She also details the mandatory guidelines issued by Apex court to all the state governments and police machinery to do the every possible needful to check the crime of eve teasing.

Fourth chapter of the this book entitled **"Eve Teasing and Patriarchy: A menace of Indian Society"** author *Parvin Sultana* discusses the role of patriarchal system of socialisation responsible for creating gender imbalance in society, She held that British colonisation of India was responsible for deprivation of women from their fundamental rights. She also compares the better status of women of north eastern states of India where tribal culture supports matrilineal system. Further, she criticises the role of Hindi cinema and media in promoting eve teasing in society through illustrating and fanaticising the youth of country. According to her, insensitive attitude of police and low conviction rate is also making the life of women miserable. She has also detailed the long term psychological consequences of eve teasing on individual and society.

Fifth chapter of the book **"Role of Media in Solving the Problem of Eve Teasing"** author *Sadhana Srivastava* has mentioned the role of media especially alternative media in solving the problem of eve teasing. According to her, films have a long lasting effect on human mind so they can be used to bring behavioural changes in offenders.

Praveen Hoogar, Ashwini Pujar and T. T. Basavanagouda authors of the sixth chapter entitled **"Eve teasing: A glance on social epidemic"** have discussed the 15 causes of eve teasing. It also focuses on the various consequences of eve teasing on women in context to restrictions on mobility, education, chances of early marriages and hindered development. Authors have tried to find out different forms of eve teasing existing in society including verbal, physical and psychological etc. They have also suggested remedies and precautions for women.

Seventh chapter of the book entitled **"Eve teasing - A social problem"** author *Ruchi Dhyani* provide precise information about eve teasing. Through data of NCRB she explores the increase in crime against women under section - 354 and 509 of IPC. With the help of various cases she proves that incidence of eve teasing can takes place with any women irrespective her social, cultural or economic background. Statements and unusual comments made by leaders of different political parties and renowned personalities of the country she suggests the attitude towards ill treatment of women which is deep rooted in our male dominated cultural background of our society.

In the eighth chapter titled **"Nature, Type and Effects of Eve Teasing"** author *Manglika Tripathi* held that eve teasing is one of the serious gender related issue. She has discussed the nature and type of eve teasing existing in society. She has also detailed the long term and short term impact of eve teasing and what women can do to overcome their consequences. With her own experiences with the incidences of eve teasing, she comes to decision that facing the teaser with courage, boldness and determination is the only solution to the problem of eve teasing.

The ninth chapter of the book entitled **"Why do they do it?"** author *Amit Kumar Dutta* attempted to establish a link between crime against women and various socio economic problems such as unemployment, poverty, lack of opportunities and unavailability of resources. He expresses that Indian society was never materialistic society but due to commerce driven consumerism today women is considered as consumable item. This chapter also focuses on the psychological impact of eve teasing on the victim and the legal remedies available to them. He also establishes the need of education and counselling for eve teasers as well as for victims.

Vishaka Shukla, author of the tenth chapter entitled **"Eve teasing - Psychology of a sick mind"** has discussed psychological aspects of eve teasers. Author held the inappropriate release of neurochemicals e.g. monoamine oxidase, epinephrine, serotonin, dopamine responsible for the psychological state of mind of eve teasers. According to the author personality disorder and developmental disorder is the main reason behind the psychology of eve teasers. She finds that lack of adequate sense of self identity and self worth leads to psychological disorders which are expressed in form of various crimes like eve teasing.

Eleventh chapter of the book entitled **"Eve Teasing: A Psychoanalytic Explication"** author *Zeba Aqil* explains the problem of eve teasing through the psychoanalytic theory of human development as developed by Sigmund Freud - a renowned psychologist. He also explains the role of male parents in family who is imitated by male child as a model. Immoral and Irresponsible activities of father and other male members of family can lead to development of negative attitude in male children. Author recommends finding out the social solution to the problem rather than legal solution through police action.

Saurabh Mishra and Deepti Mishra in the next chapter entitled **"India strict against eve teasing and Sexual harassment at work place"** authors have discussed the provisions of sexual harassment of women at work place (Prevention, Prohibition and Redressal) act 2013 and Criminal amendment act 2013 which provide enough protection to women employees against any type of sexual harassment at work place. Chapter also describe what is eve teasing as per law in India. In the last of the chapter authors have recommended some genuine steps to be initiated so that women can have a upper hand in case of violation of their rights.

Next chapter included in this book is **"Critical Evaluation of Criminal Law Amendment Act-2013 with Special Reference to Eve-Teasing in the NCT of Delhi"** in which author *Sandesh Yadav and Aayushi Chaudhary* has critically evaluated Criminal Law Amendment Act-2013 and compared pre and post status. It also discusses the factors responsible for violence against women. Along with other sections of IPC which applies in the case of harassment of women including eve teasing.

Fourteenth chapter of the book entitled **"Eve Teasing, Crime against Women: Human Rights Perspective"** author *Baij Nath* focuses on the violation of human rights of women due to eve teasing. After discussing forms, types and effects of eve teasing author has detailed the status of law in India against eve teasing with latest amendments and developments. He also explores the role of judiciary, media and NGOs in controlling the crime teasing.

The fifteenth chapter of the book entitled **"Women must protest against eve teasing"** author *Shravan* Kumar and *Ankita Singh* have discussed the continuous increase in crime against women to outrage or intent to outrage the modesty of women from year 2009 to 2013 with the help of data of NCRB. They have suggested the theory of 3E's - Encouragement, Empowerment, and Efficiency necessary for eradication of eve teasing. Chapter emphasises on requirement of women to remain prepare to face the eve teasers without hesitation equipped with self defence techniques. They also suggest the women can use mobile technology and mobile applications in the situation when they find no body to help them otherwise they can shout for help to combat the eve teasers at crowded or public place. Both the authors further add that victims must take a legal action against eve teasers by lodging a police complaint against them which can make them realise that their act is against moral, social and legal values. She tried to explore the important sections of IPC and CrPC. which provides legal remedies to victims of eve teasing. Authors have beautifully suggested some dos and don'ts for women by following they can avoid the chances of getting teased by strangers.

Next chapter of the book entitled **"Time to introspect"** author *Vidya Vati* has focused on the attitude of parents, police, society and victims towards eve teasing. It also lightens legal and constitutional aspects of eve teasing. Through a survey conducted on police officials, girls and parents on various issues she tried to explore the possible reasons and their solutions for the problem of eve teasing. She also establishes that the unrestricted exposure to internet and other media to the children are also responsible for sexual crimes and violence by teenagers in early ages. She also details about few precedents given by Apex court and High courts which guides central and state governments to take all necessary measures to stop the incidences of eve teasing.

Seventeenth chapter of the book entitled **"End Eve Teasing: Voice through Words"** authors *Manvi Yadav, Neetu Yadav, Preetu Srivastava* have stated that problem of eve teasing can only be solved by changing the attitude of our male dominated society. They further suggest that every youth must be taught essential moral values in school, colleges and universities. Chapter also discusses the role of teachers and parents in building the character of child through self demonstration. It also emphasises on the collaborative efforts of society, media, law implementing agencies and educational institutes needed to solve the problem of eve teasing in India.

In the next chapter **"Eve Teasing of the marginalised women: Experiences from Cachar (Assam)"** author *Ruman Sutradhar* has described the experiences of eve teasing faced by tribal girls and women in Cachar area of Assam. She has beautifully presented the agony faced by girls of socially and economically marginalised section. In her study she also mentions the incidences of eve teasing with mentally insane women. In the last she has suggested few measures to tackle the problem of eve teasing.

Nineteenth chapter entitled **"Eve Teasing: Outraging the Modesty of Women"** author *Deepa Awasthi* has described the intensity of eve teasing with the help of experiences shared by victims on various social media websites. She has also mentioned a list of common types of eve teasing existing in society. She has detailed about the patterns followed by eve teasers and various myths deep rooted in the mind of common man about eve teasing and the individuals responsible for that. According to her school, college, family, society, police, administration and government can together control the problem with their collaborative efforts.

In the next chapter of the book entitled **"Eve Teasing: Eradication Measures"** author *Goldy Gupta* explored the solution to the problem of eve teasing through social measures like providing quality education to children, checking the expansion of open sky culture, prohibition of use of Alcohol and Drugs, avoiding indecent outfits, appointment of censor boards for television etc. She advocates for the introduction of sex education in school curriculum at appropriate level to control gender related problems in society.

Twenty first chapter of the book entitled **"Eve teasing: How much is too much?"** written by *Fatima Rizvi* contains the detailed interview of girls expressing their personal experiences they have faced in their life. Author herself has mentioned self experience of eve teasing. Respondents also suggested that they find the attitude of their parents and friends compel them to avoid the situation after standing against the wrong doers. She has tried to explore the consequences victim faces due to this evil and their respective solutions.

Twenty second chapter of the book entitled **"Eve teasing in India and Bangladesh- a conceptual survey"** author *Rukmini U. Jamdar* has compared the status of eve teasing in India and Bangladesh along with law available in respective countries to deal with the eve teasers. According to her eve teasing is a civil torturous liability. She discusses the psychological aspects of the crime responsible for development of negative attitude in child.

In the twenty third chapter of the book entitled **"Condition of Women: A Literary Perspective"** author *Rupali Mirza* states that eve teasing is not only the part of Indian culture but it also exists in western world. Through study of various English literatures she explores the elements of eve teasing present in English Prose and Poetries. According to her literature reflects the true image of society. She criticises involving such study material in curriculum because it provoke gender bias behaviour among students.

Kaneez Mehdi Zaidi author of the twenty fourth chapter entitled **"Street harassment: The all pervasive gender discrimination problem"** has used the synonym Street harassment in place of eve teasing as the word eve teasing reflects that women themselves are responsible for the problem of eve teasing. She further discuses the causes and impacts of eve teasing, mentions that it is all pervasive gender discrimination problem. Author has explored the type of eve teasing existing in different countries and legal protection available to them in countries like USA, UK, China, Japan, Australia, Bangladesh, Pakistan and India. She further adds that the attitude of parents and society is responsible, for which victims don't come forward to report the incidences of eve teasing. She also suggests that in cases when women comes up to report the incidences administration and police do not take any initiatives considering it as crime of light nature and as something acceptable in society.

Next chapter in the book entitled **"Eve teasing, tears of girls: a study of Patiala"** written by *Palwinder Kaur,* has tried to detail all the aspects of eve teasing through a survey conducted on the university girls of Patiala city, in context to ideal time for eve teasing, ideal places for eve teasing, nature of eve teasing, reaction of victims towards the incidence, type of eve teasers etc. She has also explored the prone areas of Patiala known for the violence against women including the incidences of eve teasing. Author has established the similarity between eve teasing and sexual harassment. She considered eve teasing as first step towards sexual crime. According to her the foremost target of legislation must be to curb the problem instead of punishing the teenagers by putting them behind the bars. She has also recommended various necessary steps to put full stop on eve teasing.

Last chapter of the book entitled **"Name Calling - A Misanthropic Crude Form of Eve Teasing"** authors *Puneet Kaur Dhillion* and Ritika Goenka have detailed the Punjabi songs and their words which defaces the image of women in society, as slowly and gradually those double meaning words become the part of daily language. They also mentioned a number of popular Punjabi folk singers who used the music as platform to pace up their success by humiliating women in their folk directly or indirectly from time to time.

1

History and Tradition of Eve Teasing

Mehnaz Najmi

Abstract

Eve teasing is a word loosely used for sexual harassment of women. The term itself reflects the intensity of the offence and the psychological effects it causes on the victim. It would not be an exaggeration to say that no girl in India has been spared from eve teasing. Being subjected to many instances of eve teasing is an inseparable part of every girl's life causing much avoidable mental agony to her. The meaning of the word eve is first woman in the Bible and the meaning of tease is to laugh at somebody and make jokes about them, either in a friendly manner or in order to annoy or embarrass them. According to Wikipedia, "Eve teasing is a euphemism used in India, Pakistan, Bangladesh and Nepal for public sexual harassment, street harassment or molestation of women by men. It severely infringes the right of mobility of a woman. 90 per cent girls between the ages of Ten-eighteen are affected by eve teasing... **Historical Exposition:** Eve teasing is now accepted as a part and parcel of Indian culture. To find the solution and analyse the gravity of situation we need to delve in the past. The seed of problem lies in the history and culture itself. It is necessary to understand what lies beneath before putting any efforts to eradicate this evil....

Division of labour on the basis of physical strength pushed women towards the secondary status. Man has more physical strength as compared to woman, he could plough the land, herd sheep, gather the food but woman could not do as much of hard work due to her reproductive system.. Literature published during that time also gave legality and sanctity to such thinking, be it Vedas or Manu Smriti. Many evil social practices, like the practice of pre-puberty marriages, denial of right of women to education and also to mate selection etc were imposed on women during the periods of Brahmans and Puranas. Vedas considered male child as more important than female child....**Religion:** All religions treat women as lesser beings as compared to men. Here I want to compare two major religions namely Hinduism and Islam and their followers which are to large extent responsible for pushing women to this plight....**Role of Family and Society:** The breakdown of the value system that we carry faced sudden exposure to western cultures. Technological changes result in change of the material culture while belief systems remain the same. Holding on to the traditional Hindu "man is the lord' patriarchal belief, while the material or work culture recognises women as equal. When new values (women are equal and free) and old values ('women are only fit to be wife and mother' and 'their chastity speaks of their character') are in conflict...Role of Media and Bollywood: Media has played a very negative role as far as objectification of woman is concerned. Objectification occurs when a woman's body, parts of her body, or sexual capabilities are seen as her whole self, ignoring other attributes. Woman is shown as an object of lust. **Conclusion**

Key words: Eve-teasing, Historical Exposition, Religion, Family, Society, Media

"From watchmen to policemen, everyone on the street makes me feel uncomfortable with his looks and acts...I don't even feel safe at home".

Eve teasing is a word loosely used for sexual harassment of women. The term itself ridicules the intensity of the offence and the psychological effects it causes on the victim. It would not be an exaggeration to say that no girl in India has been spared from eve teasing. Being subjected to many instances of eve teasing is an inseparable part of every girl's life causing much avoidable mental agony to her. A lewd stare, a sly whistle, an unwarranted bump, a seemingly casual touch, a lingering look at a vulnerable time, the humming of a suggestive song, passing downright uncouth comments, cheap gestures, the display of an indecent snap or video, bikes flying close with hands stretched to grope, passing by in slow moving cars blasting loud music with many eyes inside measuring you up... all these are typical examples of eve teasing. This truth stares at the face of a girl much before she reaches adolescence. Eve teasing is a common incident, be it in buses, shopping arcades, cinema halls, shopping malls, pubs, restaurants, auto/bus-terminals, railway booking counters and every other conceivable place; but the one place where it happens with alarming frequency is on the road. It is an act of violence which needs to be treated as violence rather than an act of fun.

Definition

The meaning of the word eve is first woman in the Bible and the meaning of tease is to laugh at somebody and make jokes about them, either in a friendly manner or in order to annoy or embarrass them. According to Wikipedia, "Eve teasing is a euphemism used in India, Pakistan, Bangladesh and Nepal for public sexual harassment, street harassment or molestation of women by men. It severely infringes the right of mobility of a woman. 90 per cent girls between the ages of Ten-eighteen are affected by eve teasing. Many female students are forced to stay at home giving up their studies. Parents marry off their school and college going daughters in order to avoid this horrible situation. No government initiatives to tame the teasers have proven effective so far. Using filthy language, movement of body in dirty manner, unnecessary touching, pushing, shoving in the streets, whistling and frequent harassment at workplace by male supervisors are some of the ways to disturb women. Some even go to the extent of attacking women or throwing acid on their face.

Women are generally told to stay home or face the consequences. This is what their parents tell them. Their movements are restricted to protect the honour or *izzat* of the family which girls/women carry according to prevalent prejudices. Society has also evolved in a manner where every wrong is associated to women. Men or sons are not told to respect and treat women with dignity instead women are forced with the burden of maintaining the false pride of the family. From the day a girl is born to the day she gets married, she is told that she has to maintain the honour of the family. The situation becomes grave when maintaining pride and honour of the family turns life threatening where boys get involved into acid attacks or murdering when girl denies their advancements. Girls if complain to families about such sexual advances or eve teasing, they are blamed and their movements get restricted. They get beaten up for bringing problem and bad name to the families. They are blamed of inviting troubles. Relatives and society too blame the girls for bringing dishonour. Eventually they are forced to leave their education and are married off early. All men even property less view women as their property and think they can make woman do whatever they want by beating her (Chatra Yuva Sangharsha Vahini, Bihar, 1993).Though eve teasing is considered as a criminal activity and socially unacceptable but it still is prevalent in our society. Girls are told to stay at home when they face such trouble. Sometimes it helps but most of the times it gives boost to the confidence of the criminal. It is an irony that despite so many laws to prevent this evil from the society, it still exists. To analyse this phenomenon we need to go back to the history of women in India. We need to study the historical narratives to understand why and how woman was pushed to the sidelines.

Historical Exposition

Eve teasing is now accepted as a part and parcel of Indian culture. To find the solution and analyse the gravity of situation we need to delve in the past. The seed of problem lies in the history and culture itself. It is necessary to understand what lies beneath before putting any efforts to eradicate this evil. The problem is two dimensional. On one hand it is subjugation of woman as second gender and on the other sexualisation of woman.

Division of labour on the basis of physical strength pushed women towards the secondary status. Man has more physical strength as compared to woman, he could plough the land, herd sheep, gather the food but woman could not do as much of hard work due to her reproductive system. In the course of time her area was restricted to staying at home, rearing and bearing children and to look after house hold chores. Eventually, man started treating her as a commodity or property which he owned. Since she was not self sufficient and was dependent on male head for survival, her status and conditions kept on deteriorating. She was not allowed to participate in decision making activities or to do something that was restricted. Considering her as a commodity and a reproductive machine became a norm and to a large extent accepted law of the land. Sexualisation of woman was the direct result of commodification. It is a fact that man dominated her but he could not live without woman. For man to have woman around him was more of a necessity than need to sexually satisfy them, to rear and bear his children, to look after house hold, to take care of elderly and to make him feel like a master. Man realised early that woman is important for him, society and state therefore, every man wanted to have a woman in his house but at the same time he wanted to be the master. He wanted to control her and her sexuality in the name of purity and sometimes as a form of dominance. When one man tried to hide and dominate his women the other lusted for her. New stringent laws and regulations were made to safeguard women from lusting men. Literature published during that time also gave legality and sanctity to such thinking, be it Vedas or Manu Smriti. Many evil social practices, like the practice of pre-puberty marriages, denial of right of women to education and also to mate selection etc were imposed on women during the periods of Brahmans and Puranas. Vedas considered male child as more important than female child. We find a number of provisions in the Manu Smriti, which certainly go against her interests. Women are deprived of the Upanayana ceremony and thereby of education. Manu relegates her to an entirely subservient position. He preaches self-negation as the highest ideal of a wife. She is asked to serve and worship her husband even if he is not a person of all virtue and character. Since service and worship of the husband are the primary duties of a wife, by so performing she can hope to attain heaven. Manu deprives women of her economic rights also. He says, "A wife, a son and a Slave, these three are declared to have no property, the wealth which they earn is for him to whom they belong". It appears that Manu had a very poor opinion about women. According to him women should be guarded against her evil inclinations. Otherwise she will bring sorrow to both the families. He also observes that if a woman is chaste, it is because she has not found a proper man, place and opportunity. He, therefore, calls her a 'Pramada a temptress (Puja Mondal, Status of Women in Vedic and Post-Vedic Period). On one hand they called woman as deity and on the other hand she is called temptress. Both the ideas are beyond humanity and far from normality.

Role of Religion

Religion is an organised collection of beliefs, cultural systems, and world views that relate humanity to an order of existence (Wikipedia). Religion has played a vital role in the development and evolution of state and society. It has always been like an adhesive which binds the society and at the same time it also stops the society from moving away from the prescribed ideals. These ideals are what patriarchal society has been prescribing since ages. Religion in a way gave sanctity to them. A clear cut division of work was made with the use of religion and was declared as an ideal way of life. It suggested man to go out and work whereas women were told to stay home and look after household. The economic power eventually came into the hands of man which resulted in further degradation in the status of women. All religions treat women as lesser beings as compared to men. Here I want to compare two major religions namely Hinduism and Islam and their followers which are to large extent responsible for pushing women to this plight.

The Hindu religion or rather the Vedic religion is supposed to be *Apaurusheya,* i.e., not made by man. It has evolved over millennia of thinking by the ancient sages. It comprises of diverse philosophies, ways of worship, innumerable deities along with the 'One All Encompassing Entity called Brahma' and countless customs and rituals. But it is second to none other religion in male domination. Many Hindus claim that their religion honours women and quote the maxims like 'the hand that rocks the cradle, rules the world' or 'the deities dwell in those places where women are worshiped', etc. They proffer the examples of the erudite Gargi and Maitreyi to prove their claim that religion does not discriminate against women. But the crux of the problem lies in how they are actually treating their women today. The treatment that is meted out to women now is illustrated in the dictums, 'a shoe deserves to be put on the foot and not on the head' or 'a broom that ought to remain in the corner of the store room cannot be seated in the drawing room'. These are but the commands issued, of course in different words, by the ancient sages and thinkers and the present Jagadgurus and other sundry god men. One of the oft-quoted dictums of Manusmriti a typical male chauvinist code of conduct-says, 'a woman should always remain obedient to her father in her childhood, to her husband when married and to her son in her old age. She does not deserve freedom.' Here freedom denotes not only free movement but also freedom of thought and to do what they feel like doing. In the course of time certain dictates became dominant ideals and over the years they turned into a combined culture.

And this for the exemplary Gargi-the symbol of erudition of ancient Indian women! The sage Yadnyawalkya petulantly chastises her for asking unanswerable questions and warns and curses her, 'Do not cross your limits (perhaps as a woman) Gargi, for, if you do, your head will separate from your body and fall to the ground!' Even the somewhat liberal poet of the comparatively recent past, Tulasidas confers the license to men to beat their women. He says "Shudras, the insane, beasts and women all deserve to be beaten." Woman was kept in the category of beasts and non-humans.

If we look at the Ramayana, Sita was subjugated for being a woman. Value of her truth was lesser than the doubt of a 'washer man' (Samhita

Arni 2013). In Mahabharata, Draupadi was forced to marry five men. Duryodhan found her attractive and tried to undress her publicly along with his brothers. Reason being she was treated like property that her husbands lost in gamble and gave away to Kauravas. Krishna-the Hindu God is known for his Raas Leela that is love making, playing and teasing milk maids. There are stories how he teased them, stole their clothes and forced them to come out of water without clothes. So teasing in India is very much part of culture. Hindu mythology is replete with such examples where women were cursed or belittled by men for being who they were. Sometimes for being confident they were punished sometimes for being doormats they were tortured. As if they are commodities to be used. If this is the basis of a society, how can we imagine equal and healthy relationship between man and woman? Duty and sacrifice are the words denoted only for women (Shikhandi, Devdutt Patnaik 2014).

Islam as another or second religion entered India during 7th century. It was a religion that gave right to equality to down trodden but not to women. The condition of women only deteriorated further despite clear cut women rights described by Quran. A number of problems arose for Hindu women in the Mughal period. The first Muslim invasion took place in India in the eighth century. During this period the Hindu society was engaged in evolving, under the leadership of Sankaracharya, a technique to face the expanding Buddhism. India experienced a second Muslim invasion in the eleventh century when Mohammad Ghazni conquered India. From this period till the middle of the eighteenth century, when the British rule was established in the country the breakdown of social institutions, the vast migration of people and the economic depression in the country contributed to a general decline of social life, particularly among women.

It brought with it the Purdah system to Indian culture. Purdah means veil for women or to be precise seclusion to protect her modesty. A woman who was subjugated earlier for being a lower gender was now forced to cover her face and body irrespective of religion. She was not allowed to walk without her face covered. Women were asked to live in seclusion in sphere of their homes. Education of women in whatever form came to be stopped. Child marriage was started. During this period the inhuman practice of 'Sati Pratha was in vogue. Purdah Pratha, Sati Pratha, child marriage, girl killing, polygamy etc. were the main social evils of this period.

Religion therefore, played a role which united the society but made women more vulnerable. They became objects and commodities which men used and regulated their lives. All this made her life more miserable and degraded her status further. It also made women more dependent on male counterparts or male family members. She could not go out alone to market. She needed a male member of her family to escort her. Her forte was home and aims to become a good wife and mother. If ever she tried moving alone she would face the taunts or nasty remarks by men on roads.

Role of the Family and Society

The society changed after independence. Constitution bestowed women with equal rights and made eve teasing a criminal offence. Women started studying and working. The breakdown of the value system that we carry faced sudden exposure to western cultures. Technological changes result in change of the material culture while belief systems remain the same. Holding on to the traditional Hindu "man is the lord' patriarchal belief, while the material or work culture recognises women as equal. When new values (women are equal and free) and old values ('women are only fit to be wife and mother' and 'their chastity speaks of their character') are in conflict.

Recent example of Gauhar Khan, a TV actor, one would say, was in a space that would be ticked off as 'safe' by average standards of women's safety in India. She is a celebrity, she was on the set of a TV show produced by a popular channel, she was surrounded by people and the place was teeming with security personnel. Where could a woman possibly be safer, if not there? Yet, a man had the gall to walk up to her, deride her for her choice of clothes and then not only grope her, but slap her. If you were to consider the root of this audacity, it evidently stems from the idea that women are the second class occupants of the public space in India and can be easily shoved around as and when fancied." In the name of religion the guy came over and slapped her despite the fact that the same religion stops her from touching a woman not related to him. On the contrary he took the commandment of decent clothing in Islam seriously (duty of a woman not related in any way to him) but forgot his duty of not touching a woman and lowering his gaze. It has again proved that no matter how progressive a woman if the society is lagging behind.

A small scale survey was conducted with the students and Professors of Galgotias University to establish their views, apprehensions and gender biases in society. The age group for students is 17-25 and for Professors it is 35-60 years. A group of 30 girl students and 30 Professors was studied.

Comparative Analysis of Women age Groups 17-25 and 35-60

	Age Group 17-25		Age Group 35-45	
Questions	Yes	No	Yes	No
Do you feel safe walking alone during day time?	27	03	28	02
Do you feel safe walking alone at night?	02	28	05	25
Have you ever faced sexual harassment or eve teasing on road or workplace or educational institute?	28	02	27	03
Have you ever complained about eve teasing to your parents?	14	16	2	28
Did you ever go to the Police station to file F.I.R against the miscreants?	2	28	1	29
Has anybody threatened you if ever reiterated or objected to their misbehaviour?	2	28	1	29
Do you think this problem has increased as compared to earlier days?	30	00	30	00

If we compare the data received from women belonging to two different generations, we find that the problem persisted since ages but it has now increased at an alarming rate. Earlier women were not as outspoken as they are today. Similarly men were not as outrageous as they are today. It is true that most of the girls today would rather face the worst consequence than bring such issues to the notice of the parents as they would dissect this instance of eve teasing in a manner that is bound to cause detriment to her. A girl student said parent's reaction would be: "Who asked you to be there at that time of the night?" or "I told you earlier that what you were wearing was not appropriate!" and finally "Before I blame someone else, you should check how you have contributed to it and brought this upon yourself!" This sort of reaction will make the girl decide that if she ever walks up to her parents with a genuine instance of eve teasing she will first be accused of contributing to the act and it will finally culminate in a statement on the lines of '"That's it! Henceforth you shall not be out after eight pm." or some such stringent step taken against the victim...asked the girl. Girls/women are still apprehensive about complaining or reporting the matter to Police due to insensitivity towards women. Sometimes police starts misbehaving with them and other times they turn into moral brigade finding faults with the victims.

We can say from above analysis that women still are apprehensive and do not have confidence in their families and society. They are scared that if they complaint about eve teasing to their families their movement will be restricted. They have to face the music for something that they have not even done. Leave aside outsiders, there are relatives or family members who misbehave with woman in the name of mazaq (teasing) but such events are appreciated instead of being denounced. Be it jeeja-Sali (Brother-in-law misbehaving with the woman) or other male relative.

Role of Media and Bollywood

Media has played a very negative role as far as objectification of woman is concerned. Objectification occurs when a woman's body, parts of her body, or sexual capabilities are seen as her whole self, ignoring other attributes. Woman is shown as an object of lust. In advertisements she is shown as a commodity for market forces. Why is there a need of semi-naked woman in the advertisement of shaving cream or blade? Even when an ad of car comes, woman is never shown as owner of car but a scantily clad woman waiting for lift. She is always selling washing powder or corn flakes or diapers on TV. Why such roles are so defined? Why can't men be in these ads? Does media too wants to re-affirm these prejudiced boundaries? There are soap operas on TV where a woman called Tulsi happily lived with her bigamous husband and even went on to the extent of upbringing his children from other woman. She lived happily in a joint family tolerating all the cruelties ranging from physical to emotional but never ever raised her voice. This is the portrayal of Indian woman on TV. This is the ideal that media is presenting to 21st century women. Again history is repeating itself. On one hand there is deity or goddess like Tulsi and on the other there are temptresses selling shaving creams. Why can't they show woman of today and her real problems and issues? There is a comedy show where host keeps on making fun of his wife and her looks. Audience find it all very interesting and clap every time he utters foul language for his on screen wife. This is the kind of respect and dignity with which women are portrayed on TV.

Bollywood has also played a major role in objectifying the woman by portraying her as docile and brainless. They get charmed by their oppressor. He irritates her, tease her and do every possible thing to woe her. Finally she says yes to him and there is victory of love. Movies like Dar showed eve teasers stalking woman who stand up against them and goes to the extent of hurting her and her family members. What he did was wrong but people liked his act. No matter how wrong he was.

Young and adolescent boys take TV and movies very seriously. They follow the actors and try imitating their mannerisms. They get influenced by their on screen portrayals. They too start behaving in a fashion their heroes do. Therefore, it is high time they start taking and sharing responsibility as a stake holder in society.

Conclusion

The term 'eve teasing' has origin in South Asia. It is used to suggest the violence against women but the term itself is faulty because "Eve" represents temptress and the term actually signifies that eves (women) tempt or provoke males for vulgar comments and behaviours. Ironically, that also means women cause the problem and are also a victim to it. But that is almost like blaming the victims for their sufferings. It also depicts an element of male chauvinism. The structure of Indian society has always been male dominated. But in the modern era, women tried to break the centuries of shackles by venturing into male dominated areas. Though, we have grown by leaps and bounds yet the most basic structure of society is showing no signs of improvement.

We call ourselves modern by aping the west but we are still carrying the burden of prejudices. Woman being a 'temptress' is the notion accepted by one and all. Even women follow this idea. They are some commodity to be hidden. They need to be protected. They are the care takers of family honor. Such are the ideas that a girl learns from her family. One of the first lessons most adolescent girls are administered by mother are ways to dodge-not essentially fight-the predatory male gaze in crowded public spaces in the country. Carry a big bag, no eye contact, don't look lost, walk fast - the list of survival tricks for a woman in a public space, to which she has an equal right as men, is both exhaustive and exhausting. Such mindsets and prejudices against women are to a larger extent responsible for the pathetic conditions from which women are suffering today. A person is viewed as a thing for others' sexual use, rather than as a human being.

She is teased, she is used, she is attacked, she is victimised and she is murdered. We cannot change the society without changing ourselves. If we really want to change the society then we must start by changing the perception and traditions which effect woman. We need to come out of the bonded past. We need to treat her as equal. We need to accept that she is neither temptress nor a goddess. Parents need to become the pillar of strength for girls because any instance of eve teasing has two aspects to it, the first being the deplorable act of eve teasing and the second and more decisive factor in terms of the reaction to it by the woman or women concerned. It is seen that many women react instinctively when accosted by an eve teaser. This instinct may provoke her to rebuke the eve-teaser's acts or persuade her to silently get away from the eve-teaser. When girls report instances of eve teasing at home, they are asked to avoid any further conflict with eve-teasers and are reminded that every act of theirs would only go to encourage eve-teasers; thus they are advised to be safe than sorry. The above norm is followed by most victims of eve teasing and has contributed to a great extent in encouraging eve-teasers to cover further ground and crystallise even rank amateurs to become hardcore deviants who will indulge in all possible offences against women, thanks to the inaction and lack of resistance they witness. There are some girls who do not react to eve teasing when they faces it, as they are shocked for a moment and caught unawares by an eve teaser. Even though they have the courage to stand up for their dignity right then, they fail to do so as they are unsure as to how to react. It is the duty of parents to constantly remain on guard when it comes to protecting the girl child. They have to be on the lookout for any sign, however insignificant it may be, that will lead them to a dark incident that a girl child has experienced and is unsure as to how to react. They need to develop the confidence in girls that it is not their fault. The boy/man involved in this act is wrong not the girl. They have to keep reassuring the girl child that she can talk to them in case of even the slightest discomfort that she might be facing. They have to provide the necessary strength and support that their daughter seeks, especially so in the age of adolescence when she is not even able to identify an instance of eve teasing and label it so. They also have to thrust upon themselves the task of ensuring that the girl child has a healthy relationship with them and that she is so very comfortable that she would approach them first to seek advice on any issue - however minor it be. The girl child should be made to realise that the parents are not fighting with her but are fighting for her everyday, trying to genuinely look at the interests of the girl at all costs. The eve teaser will not openly admit that he indulged in such a depraved act. It is pertinent to note here that an eve-teaser when apprehended will admit to having committed any crime in this world rather than admitting that he has teased a woman, for fear of earning eternal disrespect from society, his friends, and worst of all, his own family. While committing the act of eve teasing there is an attitude of proving male supremacy in the eve-teaser but once apprehended, even a first time eve teaser is ashamed that his family will come to know that he has been apprehended for eve teasing. The hardened eve-teaser is all the more scared when his family is brought into the picture as he would not have painted a far different picture in front of them. His cowardly nature will disallow him from openly admitting his vices and standing by them.

Religion should be used as a tool of emancipation for woman and not as a shackle. Prejudices and age old customs should be stopped. People should be educated about such customs. Age old ideas like treating girls as *Paraya Dhan* or unequal to man or giving right to burn funeral pyre only to son needs to be questioned. Such traditions are as much responsible for the deteriorating conditions of women in India as old ideals.

Media and Bollywood also need to be censored. They must stop commodification of woman. It is time to stop and say NO to what is wrong-morally and ethically. They must realise that woman should not be used as a commodity by market forces. Portrayal of girls as 'item' in vulgar songs where women is equated with roasted chicken to be chewed and swallowed with alcohol must be stopped. All abuses and swear words have demeaning words for women, which are severely used in songs these days. They need to be questioned and censored.

Eve-teasing is an evil that needs to be eradicated from the society. For which a positive approach and attitude is required from the law makers, society and the family. Stringent laws need to be made to fight this evil. Considering it as childish, joke and boys will be boys type attitude needs to be changed. Girls should be made more independent and self dependent to fight for their own selves. We need to analyse the historical facts which are responsible for making women oppressed, repressed and suppressed. We must change and break such value system which is derogatory towards women. Parents need to take the first positive step towards upliftment of their girls. They need to build confidence among their girl child that they are trusted and if a man on street misbehaves with them, it is not their fault.

References

- Ahuja, Ram,Violence against women, New Delhi and Jaipur, 1998. Ahuja, Ram, Social problems in India, Rawat publication, New Delhi and Jaipur, 1992.
- Arni, Samhita, The Missing Queen, Zubaan Books, 2013. Bhasin Kamala and Aggarwal Bina eds- Women and Media: Analysis, Alternative and Action, Kali for Women, New Delhi, 1984.
- Desai Neera and Thakkar Usha, Women in Indian Society,National Book Trust, New Delhi, 2003. Patnaik, Devdutt, Shikhandi And Other Tales They Don't Tell You, Penguin, New Delhi, 2014.
- Flood, Gavin, An Introduction to Hinduism, Cambridge, Cambridge University Press, 1996.
- Greenberg, Julie A and Rierson Sandra L, Women in Politics: The Role of Gender in Political Decision Making, Eighth Annual Women and the Law Conference, 2008.
- Integration of the human rights of women and gender perspective, violence against women, United nations Economic and Social Council.
- Kumari, Rama, Women Welfare Programmes, Bookink Corporation New Delhi, 2000.
- Zaidi, Annie, The Good Indian Girl, Zubaan Books, 2014.
  http://www.yourarticlelibrary.com/society/status-of-women-in-vedic-and-post-vedic-period/4397/
  http://encyclopedia.thefreedictionary.com/Eve%20teasing
  http://www.fact-index.com/e/ev/eve_teasing.html
  http://www.wordiq.com/definition/Eve_teasing
  http://www.wordwebonline.com/en/EVETEASING
  http://en.wikipedia.org/wiki/Eve_teasing
  http://encyclozine.com/Eve_teasing
  http://www.indiaparenting.com/raisingchild/data/raisingchild203book.shtml
  http://www.manipuronline.com/Editorials/December%202002/december23_6.htm
  http://www-personal.umich.edu/~jlawler/aue/indian.html
  http://www.chowk.com/show_article.cgiaid=00001547andchannel=gulberg&start=0&end=9&chapter=1&page=1
  http://www.mouthshut.com/readreview/42355-1.html

http://www.mail-archive.com/goanews@goacom.com/msg00421.html
http://www.madhoo.com/archives/000441.php
http://foxx1.rediffblogs.com/
http://www.evesindia.com/xylane/fireandfury/eve_teasing.html
www.bluejeanonline.com/features/
Articles In Hindu, TOI, Hindustan Times, Deccan Hearld

2

Eve Teasing: Hurdle for Women's Upgradation

Chhaya Soni

Abstract

Pandit Jawaharlal Nehru aptly remarked that, "*To awaken the society it is the women who must be awakened. Once she is on the move the family moves, the village moves and the nation moves.*"Indian women are a typical social character. She has to play a vital role in family, society and life, as a whole. During Vedic period, women enjoyed better status as compared to later times as the position of women had declined in the post-Vedic period. Particularly during the medieval period, women suffered a lot and their position discriminated on the basis of sex and biological weakness. But our observation shows that, yet women are not recognised as equal to men and they are discriminated and treated inferior to men apparently it seems that due to the total development of a country, development of both male and female are going in a same direction and a same level of equality. Still there lies lots of open and hidden problems, which are responsible for gender inequality in society. One curler hidden problem seems to Indian society, i.e., violence against women. Eve-teasing is one of them. "Eve-teasing" refers to public sexual harassment or street harassment to a girl by a boy, when it turns into a serious issue. This chapter deals with various factors which act as barriers of women's growth. It also discusses the present situation of women in India and suggestion to remove mental haze problem.

Key Words: Eve-teasing, Origin of eve-teasing, Teasers, Aspect of eve-teasing, Upgradation, Hurdles, Situation of women, Suggestions

Introduction

Pandit Jawaharlal Nehru aptly remarked that, *"To awaken the society it is the women who must be awakened. Once she is on the move the family moves, the village moves and the nation moves."*

Indian women are a typical social character, quite different from her community members outside sub-continent. She has to play a vital role in family, society and life, as a whole. She is mother, sister, wife and daughter, all rolled into one and she has to act and perform in all these capacities in a single life time. To think and imagine, it's really great to do that much in a few decades time.

Irony of the situation, despite all significance attached to the women that she has never given her due share or status in life and society. Observing, studying and depicting women in poetry, writing, painting and sculpture is a very old business. In fact, the woman has been a sort of obsession for all the philosophers, thinkers, authors and artists. Women, as an entity, have been the focal point for all of them.

Women constitute about half of the total population of India. During Vedic period, women enjoyed better status as compared to later times as the position of women had declined in the post-Vedic period. Particularly during the medieval period, women suffered a lot and their position discriminated on the basis of sex and biological weakness. Consequently, their position was weakened and they were relegated to a low status in the society, which is one of the major reasons for their low level of education or illiteracy. Nevertheless, during the later period of 19th century and early 20th century women's education had received enormous encouragement from social reformers like Raja Ram Mohan Rai, Mahatma Gandhi, Bal Gangadhar Tilak and others. But, it was only after independence, women's education had received prominence and huge budgets in the advocacy and propagation of universalisation of education. However, due to availability of school in nearby areas and the reservation of seats for girls in educational institutions have opened the ways for women to receive education and thus improve their socio-economic status. In addition to this number of women welfare and social welfare programmes were also introduced. Accordingly, the laws were enacted to raise the socio-economic and political status of women in India.

But our observation shows that, yet women are not recognised as equal to men and they are discriminated and treated as inferior to men. For example, a daughter is considered as liability and son as an asset. In case of marriage, certain amount of dowry has to be given to the bridegroom by the bride's parents. Studies show that due to socio-economic and cultural barriers women are not given equal importance as compared to men.

In this situation, the suitable direction to get rid of the above said socio-economic and cultural barriers of women is to bring the revolution of women's education like green revolution because all these drawbacks are associated with education and economic development. Educational and economic development will lead to political freedom and cultural change which in turn brings the change in beliefs, customs, tradition, superstitions and makes us accept the changes associated with modernisation and urbanisation which have the rational and scientific base.

Violence against women is a manifestation of the historically unequal power relations between men and women, which have led to domination over and discrimination against women by men and to the prevention of full advancement of women (United Nations, 1993). Traditional philosophical views emphasised men's superiority over women. These views create many types of violence against women. Among these violence some are visible some are invisible, some are named and some are unnamed. Eve-teasing is one of them which may be regarded as one of the forms of gender based crimes against women. It is undeniable that women in India are now living in a fearful time as eve-teasing is on the rise. In spite of the fact that women's rights are the subject of a growing public awareness, eve-teasing still continues to be a prominent form of sexual offence.

Eve-teasing has remained a concern since many years, but at present it is strongly identified, previously it was not named and defined. With the development of the country, people are thinking in a distinctive way, especially the women working in the NGOs and dealing with violence and legal matters brought the issue of eve-teasing in a separate entity of violence. Eve-teasing has become the burning issue for the country because of its adverse long term effects on the young girls of India.

Eve-teasing or non-euphemistically sexual harassment or molestation of women in public places is a growing concern in India and this sub-continent at present. It is appalling and in some cases an extremely perilous practice. This is something that the women are supposed to either just tolerate or are even accused of bringing it upon themselves. But the fact is that the act of eve-teasing is widely condemned and considered a nuisance by the public and is also punishable.

Origin of Eve Teasing

The origin of this attitude probably lies in our socialisation process. From childhood, parents bring up their sons and daughters by two completely different rules of censorship on their movement. One set of rules for boys and one set of rules for girls. This defective socialisation process reminds the boys about their masculinity and their relaxed approach to eve-teasing. Women on the other hand considers eve-teasing as normal, harmless and something, which is often worthy of their gender.

What is Eve Teasing?

The Semantic meaning of crime against women is direct or indirect physical or mental cruelty to women. Crimes which are directed specifically against women and in which only women are victims are characterised as Crime against Women. Violence is also known as abuse and includes any sort of physical aggression or misbehaves. In broad terms, it includes threats, sexual abuse, emotional abuse, controlling or domineering, intimidation, stalking, passive/covert abuse and economic deprivation, rape, abduction, kidnapping, murder.

Eminent sociologist Pratikha Baxi of India has stated Eve-teasing is a euphemistic expression that lives in post-colonial India and refers largely to sexual harassment of women in public spaces, thereby constituting women as 'eve', temptresses who provoke men into states of sexual titillation.

This popular perception of sexual harassment posits the phenomenon as a joke where women are both a tease and deserve to be teased. Eve-teasing ranges in severity from sexually-coloured remarks to outright groping. Eve-teasing is normally meant as teasing a girl or woman. "Eve-teasing" refers to public sexual harassment or street harassment to a girl by a boy, when it turns into a serious issue.

Different Aspects of Eve Teasing

Eve-teasing is not only a social problem, but also a psychological problem. According to Sheila Gupta, eminent psychiatrist, men who harass girls suffer from psychological problem and seek out a strange pleasure by passing vulgar and bawdy comments. (Rachana, 2008). Though the boys consider the phenomenon of eve-teasing as something usual, but according to many psychologists sex, love or fun is not only the sole motive which encourages men to indulge in eve-teasing behaviour. They believe that eve-teasing behaviour occurs due to the non-fulfilment of psychological, social and emotional needs. Thus, social scientists believe eve-teasing to be a result of the frustrations suffered by a majority of youth.

This type of violence has no boundary no definite form, as a hidden way eve-teasing is becoming the grave issue for the young girl which throwing to them in the dark world of fear, disrupted education, social stigma which sometimes bound them to commit suicide. Eve-teasing is a hidden and most dangerous form of violence which many of the close people of the girls come to know when it is public in the newspaper.

Who is Teaser?

Eve teaser is any person on the street, in front of schools and colleges, in the bus, train, lift, shopping mall anywhere teases girls in any form of vocabulary, gesture, or directly physical assault. Among the eve teasers from rich to poor, being illiterate to educated, being young to middle age men are included. They could be teenage boys, traffic police, rickshaw pullers, bus drivers, supervisors or colleagues of the working women.

1. **Teasing by Mobile Phone:** The teaser sends an SMS in an ornamental, romantic and rhetorical language; as a result the adolescent girls are easily trapped with the false appreciation of the teasers. The girls sometimes take it as a love with the boy and become the victim. The boy capitalises the innocence of the girl by using mobile camera or video recorder, some intimate moments or dialogue.
2. **Sexual Abuse through Internet:** In the face book or in chatting young boys and girls are coming closer to each other. Sometimes the boys exploit the girls with some photograph by insert with modern technology, blackmail them, sometimes the boys encourage the girls to watch some porn website as a result they fall victim of the sexual extreme world.

Eve Teasing as a Hurdle

Different types of issues among other forms of violence, eve-teasing is one of them. It is not a recent phenomenon, it was there and it is and it will be but the pattern, definition and intervention are changing. With the advancement of technology the mechanism to tease the girls are changing. The young boys browse many restricted site on internet, adopt many things from there, afterwards out of curiosity they apply the behaviour in the form of eve-teasing to the young girls.

Eve-teasing mainly occurs due to attitude towards girls, family culture, education and loss of morality. Eve-teasing has no specific law because sometimes it becomes very difficult to judge whether it is eve-teasing or not. It is very complicated in nature. Sometimes too much restriction and religious fundamentalism not to intermix with the girls make the boys more curious towards the young girls. From experience and common understanding, some factors responsible for Eve teasing are-

1. Misuse of technology
2. Influence of electronic media and film
3. Having a curious attraction to opposite sex
4. Time passing because they have no job to do
5. Drug addicted due to frustration or bad company
6. Lack of family education and culture.
7. Attitude towards girls and no respect for them
8. Loss of morality and lack of ethical sense.
9. Lack of social values
10. Women's subordination
11. Bad impact of electronic media
12. Lack of security for women
13. Flaws in existing special laws
14. Absence of proportionate punishment
15. Improper socialisation
16. Lack of consciousness about the legal provision
17. Lack of knowledge
18. Girls coping strategy

Eve teasing acts as a control on women by repressing their general mobility and accessibility to public spaces, thereby affecting their sense of personhood and security. As Shah writes, "for women learning to avoid being hustled in the street is as much a part of living in the city as learning to cope with public transportation" (Shah, 2000). The UN Special Report on Violence against Women views eve-teasing as;

"A personal attack on woman's mind and body, instilling fear and violating a woman's right to bodily integrity, education and freedom of movement. It is utilised as a powerful mechanism of control and intimidation, through which women's subordinate social status is maintained. The immeasurable damage to a woman's self-esteem and the subsequent avoidance of public places by single women could hardly take us on the way to achieve gender equality."

Gender biased socialisation and social control at the family and societal level is at the root of sexual violence against women. Therefore eve-teasing can be perceived as an outgrowth of the gender biased socialisation process and a mechanism by which men assert power and dominance over women. There are many facts, which shows that women are not going forward, it is clear from following points.

1. ***Drop out from the Educational Institution:*** As a result of eveteasing many young girls are depriving from their basic rights to education. And ultimately they are becoming burden to family and society because without economic independence no one could be empowered. They ultimately become parasite in nature. Most of the time eve-teasing occurs near girl's school. Adolescent's boys wait there, sometimes for particular targeted girl sometimes generally. Normally the boys follow the girls from their house when they started for school. Sometimes they pass bad comments; sometimes they throw a letter with bad proposal, sometimes the teaser force and threat the girls to make a relationship with them, sometimes they propose the girl for marry. If any girl refuses, they are threat to be raped or kidnapped. As a result the girl has to leave the school.
2. ***Reduce the Mobility:*** Due to threat of eve-teasing young girls are getting confined within the four walls, devoid of enjoying education, entertainment, outside work. By reducing physical mobility, they are losing their mental mobility also; they are staying within a limited and narrower mental state which ultimately destroys their mental clarity and independent thinking for development.
3. ***Early Marriage:*** Early marriage destroys the dream and life of the girls. Due to early pregnancy and too many responsibilities in household work their physical and mental health becomes very week. Neither can she take care of herself, nor to her children and family.

4. ***Psychological Problem:*** Many girls become psychologically abnormal out of fear and social security. Sometimes they do not get support from family due to mistrust. All these causes frustration and leads many girls towards committing suicide.
5. ***Curtailed Education:*** Sexual harassment increases girls drop-out rate from school. Parents concerned about their daughter's honour and safety sometimes keep their daughters at home and marry them at an early age.
6. **Hindered Development:** Eve-teasing contributes to perpetuating the low status of women. It also hinders women from participating in the formal employment sector. As nearly half of the population of the country are women, for the economic development of the country their participation in employment is a must.

Eve Teasing and the Situation of the Women in India

This situation is becoming alarming that, in general, it can be argued that at present no girls have been spared from being a victim of eve-teasing in one form or another. Teasing young girls is not a new phenomenon. From electronic media to our nearby street, we are almost used to seeing girls subjected to teasing. Even middle age women go outside of home, they are more likely to become a victim of indecent verbal comments or physical gestures, anytime, anywhere and by anybody. In the contemporary development context, eve-teasing is being recognised as formidable challenge to women's mobility as well as to the overall development of the society. Eve-teasing causes different unpleasant situations to women at individual and social level. There can be found numerous instances where due to teasing girls are forced to discontinue their education, or to quit their job.

Almost every young girl is a victim of teasing. The most of the people may avoid it as a common matter with young generation. It is surely a social problem. These days, many girls have committed suicide only to save themselves from eve-teasing. That means, eve-teasing in India has reached its maximum range. The teasers wait outside schools, colleges or house gate and as soon as girls walk passed by them they start teasing with ribald comments, smutty jokes, coarse laughter, sly whistles and even indecent exposure.

There are some parents in our society who do not believe in equality of men and women. Girls are taught to avoid such situation and not to give much thought into the matter. It is also seems, that, Women are not safe in any social setting; they are denied free movement wherever they go. They are victimised on buses, busy markets, inside and outside educational institutions, at picnic spots and are not spared even in social gatherings like marriages etc.

Every year new girls are humiliated and brutalised, many are maimed for life, many drop out to escape the physical, mental and sexual torture and some are forced by their parents to get married according to their choice, several suffer from severe stress disorder and even some are driven to commit suicide. Actually, eve-teasing violates a women's right to live with dignity.

An economically and educationally empowered woman is also susceptible to eve-teasing and harassment by their colleagues at workplace or friends/classmates at colleges. Women in Indian society have been victims of humiliation, torture and exploitation since long. There are many records about episodes like abduction, rape and murder etc. of women.

It was not that acute problem in India till 1980s. However, from the 1980s when girls and women especially in rural areas started going out for education and employment on a large scale, eve-teasing with its sharp jaws has started to pollute our social fabric. The women of the world have been exposed to greater insecurity owing to war, violence, terror and atrocities wherever peace has eluded giving place to conflict. The women of the world have been affected more by poverty; lack of opportunities and facilities owing to the innate discrimination prevalent in all societies.

Suggestions for Removing Hurdles

This gender inequality has resulted in eve-teasing and all other forms of atrocities against women. A change in attitude is need of the hour. Any change is possible only when we are able to identify the real facts behind eve-teasing. Educational institutions build human resources and educate the future generation in forming ethics and behaviour, our approach towards the society.

1. Empower the organisation like National commission for women (NCW) so that justice would be delivered to the victims at the earliest.
2. Police officers, especially females, should be stationed in plain clothes at places often in complaints.
3. Special anti- eve-teasing cells should be established to confront the menace in an effective manner.
4. The employers should allow female employees to leave at eight pm or arrange adequate transport facility for them so that they can reach home before it's too dark especially in winters.

5. Parents should be involved into daily activities of children and also provide moral education to them, to keep them on right track. Parents should spend quality and quantity time with their children, as it helps them to share healthy relationship with each other.
6. Ulema also have a role to play in curbing social crime. Besides, delivering sermons and speeches, they should encourage people for setting up of "Mohalla committee" in each and every locality for the every act of arresting and bringing the culprit to book that will surely help in bringing an end to this ever growing social evil.
7. At the legal level, strict implementation of regulations prohibiting overloading on buses and maintenance of separate seats reserved in buses for women would be very effective measure for protecting them from physical assault; police should perform their duty honestly and special police forces should be employed for such offences which would take on spot action and more importantly would serve the purpose of putting constraints to potential offenders. Who so ever is found guilty must be punished. As far as the remedial measures at personal level are concerned, women should avoid wearing indecent and revealing outfits.
8. Co-education system of education should be encouraged and all the male and female students should be allowed and motivated to participate in games and sports, cultural activities and literary activities to release their tensions.
9. Social awareness about eve-teasing should be increased manifold through skits, drama, debates, seminar etc. held exclusively in colleges and universities.
10. Enforcement of law specific to eve-teasing and other forms of sexual harassment should be implemented by women police officers. This would enable the victim to take the course of law without any hesitation.

Conclusion

To state precisely, eve-teasing is not a problem rather, it is a collection of problems that shows a typical failure of the society we live in. Two types of mentality exist in Indian society one which has positive thoughts about women and another which has negative thoughts. Mainly eve-teasing is related to second types of thoughts. They are narrow minded and cannot tolerate progressive women. So they try to create hurdles and obstacles in their path, So that the women get demotivated and stop the effort for their upliftment. This problem needs a collective active role from the entire country in addition to the legislation and their strict implementation.

References

- Akhtar, C. (2013). Eve-teasing as A Form of Violence Against Women: A Case Study of District Srinagar, Kashmir. International Journal of Sociology and Anthropology. 5(5). http://www.academicjournals.org/article/article 13797. retrieved on October 01. 2014.
- Akhter, Z. (2013). Eve-teasing, Tears of the Girls: Bangladesh Open University Towards Women Empowerment. International Women Online Journal of Distance Education. 2(4,1). http://www.wojde.rrg/file upload/bs 295854/file/01_2. retrieved on October 16, 2014.
- Apte, J.S. (1995). Education and Women's Empowerment. Indian Journal of Adult Education 65(3).
- Altaker, A.S. (1959). The Position of Women in Hindu Cvilisation.
- Bakshi, S.R. and Sharma, S.R. (2009). Modern History and Social Status of Women. Jaipur: Sublime Publication.
- Bano, A. (2003). Indian Women the Changing Face. New Delhi: Kilaso Books.
- Bashir, A. and Khurshid, S. (2013). Eve-Teasing and Molestation-A Case Study of District Srinagar. International Journal of Science and Research. 2(12). www.ijsr.net/archive/v2i12. retrieved on November 05.2014.
- Faruq, F. (2011). Eve-Teasing: A Social Disaster for Women in Bangladesh. Eastern University Journal. 3(3). http://gsdl.easternuni.edu.bd/greenstone/collect/2euj. retrieved on October 23.2014.
- Ghosh, D. (2011). Eve-teasing: Role of The Patriarchal System of the Society. Journal of the Indian Academy of Applied Psychology. 37(100-107). medind.nic.in/jak/t11/i2/jakt. retrieved on November 03.2014.
- Indian Association For Women's Studies (1993). The 6th National Conference University of Mysore, Karanataka.
- Mathur, S.S. and Mathur, A. (2001). Socio-psychological Dimensions of Women Education. New Delhi: Gyan Publishing House.
- Pillai, J. K. (June 5, 1989). Strategies for Empowerment of Women. University News.
- Rachna, (2008). Eve-Teaching: Rising Culture. www.inspablogs.com, retrieved on October 23.2014

- Shah, B. (2002). Women Higher Education and Empowerment (Challenges and Prospects). Agra: Y.K. Publishers.
- Shah, G. (2000). Crime Against Women and Police, New Delhi.
- Singh, K. A. and Choudhary, J. (2012) : Violence Against Women and Children-Issues and concerns. New Delhi, Serials Publication.
- The United Nations, (1993). Deceleration on the Elimination of Violence Against Women, General Assembly Resolution.
- Trivedi, J.H. (Aug. 7, 1989). Future Images of Women's University. University News.
- Prasad, J. and Kaushik, V.K. (1995). Women Education and Development, A New Perspective. New Delhi: Kanishka Publisher.

3

Eve Teasing: An Extensive Social Evil in India

Nalini Mishra

Abstract

Eve-teasing to-day has become pernicious, horrid and disgusting practice. Not only girls of the society but even parents feel unsafe and insecure sending their daughters out to colleges and for higher studies. This unwelcome masculine behaviour has caused many parents to forcefully give an end to their daughter's education. Every citizen in this country has right to live with dignity and honour which is a fundamental right guaranteed under Article 21 of the Constitution of India. Everyone would agree that sexual and violent crimes should be brought to justice, but this can't happen when official processes prevent victims from speaking up for themselves, or where rape and violence are constructed as some isolated, foreign event, making survivors too afraid to report their experiences to the police. The mindset, an under developed sick mind, a mind with indifferent attitude towards other's comfortableness, is actually graduated into the phenomenon of eve teasing and when it is reflected along with their sexual perversion, it is taken as a substance having no appeal for serious consideration. Sexual harassment like eve-teasing of women amounts to violation of rights guaranteed under Article 14 and 15. No one thinks that this kind of harassment is directly hampering the social, emotional, as well as moral sentiments of a woman that may even lead to suicide. It's very important to educate people on this issue and create awareness amongst people so that women of our society can live a hassle-free and joyful life without having any kind of psychological mark on their hearts and minds.

Key Words: Attitude, Rights, Perversion

Introduction

Eve-teasing is a term used in India for public sexual harassment or molestation of women by men, where Eve alludes to the very first woman, according to the biblical creation story. Eve-teasing encompasses any act or words by which a man makes a woman feel uncomfortable and anxious. Considered a problem related to delinquency in youth, it is a form of sexual aggression that ranges in severity from sexually suggestive remarks, brushing in public places and catcalls to groping. Sometimes it is referred to with a coy suggestion of innocent fun, making it appear innocuous with no resulting liability on the part of the perpetrator. Some non-governmental organisations have suggested that the expression be replaced by a more appropriate term. According to them, considering the semantic roots of the term in Indian English, Eve teasing refers to the temptress nature of Eve, placing responsibility on the woman as a tease.

Eve teasing is an extensive social evil in India that has taken away the right of women to live a dignified life. The issue has become persistent making women the victims irrespective of their age, caste, creed, and facial features. The worst aspect is that even educated men and youth don't think about desisting themselves from this uncouth behaviour and attitude. No one thinks that the kind of harassment is directly hampering the social, emotional, as well as moral sentiments of a woman that may even lead to suicide.

Basic reasons behind the problems faced by female can be compiled as follows:

1. Gender discrimination in the society
2. Less importance to girl education or inadequate education
3. Disobedience to social values
4. More mechanical way of living
5. Shrinking human values

Difference Between Sexual Harassment and Eve-Teasing

There is considerable overlap between sexual harassment and eve-teasing, with the main difference lying in the intensity of the acts. Eve teasing being milder while sexual harassment can be preceded by a history of interaction and usually involves a known target, eve-teasers zone in on their target on the spot and look for random opportunities. In a majority, but not in all cases, sexual harassment tends to take place in closed spaces and the identity of the culprit is usually known; eve-teasing is generally experienced outdoors, usually in the marketplace or on the streets, and the teaser is an unknown male. In sexual harassment the harasser usually takes advantage of a higher rank, powerful position or physical strength. On the other hand, eve-teasing is almost a recreational activity. It is 'fun' for the boys. It is a difficult crime to prove and the eve-teaser takes advantage of his gender. Finally, in sexual harassment, the harasser and the victim most of the times tend to have an established contact, for example boss and employee, uncle and niece, whereas in eve-teasing, it is often their first and only encounter.

Consequences of Eve-Teasing

Eve-teasing to-day has become pernicious, horrid and disgusting practice. An eve-teased female feels weak and frustrated and may experience depression and low self-esteem. Being harassed on the streets can prompt her to withdraw or become constantly anxious. There are many instances where girls at young age are being harassed, which sometimes may lead to serious psychological problems and even committing suicide. The consequences of Eve-teasing leave untold misery and unhappiness on women which can be summarised as follows:

1. The morale of women suffers
2. Physical and mental impairment
3. Lose of faith in family and society
4. Desperate step of suicide

The Psychology Behind Eve Teasing

Many psychologists believe that sex, love or fun is not the only motive that men indulge in this behaviour. Eve teasing is closely related to the patriarchal mindset of the Indian male. Men are raised to believe that they are more powerful physically and emotionally than women. They feel that they are doing nothing wrong just having some fun. Women on the other hand are made to feel vulnerable and the weaker sex.

Teachers of psychology and social scientists believe eve teasing to be a result of the frustrations suffered by a majority of youth. Disappointed by the unbecoming attitude of teachers and indifferent parents, they yearn for an outlet to vent their aggression and depression. Individuals who do not inherit good values tend to indulge in acts of sexual harassment.

Eve teasing can be seen as a right of passage for boys on their way to becoming men. Considering that sex is not the only motive, it would be reasonable to conclude that the psychodynamics of eve teasing are closely linked to the issue of masculinity and the masculine agenda.

At the risk of over simplifying a complex phenomenon, it would not be imprudent to say that in our country, the construct of masculinity is usually equated with patriarchy. In other words , masculinity is experienced not so much as a set of emotional or behavioural characteristics unique to the male gender, but more in terms of hierarchical domination over the feminine gender, so that the most man gets a socially dominant position over his female counterpart.

Gender segregation from childhood, lopsided parental relationships as well as the representation of man-woman relationship in literature and popular cinema, all serve to reinforce the patriarchal model of masculinity in the mind of the growing male child.

It may appear paradoxical that in a country like India where the mother is generally deified, the growing male child does not learn to respect the members of his mother's gender. But it is because of this deification that the boy finds it easy to slip into the patriarchal mode, for he does not relate to his mother as a woman, but as a helpless and martyred dependent who needs to be pitied and cared for.

The vocal emergence of feminism has also pushed the contemporary male a little on the back foot, not only the women are threatening to encroach on his male dominion, but also because he does not have any idea about how he can counter encroach on hers. So he moves squarely into the adversarial position, something he is instinctively comfortable with and, during adolescence, focuses not just on how he can express himself sexually, but also on how he can claim his patriarchal right. As part of his evolution into the patriarchal role, an arena is required in which his valour can be expressed. Organised sport and cultural activities are examples of these, but require some talent and application. Whereas standing with a group of peers at a bus stop or in a Cineplex, passing lewd remarks, gesticulating lasciviously and generally behaving obnoxiously requires mere numbers, and when the halpless girl is in no position to defend her despite visible evidence of distress, domination gets established.

Necessity of Proper Legislation to Curb Eve Teasing

Not only girls of the society but even parents feel unsafe and insecure sending their daughters out to colleges and for higher studies. This unwelcome masculine behaviour has caused many parents to forcefully give an end to their daughter's education.

Whatever the cause the reason be, there should definitely be an end to this social issue. The simple answer to this solution is education. It's very important to educate people on this issue and create awareness amongst people so that women of our society can live a hassle-free and joyful life without having any kind of psychological mark on their hearts and minds.

For reasons not easily comprehensible, offences committed to invade other's privacy are not at all considered crimes in India. Neither law nor law enforcing agencies does accept the concept of 'invading personal spheres'. The mindset, an under developed sick mind, a mind with indifferent attitude towards other's comfortableness, is actually graduated into the phenomenon of eve teasing and when it is reflected along with their sexual perversion, it is taken as a substance having no appeal for serious consideration. When things go beyond normal apprehension- say, girl who is eve teased, molested, raped, commits suicide, or her helpers being brutally killed by the goons- then it becomes serious issue and everyone would start talking about strong law against eve teasing. Addressing a problem at the matured stage will not help. The persons who are not punished for interfering in others' privacy can easily escape the claws of law too if the girl concerned does not commit suicide or nobody is killed in the attempt of rescuing girls!!! Our law will not punish anyone until a murder or suicide takes place. Till then the state of affairs will remain same. Until our society becomes sensitive enough to respect one's privacy through its strong law, it cannot hope to address other bigger issues emanating from similar circumstances. In European countries, such incidents are much lower in number due to the presence of strong laws which seriously consider punitive action against someone if he/she violates other's privacy.

Guidelines Issued by apex Court

Every citizen in this country has right to live with dignity and honour which is a fundamental right guaranteed under Article 21 of the Constitution of India. Sexual harassment like eve-teasing of women amounts to violation of rights guaranteed under Article 14 and 15. The imperative tone of the mandate of the directives of the Supreme-Court which is binding on all under Article 141 of the Constitution obligates the State Government and concerned authorities to implement the directives in letter and spirit without any exception to curb the eve-teasing :

The following directions are given in order to curb eve-teasing -

(1) All the State Governments and Union Territories are directed to depute plain clothed female police officers in the precincts of bus stands and stops, railway stations, metro stations, cinema theatres, shopping malls, parks, beaches, public service vehicles, places of worship etc. so as to monitor and supervise incidents of eve-teasing.

(2) There will be a further direction to the State Government and Union Territories to install CCTV in strategic positions which itself would be a deterrent and if detected, the offender could be caught.

(3) Persons in-charge of the educational institutions, places of worship, cinema theatres, railway stations, bus-stands have to take steps as they deem fit to prevent eve-teasing, within their precincts and, on a complaint being made, they must pass on the information to the nearest police station or the WOMEN'S HELPLINE.

(4) Where any incident of eve-teasing is committed in a public service vehicle either by the passengers or the persons in charge of the vehicle, the crew of such vehicle shall, on a complaint made by the aggrieved person, take such vehicle to the nearest police station and give information to the police. Failure to do so should lead to cancellation of the permit to ply.

(5) State Governments and Union Territories are directed to establish WOMEN HELPLINE in various cities and towns, so as to curb eve teasing.

(6) Suitable boards cautioning such act of eve-teasing be exhibited in all public places including precincts of educational institutions, bus stands, railway stations, cinema theatres, parks, beaches, public service vehicles, places of worship etc.

(7) Responsibility is also on the passers-by and on noticing such incident, they should also report the same to the nearest police station or to WOMEN HELPLINE to save the victims from such crimes.

(8) The State Governments and Union Territories of India would take adequate and effective measures by issuing suitable instructions to the concerned authorities including the District collectors and District Superintendent of Police so as to take effective and proper measures to curb such incidents of eve-teasing.

In the Indian Penal Code, the word 'eve-teasing' does not exist. Eve teasing is an attitude, a mindset, a set of behaviours that is construed as an insult and an act of humiliation of the female sex. However, victims of eve teasing could take recourse to certain sections of the IPC. Section 298 (A) and (B) of the Indian Penal Code sentences a man found guilty of making a girl or woman the target of obscene gestures, remarks, songs or recitation for a maximum tenure of three months.

Section 292 of the IPC clearly spells out that showing pornographic or obscene pictures, books or slips to a woman or girl draws a fine of Rs. 2000 with two years of rigorous imprisonment for first offenders. In case of repeated offence, when and if proved, the offender will be slapped with a fine of Rs. 5000 with five years imprisonment.

Under Section 509 of the IPC, obscene gestures, indecent body language and acidic comments directed at any woman or girl carries a penalty of rigorous imprisonment for one year or a fine or both.

Suggestions to Curb Eve Teasing

Every man needs to be aware of 'how to treat a woman'. Eve teasing in India has to do with women empowerment and girl education. What's the point of education if the people are not even willing to respect women? The answer lies in changing the mindset and inculcating moral values in our education system.

There are plenty of NGOs in India who are working for the cause of women empowerment. They are teaching women on how to deal with difficult people and how to fight back against the harassment at workplace. Workplace gender discrimination is not a new thing but some prominent organisations are leading the way to rectify the situation. Dealing with eve teasing has been made further easy by some charity organisations that help women with harassment problems. We still have to go a long way to completely rectify the situation.

The following measures can help in changing the mindsets of the people that can ultimately help in reducing plights of women including Eve-teasing:

1. Boys and girls in families should be treated equally and boys should be taught that their sisters have the same rights as they do.
2. Girls should be allowed to participate in outdoor games more freely, thus dispelling the myth that they are the 'weaker sex.'

3. School curriculum should include gender related studies that highlight the achievements of women and their capabilities.
4. Sex education should include understanding the emotions, needs and behaviour of the opposite gender.
5. The concept of 'boys will be boys' should be curbed right at the beginning. Small pranks against girls (or even in general) that are tolerated since they appear to be harmless lay the seeds for much more unacceptable behaviour in later years.
6. Bystanders should not remain mute witnesses whenever any incident of eve-teasing takes place, because such inactivity not only encourages the abuser but also gives wrong signals to prospective abusers.
7. 'Gentlemanly' behaviour should be encouraged and rewarded, particularly among adolescent boys and they should be projected as role models.

Public education on this issue means working with law enforcement officials to support their work with local communities, to help them establish empathy and rapport, so that victims might feel more confident in coming forward. Sociologists can also work to connect community support groups, government agencies, police, schools and workplaces. Applied sociologists are especially adept at facilitating social exchange between different public and professional bodies. We are in a prime position to shape social policy through considered engagement with decision-makers. Everyone would agree that sexual and violent crimes should be brought to justice, but this can't happen when official processes prevent victims from speaking up for themselves, or where rape and violence are constructed as some isolated, foreign event, making survivors too afraid to report their experiences to the police.

It's a real shame that inspite of the amount of development happening all around the world, the so called "civilised world" behaves in an "uncivilised manner" with the fairer sex. What is required is real action. It is now high time to include eve teasing as a separate Tort so that this injustice and crime against the honour and dignity of the women can be stopped.

References

- en.wikipedia.org
- www.banwasi.com
- www.lawyersclubindia.com
- www.academicjournals.org
- www.smartindianwomen.com
- https://aamjanata.com

4

Eve Teasing and Patriarchy: A Menace of Indian Society

Parvin Sultana

Abstract

Eve teasing a euphemism means sexual harassment in the public spaces. While Violence against women has become wide spread, the solutions have often failed to reduce the number of cases. There is a tendency to compare the problem of eve teasing to a law and order problem or to transgressions made by women. What is often overlooked is the mindset that actually makes such behaviour acceptable and something less than a crime. There is a need to target the ideology behind such behaviour i.e., the ideology of patriarchy which puts in place a belief that men are superior to women. This ideology needs to be questioned and countered. The solution for eve teasing must address the misconceptions promoted by such an ideology. Multi pronged strategies needs to be initiated which will not only work on betterment of law and order situation but also change the attitude of people towards violence against women. So change needs to be initiated at the ideology level first.

Keywords: Patriarchy, Sexual division of labour, Gendered spaces, Media, Tradition.

Eve teasing or sexual harassment in public spaces is one of the many menaces that Indian society suffers from. Feminist scholars have long realised that Indian women are disadvantaged by widely shared gender ideologies that restrict women's movements outside the home and their interactions within the family. Restrictions on women's activities are closely intertwined with the notions of honour and shame. To understand the different parameters of restriction of women's movement, we need to start with situating the ideas of private and public spaces. After looking at such gendered notion of spaces, this chapter will move on to the idea of role playing earmarked by the behaviour and body language of both the sexes in specific spaces. Through such understanding the chapter will try to state that eve teasing is not merely a sexual act but a play out of power dynamics. It is one of the many tools used to show women where they belong and re-entrench the gender division of space and labour. Eve teasing is closely related to the fundamental beliefs of patriarchy which dehumanizes, objectifies women and put them in a subservient position. As such, mere laws cannot fight this menace and what is required is a socialisation of values of gender equality. Eve teasing is the manifestation of patriarchy and countering it must start with taking patriarchy head on.

Gendered Spaces in India

Spaces continue to be gendered and male dominance in India is rooted in the gender division of labour. Men continue to work primarily in the public sphere whether such work involves managing agriculture or earning money. Women's work often remains restricted to hours of toil in the "domestic sphere". (Mukhopadhyay and Seymar 1994, Kishwar 1991) Many scholars argue that under the "classic patriarchy" of North Africa, Middle East, China, India, male dominance is rooted in the operation of patrilocally extended households. Under classic patriarchy, girls are given away in marriage at a very young age into households headed by their husband's father. There, they are not only subordinate to all the men but also to the more senior women, especially her mother-in-law. Her work and life is regulated by these hierarchical relationships. Her body language is regulated by the parameters set by the elderly women of the family. These women often act as agents of patriarchy. Their status in family is closely intertwined with how well they reinforce patriarchal values.

A gender division of labour is accompanied by a gender ideology that justifies it. In India, an integral part of gender division of labour is an ideology of appropriate female behaviour that emphasises modesty, obedience, self sacrifice and attachment to the home. Spaces become important markers of gendered division. This spatial differentiation became re-entrenched during the colonial period in India. Victorian views of gender and sexuality greatly influenced new ideals of the Indian women at the turn of the century. Women were "...conceived of as bulwarks protecting what has been seen as the 'uncolonised' space of the home against an outside world dominated by colonial values". The colonial atmosphere outside the home resulted in Indians creating a purely traditional and religious atmosphere inside the home. This meant a protectionist attitude which in fact reinforced conservative views of sexuality.

Colonialism also led to the rise of Occidentalism or cultural superiority and uniqueness of India. This cultural superiority was played out in the private sphere. While British under the garb of "White man's burden" tried to play the inferiority and barbarity of Indian culture to dominate the sub continent, Indian nationalists responded by asserting the superiority of the Indian culture. The domination by British often took political form when certain traditional practices were criticised and then banned. These practices included sati (widow burning), child marriage etc. The British government also allowed widow re-marriage. All these were seen as nothing less than encroaching on the private sphere by the nationalists.

This encroachment actually met with a stronger assertion. There was a rise in the number of cases of Sati. The British's political attack on Indian traditional practices only worsened the repression of women in India and in many ways helped to stunt the growth of the Indian mentality about gender roles. According to Ashish Nandy, the British actually helped to crystallise traditional concepts of women and womanhood. Hence the British colonialism stunted the social growth of women. In direct reaction towards the marginalisation that Indian men felt from Colonialists, they started using traditional gender roles of Indian women as a psychological rebellion to British rule. Women were used to assert the superiority of Indian tradition. This actually restricted women on many respects and limited their freedom.

Women's role was not only politicised to support the national movement but essentially caught within the framework of a patriarchal structure. These patriarchal perceptions were further expanded by the Nationalist Movement. When Gandhi spoke of the woman's role in the national movement, he romanticised their submissive traditional roles. Gandhi however also supported the idea of rights of women. While his support for the women's movement was not informed by a feminist perspective, rather from the point of view of the needs of the national movement for swarajya. The freedom movement portrayed women as the carrier and marker of cultural values. Women became the symbol of traditional values of the country. The ideal Indian woman was 'educated but respectable according to the model set out by government and missionary, but in dramatic contrast to those models, they were also to be upholders of their sacred religious traditions'. Hence by controlling women, Indian men thought they could stop any transgression in the cultural sphere. Mobility of women was to be restricted to the private sphere. One way of differentiating 'our' women from 'their' women was earmarking the limited spaces accessible to women. When women entered public space, the frustration of men expressed itself in the form of eve teasing also. This was because notion of good women being in the private space was still intact. Women entering public space as labour force seemed to challenge the dominance of men in their traditional strong hold.

Eve Teasing in India

Eve teasing is an expression that is ubiquitous in post-colonial India and which refers to sexual harassment of women in public places. The word 'eve' here refers to women and has been derived from the biblical story where Eve was named as the first woman. The term 'eve teasing' is frivolous in describing a serious offence like sexual harassment. It is a euphemism. The term 'eve teasing' is not accepted by many human rights groups, activists and feminists, despite extensive use of the phrase by some media and the police. The reason for rejection of this phrase is that it minimises the serious nature and dismisses sexual and gender violence. Many even find the practice harmless and inoffensive. One of the other problems with this term is that in the Indian Penal Code, the word 'eve-teasing' does not exist. Eve teasing is an attitude, a mindset, a set of behaviours that is construed as an insult and an act of humiliation of the female sex. Eve teasing is considered as a growing problem throughout the sub-continent which ranges in severity from sexually coloured remarks to outright groping. It includes stares, comments or remarks, verbal abuse, suggestive songs, lyrics typically targeted at the girl in question, an unwelcome touch, sexual in nature, physical abuse–beating, flashing which is accompanied by masturbation–or an act of exposing one's genitals etc. Although eve teasing is quite common in India, only one in 10,000 cases is reported. Not only reporting even conviction rate is dismally low. Moreover eve teasing is often viewed as normal, romantic and a moderate crime unlike rape or murder even by the authorities despite the fact that it violates women's basic right to live with dignity. Furthermore, eve teasing can often escalate into a violent crime, such as rape or murder. Eve teasing can at least be the tip of an iceberg and point to a patriarchal structure where systemic violence against women is promoted.

Ordeal against women in our society is manifested in different shades. Eve teasing is just one such phenomenon, which reminds the female gender about their vulnerability, susceptibility, timidity and the tag of 'weaker sections of the society'. Eve teasing is closely related to the patriarchal set up of the society. The origin of this attitude probably lies in our socialisation process. From childhood, sons and daughters are brought up by completely different rules of censorship on their movements their house. Gender inequality is a form of inequality which is distinct from other forms of social and economic inequalities. It is both subtle and direct, and is borne out of the patriarchal values operating in society. It stems not only from pre-existing differences in economic endowments between men and women but also from pre-existing gendered social norms and social perceptions.

Causes and Consequences

Many studies have tried to pinpoint the causes of the increasing cases of eve teasing. The factors which can be said to be mainly responsible are patriarchal mentality of men, improper socialisation, media's role, lack of consciousness about the legal provisions to punish sexual abusers, lack of knowledge, economic insecurity amongst women and a tendency to accept such harassment etc.

Our patriarchal mindset is an important factor that is the source of eve teasing. Men are raised to believe that they are more powerful–physically and emotionally than women. Women on the other hand are made to feel vulnerable and the weaker sex. The discrepancy between the norms, values, expectations and sanctions imposed on girls and those on boys because of the socially structured gender inequality is a critical factor. Men are given unlimited freedom as opposed to sanctions being implemented on women. Men are made to believe that women belong to the private sphere and men belong to the public sphere. And hence women who step out of home are available for such kind of lewd remarks. For men most acts of sexual harassment have to do with power relations or the urge to show women their place. Eve teasing is re-entrenching the idea that women are objects to be desired and explicit expression of male desire is acceptable. Hence eve teasing can be perceived as an outgrowth of the gender biased socialisation process and a mechanism by which men assert power and dominance over women.

Media also plays an important role in shaping our notions about gender roles. The portrayal of violence against women in any of the media–advertising, films, and newspapers reporting of sexual offences–is one of the most insidious as well as effective way of showing where power lies in the society. In TV shows and films the demarcating line between a stalker and a lover is too blurred. In most programmes eve teasing is used frequently to settle a relationship. This reinforces the misconception that eve teasing can be an expression of love as well. Normally the eve teaser is portrayed as the male protagonist who finally succeeds in winning over the girl's love.

If the Indian media makes light of sexual harassment by using a euphemism, Indian popular cinema encourages such behaviour. The portrayal of sex in Bollywood has long been euphemistic. The couple kisses behind a tree, intertwined feet indicate sexual intercourse, a rape is denoted by a flock of raucous birds disturbed from their peace and rising into the sky. The rape victim is portrayed as fallen, devastated, hopeless and isolated. She has only two choices–either she marries the man who raped her or she commits suicide–both to prevent further shame on her family. While the use of euphemisms may be acceptable in some situations such as a private conversation or artistic representation, it can be obstructive and destructive in the public discourse of a serious issue where the aim is to bring about change.

One can see such blatant sexist reinforcement in Hindi films very often. Taking the example of Ranjhnaa, many film critics pointed out how stalking has been romanticised in the film. It completely scuttles the space for consent. Stalking and obsession is dressed up as love. This film which tried to be different and portray the lives of people in small towns again fell into the trap of misogyny. The hero's love was following the girl around, staring at her, holding her hand forcefully, cutting his wrists to force her say yes. Such relationship had no space for the consent of women.

Apart from factors that shape the attitude of people towards sexual harassment, there are some other issues that contribute to the continued problem. The last few years have seen heinous sexual violence against women, one being the New Delhi gang rape case. One of the major causes of continued cases of eve teasing and very low rate of conviction is the presence of very few female police officers. Many studies have shown police officials as being highly insensitive to gender violence. The presence of too few women officials has just worsened the situation. Complaints of eve teasing are not even taken seriously. The popular attitude have often pinned the blame of sexual violence on the attire of the victim. This actually discourages women to raise their voice against such violence.

There is a lack of public safety. Women aren't protected outside their homes. Moreover women who drink, go to pubs are widely seen in Indian society as morally loose and in some ways deserving sexual harassment. Moral policing is so rampant in India and dressing it up in the name of Indian tradition, such outfits re-entrench the dichotomy of 'good' woman and 'bad' woman. So the fingers are raised at women first. In many cases insensitive onlookers expect women to compromise and marry one of their attackers. Moreover too few convictions (as low as 26 per cent), a sluggish judiciary, the social stigma associated to the victim, discourages women to speak out against such cases. However the main cause continues to be the low social status of women in the Indian society. Less importance, value attached to a woman portrays them as lesser human beings.

The consequence of this heinous activity is that it hampers the development of an entire community. It not only is a setback to women who try to break free of traditional bondages and go for higher studies or take up jobs, it also has a long term psychological impact. Women often suffer from self loathing. The patriarchal society often puts the blames on women. As a result the problem is not only the misogynist mentality of men but also women transgressing traditional boundaries. Women trapped in a patriarchal society often internalise male perceptions of sexual harassment and blame themselves for having brought on the harassment. They not only doubt the validity of their own experiences but begin to believe that they themselves must be abnormal, cheap, indecent and deserving the violence that comes their way. Many have opined that this experience have impacted their academic performance. It not only leads to a low self esteem but also hampers a woman's basic right to a life with dignity.

Eve Teasing and Patriarchy

Of all the forms that violence against women can assume, eve teasing is the most ubiquitous and insidious as it is considered 'normal' behaviour and not an assault to females. Every single day in their lives, women face what can be described as a systematic assault on their fundamental right to free movement and right to personal dignity. The sexual harassment that women are subjected to on the streets, in buses, and in other public places constitute a serious infringement of women's basic rights which are unique to them. The only comparison can be with untouchables and the humiliation that they suffer on a day to day basis. Women and Olga untouchables were traditionally categorised together. These groups were the marginalised lot. The social reformer Jyotiba Phule called this category *Streeshudratishudra* and said that their emancipation was interconnected.

Eve teasing to an extent controls women's lives. As Shah writes, "for women learning to avoid being hustled in the streets is as much a part of living in the city as learning to cope with public transportation". (Shah, 2000) The act of eve teasing was to tell women that their place was in home, not in the public. Historically speaking, "Indian women in the 19th century who were sexually harassed in public places whether unmarried, married or widowed, were often women who had broken with tradition by seeking public roles". The women's movement in India also did not try to restructure the patriarchal society. Rather their demands have often been reformist.

Post Beijing Platform for Action (1995), rape and sexual harassment are recognised as inhumane crimes against women at a global level. While Indian constitution provides a number of laws against sexual harassment, the presence of such laws does not guarantee justice for the victims. The interaction of religion, culture and social values in many countries strengthens traditional patriarchal ideals and structures contributing to the subordination of women and an increased rate of violence, particularly sexual violence against them. The promotion of patriarchal ideologies by well-known political, community and fundamentalist leaders, many of whom are involved in framing legal and social policies, is of particular concern.

Within a patriarchal culture, violence by male perpetrators against women is often perceived as an emblem of masculinity. Such violence is deemed indispensable in preserving traditional patriarchal practices and gender roles (True, 2012) through which women are perceived as carriers of traditions and not as primary actors in bringing social change (Yuval Davis, 1999). Such attitude dehumanises women and reduces them to a means to some end. Women are expected to serve certain purposes, being the biological reproducer of cultural purity, even her sexuality needs to be regulated. Those women who decide to not fit into this role are often sidelined as fallen.

Eve Teasing in the North Eastern India

The north eastern region of India which comprises of the states of Assam, Meghalaya, Mizoram, Manipur, Tripura, Arunachal Pradesh, Nagaland and Sikkim is home to a large number of tribes. Some tribes in the region continue to have a matrilineal system. In the north eastern region women enjoy greater mobility and visibility than women of other parts of the country. Practices such as dowry and bride burning are not very common in the region. The socio-political status of women is better as they have easy access to ownership of property. Women play a greater role in the economy. While women are more visible in public spaces and they don't face explicit sexual abuse, the picture is not completely rosy. Women in the region compared to their counterparts in other region enjoy greater freedom, but a closer look would suggest otherwise. Many scholars have shown how traditional and customary practices continue to push women to subservient positions. Even in the face of formal equality of the sexes, women are never allowed to represent the family or the kin group at the community level, they are not given any authority at the social level. Women may own property but men continue to be the decision makers. Even in matrilineal societies, it is the maternal uncle who holds the power.

Moreover the better social status of women is in fact corroded by the violence inflicted on the society due to insurgency and counter-insurgency. It is seen that women are the worst victims of a militarised society. Apart from being a major part of the casualties, women are targeted to subdue unruly tribes. Women's bodies are marked as body politic. Women are also left to fend for themselves and their households after the men are killed by insurgents or security forces. In a militarised society, the case of domestic violence also tends to be higher and women continue to be at the receiving end.

The Way Forward

Eve teasing is essentially a problem with the attitude of people. Deep rooted patriarchy provides a social sanction to such misogynist behaviour. Male and female politicians alike have at times denied the occurrence of such sexual violence. This reflects the patriarchal ideas of femininity and masculinity where a woman's sexuality plays a crucial role in determining her moral standards (Walby,1990). A combination of religious and cultural beliefs reinforcing traditional patriarchal values has led to the proliferation of a violent culture against women. While continued gender violence indicates that current legislation is failing to protect women, sexual violence continues to be framed in terms of women's sexuality, morality and honour relying upon the dichotomy of moral versus immoral women. These patriarchal responses serve to perpetuate such a culture that promotes violence against women.

The first step to a society with no gender violence is to start with socialisation process. Both men and women since their childhood must be spared a gendered upbringing. Essentialised gender roles and the rigidity attributed to them must be questioned. Segregation at school level on gender lines does more harm. Intermingling would normalise interaction. Gender sensitivity must be promoted through education, class participation also.

The next important role is of the family. Discrimination of girl child starts even before she is born. Along with stringent laws, the attitude of families towards girl child needs to be worked upon. Apart from the talk of a girl's marriage, her education and empowerment should be of focus. When women would feel confident about the support of family and society, we can expect them to stand up to crimes that violate their rights. And the first step is to ensure women that they are no mistakes.

Media re-entrenches certain images. It tends to not only reflect reality but shape our views about it also. They can play a pro-active role in promoting gender sensitivity. Films and TV shows must talk about the prerogatives of working women and not limit to the scheming of women in kitchens. They should promote the need for education and independence of women and not portray getting married as the only aim worth working for.

Conclusion

The problem of eve teasing should not be trivialised and reduced to a law and order situation. It is a problem of patriarchal attitude. Eve teasing as an activity re-entrenches the notion of gendered spaces. It promotes the idea that public space is accessible to women only at a price. It is men who naturally should be out there. So women who decide to transgress traditional roles and stand up for equality must bear the burden of their gender. This attitude needs to be countered at the very beginning. And the fight against sexual harassment in public spaces must begin in private spaces of home by instilling values of equality in both men and women.

References

- Anagol-McGinn, Padma. (1994). Sexual Harassment in India: A Case Study of Eve-teasing in Historical Perspective. In Clare Brant and Yun Lee Too (Ed.) *Rethinking Sexual Harassment.* London: Pluto Press.
- Buongpui, Ruth Lalsiemsang. (2013). Gender Relations and the Web of Traditions in North East India. *The NEHU Journal,* 11(2), 73-81.
- Chandoke, Deepali. Impact of Sexual Harassment on Women. Retrieved on 18th Nov, 2014 from Legal Service India: http://www.legalserviceindia.com/helpline/help6.htm

- Das, Jogesh. (2012). Women's Human Rights in North East India. *IOSR Journal of Humanities and Social Sciences,* 3(4), 34-37.
- Ghosh, Deepa. (2011). Eve Teasing: Role of the Patriarchal System of the Society. *Journal of the Indian Academy of Applied Psychology,* 37, 100-107.
- Khazan, Olga and Lakshmi, Rama. (Dec 29, 2012). "10 reasons why India has a sexual violence problem," *The Washington Post,* Retrieved on 17th Nov, 2014 from The Washington Post: http://www.washingtonpost.com/blogs/worldviews/wp/2012/12/29/india-rape-victim-dies-sexual-violence-proble/
- Kishwar, Madhu. (1991). "Introduction." In M. Kishwar and R. Vanita (Ed.) *in In Search of Answers: Indian Women's Voices from Manushi* (1-49). New Delhi: Horizon India Books
- Metcalf, Barbara D. and Thomas R. Metcalf. (2002). *A Concise History of India.* Cambridge: Cambridge University Press.
- Mohanty, Ranjani Iyer. (April 21, 2013). *The term 'Eve Teasing' Must Die.* Retrieved on 15th Nov, 2014 from The Wall Street Journal: http://blogs.wsj.com/indiarealtime/2013/04/21/the-term-eve-teasing-must-die/
- Mukhopadhyay, Carol, and Susan Seymour. (1993). "Introduction." In C. Mukhopadhyay and S. Seymour(Ed.) in *Women, Education, and Family Structure in India* (1-33). Boulder, CO: Westview.
- Nandy, Ashis. (1980). *At the Edge of Psychology: Essays in Politics and Culture.* Oxford: Oxford University Press.
- Panikkar, Sumati. (July 12, 2013). *Of Love, Stalking and Ranjhnaas in Bollywood.* Retrieved on 16th Nov, 2014 from Bargad:http://bargad.org/2013/07/12/raanjhanaa/
- Shah G (2000). *Crime against Women and Police: A Report.* New Delhi.
- Singh, Darshini. (Dec 5, 2013). *Eve teasing in India, Part* 1 Retrieved on 13th Nov, 2014 from Engaging Peace: http://engagingpeace.com/?p=7344.
- Talwar, Vir Bharat. (1999). Feminist Consciousness in Women's Journals in Hindi, 1910-20. In Kumkum Sangari and Sudesh Vaid (Ed.) *Recasting Women: Essays in Indian Colonial History* (pp. 204-232). New Brunswick: Rutgers University Press.
- True, J. (2012). *The Political Economy of Violence against Women.* New York: Oxford University Press.
- Walby, S. (1990). *Theorising Patriarchy.* UK, USA: Basil Blackwell.
- Yuval-Davis, N. (1997). *Gender and Nation.* London: Sage.

5

Role of Media in Solving the Problem of Eve Teasing

Sadhana Srivastava

Abstract

Eve teasing is a very shameless problem in India. It is a ridiculous form of enjoyment for men and physical as well as psychological torment for women. We will not able to solve this problem until women start reacting to it. Solution to this problem is awareness and women empowerment. Media which has played a vital role in women empowerment till now can also be effectively utilised to solve the problem of eve teasing for sharing their views, experiences and suggestions. This chapter focuses on the role of media in eradicating problem of eve teasing from society. Media can provide psychological solutions to victims of eve teasing at the time it can play a decisive role in preventing male members from committing the crime.

Key words: Eve teasing, Media, psychological solutions, victims.

Our Society is suffering from number of social evils at present. One of them is the Eve Teasing. Eve Teasing is a term which usually involves young men annoying or disquieting girls or women by making sexual innuendos against them in public or in work places. Eve teasing is a euphemism used in Bangladesh, India and Pakistan for public sexual harassment, street harassment or molestation of women by men. In this technology based era we can also add the teasing of women on phone or on internet by using social media sites. It is essentially need to give proper attention to these new emerging challenges. Every women in our society faces eve teasing, forms could be different depends upon cultural and economic background of eve teaser, victim and place.

According to Dr Zobaida Akhter from University of Malaya, Kuala Lumpur, Malaysia–"Eve-teasing is normally meant as teasing a girl or woman." "Eve-teasing" refers to public sexual harassment or street harassment to a girl by a boy, when it turns into a serious issue. Eve-teasing is a very common term in India, Bangladesh, Nepal and Pakistan

According to this definition we can understand that Eve-teasing is a big problem not only in India But this is universal problem, especially South Asian countries like India, Pakistan, Bangladesh, and Nepal. Unfortunately none of the countries come forward with true and effective solution to this problem till now.

While legal definitions refer to crimes that outrage the modesty or insult women. In many Indian states the category of *eve teasing* of women finds popular usage. Eve teasing (an English phrase) refers to all forms of harassment women face in public spaces that are considered trivial, funny and part of everyday life, thus acting as normal mechanisms legitimising harassment by positioning the very presence of women in public spaces as 'provocative'.

Eve teasing as a cognitive category and culturally sanctioned practice denotes the tensions that inhere in the manner in which the private and the public as gendered domains are constantly redefined. It normalises and escalates violence against women in public spaces while simultaneously making invisible forms of violence in the domestic arena as the distinction between the two domains is increasingly challenged. (Pratiksha Baxi)

Eve teasing is rampant throughout India for all young women regardless of race, nationality. At some point, spread of globalisation has also contributed to this shameful fact. Western entertainment portrays women in over the top sexual form and that has proved detrimental in case of Indian women. Eve teasing could take place in any form, right from lecherous glances to perverted touching, also stares, comments or remarks, verbal abuse, suggestive songs, lyrics typically targeted at the girl in question, an unwelcome touch, sexual in nature, physical abuse, beating, etc.

In India Constitutional and legal provision for Women is the principle of gender equality enshrined in the Indian Constitution in its preamble through fundamental rights, fundamental duties and directive principles. The Constitution not only guarantees equality to women, but also empowers the State to adopt measures of positive discrimination in favor of women for neutralising the cumulative socio economic, education and political disadvantages faced by them. Within the framework of a democratic polity, our laws, development policies, Plans and programmes have aimed at women's advancement in different spheres. India has also ratified various international conventions and human rights instruments committing to secure equal rights of women. Key among them is the ratification of the Convention on Elimination of All Forms of Discrimination against Women (CEDAW) in 1993 (Aadil Bashir, Shabana Khurshid)

One of the research held in the Chandigarh in Punjab University Campus on girls hostel students by Reena Devi and Anu Jasrotia, they find some solution regarding eve teasing. Majority of the respondents agreed that eve teasing was a common phenomenon of the university. Highest proportion of the respondents agreed that eve teasing was irritating. Maximum proportion of the respondents was fed up with the eve teasing in the campus. The study also highlighted that the respondents agreed that they did avoid going to the market during odd hours. Majority of the respondents stated that university campus should be free of eve teasing. Findings revealed that Eve-teasing was commonly committed in the evening. Further findings also stressed that market area of the university was highly prone to eve teasing, Findings stated that majority of the respondents expressed that the eve-teasers indulged more in using indecent gestures, Findings unveiled that highest proportion of the respondents reported the matter of eve teasing to the university authorities and Lastly, the findings exposed that the outsiders were generally involved in eve teasing inside the university campus.

Reasons of Eve Teasing

Who is responsible for eve teasing? Does only man is responsible? Some of the arguments suggest that girls are also responsible for the problem of eve teasing as they motivate the boys for such acts through their body language, gestures and style of dressing, but such type of suggestions fails to explain why girls of age five years and women of age more than 60 years are victimised of sexual violence. It is certainly an abnormal behaviour by men based on psychological disorder. Women can also be held responsible but their part is limited only on the terms that they usually do not react appropriately to incidence of eve teasing, they usually ignore the issue which commonly motivates the criminals.

Another strong reason for the problem of eve teasing is the structure of Indian society which has always been male dominated. But in the modern era, women tried to break the shackles of centuries by venturing into male dominated areas. Though, we have grown by leaps and bounds yet the most basic structure of society is showing no signs of improvement. Women should empower themselves to fight back. Although, you can always pretend to ignore all the lewd comments but things would be much better if you can just look straight into the eyes of the offender and speak up.

I met my friend a few days ago. She narrated me what she had to endure a few days back while returning back home from office. She was traveling in bus. Suddenly she felt a wrong touch, somebody's hand on her back. Firstly she feared, but suddenly she gathered courage and asked the man how he dares to touch. Public Supported her. Unfortunately, many girls who are abused harassed or teased, very few of them speak and fight for justice.

Mobile and social media websites has emerged as are very popular means of eve teasing among the offenders to harass the girls with being exposed to society. Eve teasing is a very different form of sexual assault. There are many forms of teasing; it could be through words, eyes, acts. All of these forms provide a moment of enjoyment to boys but annoy the victim at same time. Some of the men excuses that women also enjoys eve teasing to protect themselves from being defamed in society, they tends to oppose it, that is why they ignore it inviting the teaser to repeat their act. It is not true; tears in the eyes of a victim are enough to explain the trauma she has faced at that instant.

According to Rajesh Venkatraman (2004), "Eve-teasing is not just a college girl's problem. It leads to insecurity for parents or to even anyone whose loved one undergoes this." This unwelcome masculine attention on women subjects them to an unimaginable sexual pressure. Tucking this issue under the carpet is not a solution. A civilised society cannot afford to ignore such an issue. Eve-teasing deserves to be tackled actively. Eradicating eve-teasing will help women access public places fearlessly and will further gender equality.

Solution to the Problem of Eve Teasing

There could be number of types of eve teasing but the solution to all those is one that is awareness among girls. Once the offenders are exposed to society and family, convicted by police if necessary, they are made to realise the guilt they will surely think twice before repeating the blunder. There is need of strict implementation of laws, which can directly effective in reducing the problem of eve teasing in society. (Desh Raj Sirswal)

Role of Family

Family can play an important role in combating the issue of eve teasing. Usually eve teasers lack morality and ethical sense. If family focuses on its liability and responsibility to teach moral values than half the work is already done. On the other side family must support the innocent girls after incidence. Support of the family members will boost the confidence of girl which will help her in tackling the trauma of girl.

Role of Society

Sometime families come in support of victim but due to lack of social support they cannot carry their fight against the offender for long time. Pressure from close friends, relatives, neighbours compels them to march forward ignoring all the bad patches of life. Now it is need of the hour to change the mindsets of the community. Schools can play their effective roles in developing an environment against eve teasers in society.

Police can play an important role by creating an environment in favour of women by reacting to the complaints of victims in appropriate way. Most of the women find the police irresponsible and reluctant when comes the matter of reacting against the eve teasers. Appointment of more number of women police and deploying them on sensitive areas can really make the difference. Police must behave sensitively when some victim of eve teasing approaches them to file a complaint, they must understand that a girl only speaks up when matter reaches to zero tolerance. Instead of asking harassing questions they should listen to girls and react immediately to win the confidence of girls. One more thing police must know that every time it is not possible for the victim to provide evidence of eve teasing because during incidence it was more necessary to save her dignity rather than collective evidences, which ought to be the onus of police.

Role of Government and Administration

This is responsibility of Government and administration to provide a secure and peaceful life to all its citizens including women who are almost half of the population. First step expected from government is to legislate appropriately and timely. Next step is to do all the needful to implement the legislated laws so that they can deliver the expected results.

Role of School and College

It is very important that school and colleges must play their decisive role in combating the social issues like eve teasing because they have been allotted the most responsible task of the society–preparing citizens of the future. In recent years it is seen that educational institutes are more focused toward bookish knowledge rather than emphasising on the all round development of students. This has created a moral vacuum among youth which is the most prominent reason for increase in gender based crime in society.

Role of Girls

Girls especially victims of eve teasing are the most important instrument to tackle the problem of eve teasing. They can share their experiences with the forthcoming generation to give them confidence and courage to face the nuisance of society in better way. It is responsibility of women to come forward for sake of women.

Role of Media

Media has emerged as a master key to all social problems because it provides a platform to share the information. It can be used to promote awareness in public. Beside mainstream media like television, Radio, newspaper alternative media like film, internet, can also be used to set up an initiative to combat the evil reasons and effects of eve teasing. In this regard a number of bollywood films have been telecasted who executed their social responsibility very well. By demonstrating the image of heroine who fights against the all evil forces of society some time for her and some time for other women and wins her fight in the last. Film directly affects the psychological thinking of individual and society.

- By Creating Awareness: Every girl should be made aware that eve teasing is not a normal act, it is a punishable offence. Women must understand that eve teasing may be the crime of light nature but it provides a base for other sex related crimes like rape, abduction, prostitution etc. Though laws are available to against all the forms of eve teasing, but the need is to come forward to get the offender punished. This is only possible when public have the knowledge of such laws.

- By Bringing Behavioural Change: Media can change the thinking of Individual and society by bringing behavioural change. Everybody in society must be made to realise that every woman have equal rights in society similar to men.
- By Informing the Laws Related to Eve Teasing: Media should inform the women about laws legislated to protect their rights. Especially television, instead of telecasting "Saas–Bahu" daily episodes from morning till evening. Serials should be made and telecasted on gender related issues.
- By Motivating the Girls through Success Stories: Media can motivate the girls by telling them the real success stories of the victims. These stories will not only motivate them but teach them lessons to deal with the problematic guys in society. Experiences, interviews, stories, dramatised play can help in developing the environments in favour of women.
- By Exposing the Eve Teasers: It is responsibility of media to expose the eve teasers by deploying their hidden cameras and cameramen at teasing prone areas to expose the eve teasers who always try to remain their identity after committing the crimes against women. Media can also take the help of common man who can take the photographs and provide it to media for shake of exposing the offenders.

References

- http://www.assignmentpoint.com/arts/assignment-eve-teasing.html
- http://www.wojde.org/FileUpload/bs295854/File/01_24.pdf
- http://www.undp.org/content/dam/india/docs/sexual_harassment.pdf
- http://lex-warrier.in/2012/12/eve-teasing.
- http://www.tarj.in/images/download/ajmr/AJMR%20%20AUGUST%202013%20COMPLETE%20PDF/8.12,%20Reena%20Chauhan.pdf
- http://www.ijsr.net/archive/v2i12/MDIwMTM1NTM%3D.pdf
- http://www.tarj.in/images/download/ajmr/AJMR%20%20AUGUST%202013%20COMPLETE%20PDF/8.12,%20Reena%20Chauhan.pdf
- http://ken-foundation-awareness2.blogspot.in/p/eve-teasing-evils.html
- http://ken-foundation-awareness2.blogspot.in/p/eve-teasing-evils.html

- http://www.thehindu.com/op/2004/04/13/stories/2004041300121800.htm
- https://www.causes.com/actions/1714214-save-indian-society-from-the-evil-of-eve-teasing
- http://www.tarj.in/images/download/ajmr/AJMR%20%20AUGUST%202013%20COMPLETE%20PDF/8.12,%20Reena%20Chauhan.pdf
- http://www.mightylaws.in/799/menace-eve-teasing-problem-solutionhttp://www.tarj.in/images/download/ajmr/AJMR%20%20AUGUST%202013%20COMPLETE%20PDF/8.12,%20Reena%20Chauhan.pdf
- http://www.mightylaws.in/799/menace-eve-teasing-problem-solution

6

Eve Teasing : A Glance on Social Epidemic

Praveen Hoogar, Ashwini Pujar and T. T. Basavanagouda

Abstract

Eve teasing is an expression that is ubiquitous in post colonial India which refers to sexual harassment of women in public places. Eve teasing is an attitude, mind set and set of behaviours that is constructed as an insult and an act of humiliation of the female sex (Ghosh, 2011). At present it has become a big problem across the world, especially in south Asian countries such as India, Nepal, Pakistan, and Bangladesh etc. Present chapter entitled 'Eve Teasing: A Glance on Social Epidemic' encompasses most of the aspects of the problem to be discussed in any burning social issue. Firstly it is having Introduction parts, brief explanation about various types of violence. Below given topics have been also discussed under this chapter.

- Definition of eve teasing
- Eve teasers and Victims
- Causes for eve teasing
- Forms of eve teasing
- Consequences of eve teasing

- Remedies and precautions
- Conclusion

Key Words: Molestation, Violence, Causes, Remedies, Precautions.

Introduction

Eve teasing, very words themselves denote that action or process of teas on eves mean women. All of us are aware that biblical explanation about life where this Eve comes into scenario. According to bible life has been started with Eve and Adam. Whereas Eve was a women and Adam was a man, by whom this present human stock originated and till continuing. All humans are descendents of that Eve and Adam. Here Eve is nothing but a women or young girl. So, whichever act, behaviour, circumstance, affects badly to a women or young girl by men is said to be eve teasing. It is considered as crime. The semantic meaning of crime against women is direct or indirect physical or mental cruelty to women. Crimes which are directed specifically against women and in which only women are victims are characterised as Crime against Women". Clarifying the concept of violence against women is also equally important. Violence is behaviour involving physical force intended to hurt, damage or kill (Pocket Oxford Dictionary, 2005). This is also known as abuse and includes any sort of physical aggression or misbehaves.

As stated in earlier line it is very important to clarify the concept of violence against women because of their nature and type of abuse. For the sake of understanding those are given as below;

1. Domestic Violence

Any abuse committed or happened at home may be called as Domestic Violence. It involves family members viz. Children, spouse, parents or servants. This type of violence may involve different means such as hitting, kicking, biting, shoving, restraining, throwing objects, etc.

2. Social Violence

This is also very serious type of crime as any other. Name itself suggests that abuses committed or happened at society or public places may be called as social violence. Eve teasing is one of the forms of social violence.

In broad terms, it includes threats, sexual abuse, emotional abuse, controlling or domineering, intimidation, stalking, passive/covert, abuse and economic deprivation, rape, abduction, kidnapping, murder (all cases of criminal violence, dowry death, wife battering, sexual abuse, maltreatment of a widow and for an elderly women are considered as the cases of domestic violence and eve teasing, forcing wife/daughter-in-law to go for feticide, forcing a young widow to commit sati, etc., are considered as social violence, which affect a large section of society(Singh and Choudary,2012).

Definition of Eve Teasing

The meaning of the word "eve" is 'First woman in bible: in the Bible, the first woman created by God, and Adam's companion in the Garden of Eden' (Microsoft Encarta 2007). And the meaning of "tease" is 'playfully make fun of, attempt to provoke or tempt sexually (Pocket Oxford English Dictionary, 2005). Tease is 'to laugh at somebody and make jokes about them, either in a friendly way or in order to annoy or embarrass them'(Oxford Advanced Learner's Dictionary, 2012). According to Krug et., Al., Violence against women is experienced by women of all ages and social classes, all races, religions and nationalities, all over the world. It is overwhelmingly perpetrated by men (2002). Some non-governmental organisations have suggested that the expression be replaced by a more appropriate term. According to them, considering the semantic roots of the term in Indian English, Eve teasing refers to the temptress nature of Eve, placing responsibility on the woman as a tease.

Who are the Eve Teasers and Victims?

It is very difficult to identify or confine specifically a person as eve teaser and as victim. Because it is not confined with any age group, occupation, status, business and literacy, it spreads all over the sections of society. According to Irin Khan an international spokesman says the eve teasers are school students, college students, university students, jobless young man, rickshaw pullers, street traders, bus drivers, bus conductors, labours, security guards etc., are involved in eve-teasing. Young and adult, rich and poor, educated or uneducated all classes are involved in this heinous act. The victims are also from various classes like factory workers, domestic workers, students and high class professional women. Eve-teasing may be cores for poor income group, but richness does not guarantee free from eve teasing. (Irin Khan, 2010).

Causes for Eve Teasing

It is very difficult to define causes for the eve teasing because there are no such specific reasons or causes behind it. It is a social issue and one of the type of violence. It is not a recent occurrence; it was in past, it is in present and it will be in future but it has a tendency of changing its definition, nature, pattern and intervention. For example;

Presently, we are living in Information and Technological era. With the advancement in information and technology the apparatus to tease the girls are changing. However it's widened awful implications becomes a social ailment all over the world. It has become one of the burning issues of present days. Obviously it has got more attention from various Social scientists, researchers, thinkers, Law persons, and organisations etc. As a result of rigorous attention from concerned prominent persons and organisations among the others eight major causes of eve teasing found out. These are: family and social causes, unemployment facimisism, open sky culture, political atmosphere, administrative carelessness, social cultural activities, demonstration effect, Lacking of respect to each other (Najneen Akhter, Daily Janakontha, 2010).

Apart from above mentioned causes Muhammad Aminul Hoque (2013) explains about 15 causes which are responsible for eve teasing. Those are;

1. Natural Attraction to each other
2. Lack of religious education
3. Unmindful about religions
4. Unfair dress
5. Open sky culture
6. Absence of family education
7. Political patronise
8. Cultural Aggression
9. Absence of Law
10. Alcoholism and drug addiction
11. Unemployment
12. Lack of Social bondage
13. Computer and Mobile etc...
14. Obscene cinema, drama and songs
15. Environment

Forms of Eve Teasing

There are a lot of ways by which women are harassed. Some of the typical examples would be a vulgar stare, a wink, an opportune clap, a sly whistle, a needless collision, an apparent casual touch, a persistent stare, passing uncouth comments, the purring of an evocative song, despicable gestures, bikes soaring close with hands stretched intending to take a feel of the girl's body, passing by in slow moving cars with loud music with an number of boys inside eyeing the girls in order to measure her up (Hoque, 2013).

We can classify eve teasing into three form, those are;

1. **Physical** : Physical form includes kissing, push away, pull near, Shoving, needless collision and unusual touch etc.
2. **Verbal and Non-verbal** : This form of eve teasing includes whistle, passing bad comment, wink, clap, and passing uncouth comments
3. **Visual :** Visual form of eve teasing includes action of flying kiss, seducing gestures, sending vulgar SMS, sending uneven MMS, posting bad comments posters, photos in Social Medias like Facebook, Whats app, We Chat etc...

In present days whistling, passing uncouth comments and posting vulgar contained sms, mms, and photos are the most frequently using forms to eve teasing.

Consequences of Eve Teasing

It is the most pervasive violation of human rights in the world today. Its forms are both subtle and blatant. Its impact or consequences are multiple in numbers. Its impact on victim or women is in both Physical means physical impairment, even death at the hands of spouses may occur, and Psychological means high levels of stress, even mental disorders may appear. Some of the often consequences of eve teasing are given below.

A. Curtailed Education

Sexual harassment increases girl's drop-out rate from school. Parent concerned about their daughter's honour and safety, they are ready to take any rigid decision like they may keep their daughter at home or marry them of at an early age. As a result many young girls are depriving from their basic right to education. And ultimately they are becoming burden to family and society because without economic independence no one could be empowered. They ultimately become parasite in nature. Anything that results in girls not being educated is disaster for all.

B. Reduction of Mobility

As this name itself suggest, it is the process which reduces the ability to move or be moved freely or easily by a women or young girl. We can find two types of mobility one is Physical Mobility, and another one is Mental Mobility, both are one are in the way inter dependents and having subsequent impacts on each other. Due to menace of eve teasing young girls are getting confined within the four walls, devoid of enjoying education, entertainment, outside work. It can be called as reduction in physical mobility of a girl. By reducing physical mobility, they are also losing their metal mobility. They are staying within limited and narrower mental states which ultimately destroy their mental clarity and independent thinking for any development.

C. Early Marriage

Though the same process in which eve teasing pushes girls out of schools, girls who are harassed are also pushed into marriage before they attain physical and mental maturation. This early marriage destroys the dream life of the girls. Due to early pregnancy and too many responsibilities in household work their physical and mental health becomes very week. Neither she can take care of herself, nor her children and family. Early marriage results in early pregnancy, and it have further implications such as high incidents of maternal and child mortality, malnutrition etc., this cycle continues with no respite in sight.

D. Ruined Atmosphere

Because of this social evil total social atmosphere has been ruining. Social atmosphere such as academic, work and public spheres have got botch for their reputation along with the bankruptcy of moral values among youths, upon whom the future of our country rests; workers of any industry or area, upon whom the growth and development of industry interns nations is relay; upon whom public peace and betterment is dependent.

E. Hindered Development

Many reasons such as mentioned above Curtailed education of women, early marriage, reduction in mobility of women, ruined atmosphere are somehow by products of eve teasing. By which ultimately results in obstruct development of women and also nations. Eve teasing contributes to perpetuating the low status of women. It also hinders women from participating in the formal employment sector. Nearly half of the population of the any country are women, for the overall development of the any country especially for the economic development their participation in all employment sector is must.

Remedies and Precautions

- Girls have to be move forward with enthusiasm in their life.
- Every girl has to learn self defensive techniques. It is a prime necessity for all girls and women.
- Girls should be supported positively by all people and society, at least by their family members. It's very necessary to a girl who is not subjected to eve teasing as well as victim.
- Victim should be provided moral support along with enough monetary compensation.
- Offender should be humiliated in public through this that offender will get on spot and shameful punishment and also brings fear in other hidden eve teasers or offenders.
- Strong law and executive powers should be generated and given to an appropriate person or agency. He or that agency should take these type of issues very seriously and execute them in as much as shorter period, by this offender will be punished in right time and victims will get quick relief.

Conclusion

There is no doubt Eve Teasing is a social epidemic. Being a hushed slayer, it disturbs many systems in society. Its consequences and implications are having unexpected levels of awfulness. Because all over social; systems interrelated and interdependent. At the same time eve teasing is the outcome of various social factors. Undoubtedly eve teasing is a traumatic experience which can leave deep psychological scares and negative consequences for the greater community. There is an immediate need to bring eve teasing as a head of liability under the law of Torts. There should be a provision for a strong punishment for eve teasers. There is a great responsibility on all to keep our own society peacefully and prosperously. Achieving equality in all sense (viz.., social, Economical, Educational, Political, and Occupational etc…) is the prime need of our present societies all over the world and respect towards everybody irrespective of race, religion, caste, gender and any economic status is the fundamental thing to be necessitated now.

References

- Chesfeeda, A. (2013). Eve teasing as a form of violence against women: A case study of District Srinagar, Kashmir, *International Journal of Sociology and Anthropology* (IJSA), 5(5). Pp. 168-178, ISSN 2006-988X
- Ghosh, D. (2011). Eve Teasing: Role of the Patriarchal System of the Society. *Journal of the Indian Academy of Applied Psychology,* 37 (Special), Pp: 100-107
- Hoque, M. A. (2013). Eve Teasing in Bangladesh: Causes and Impact on Society, A Study from Islamic Perspective. The *International Journal of Social Sciences,* 15(1), pp. 1-11.
- Khan, I. (2010). "Eve teasing or Adam terrorising?" The Daily Prothom Alo, Dhaka: June 26, 2010. P 01.
- Krug, E., Dahlberg, L., Mercy, J., Zwi, A., Lozano, R. (2002). World report on violence and health. Geneva: WHO.
- Microsoft Encarta (2007). Microsoft Corporation. See word: eve-teasing.
- Najnin, A. (2010). "Eve teasing-01" The Daily Janakantha, Dhaka: May 29, 2010. Pp. 01
- Oxford Advanced Learners Dictionary (8th Ed, online version).Oxford: Oxford University Press. http://oald8.oxfordlearnersdictionaries.com/dictionary/tease. (Retrieved October 10, 2012)
- Rashed, M., (2005). Should eve teasing go unpunished? Dhaka, Bangladesh
- Singh, K. A., and Choudhary, J. (2012). Violence against Women and Children-Issues and Concerns. New Delhi, Serials Publications, p.13.
- Gangoli, G. (2007). Sexual Harassment Indian Feminisms: Law, Patriarchies and Violence in India, Ashgate Publishing, Ltd. ISBN 0-7546-4604-1. Page 63-64.
- Farah, F. and, Rajagopalan, S. (2005). In Public Spaces: Security in the Street and in the Chowk Women, Security, South Asia: A Clearing in the Thicket. SAGE publication, ISBN 0-7619-3387-5. Page 45.

- Akhter, Z. (2013). Eve Teasing, Tears of the Girls: Bangladesh Open University towards Women Empowerment, *International Women Online Journal of Distance Education* Vol: 2 Issue: 4, Pp: 1-23, ISSN: 2147-0367.
- Sheikh, W. and Mostofa, S. M. (2013). A Study of Eve Teasing In Bangladesh, *BEST: International Journal of Humanities, Arts, Medicine and Sciences* (BEST: IJHAMS) Vol. 1, Issue 3, Pp: 85-104.

7

Eve Teasing : A Social Problem

Ruchi Dhyani

Abstract

Men and women are the two pillars, on which the whole world finds its foundation, so how can we give more importance to men than women? A woman, the creator of this world, always becomes the victim of violence in the hands of so called male dominant society. Rape, eve teasing, domestic violence, dowry deaths, exploitation, sexual harassment at workplaces and acid attack are now becoming the headlines of newspapers and news channels every day. No woman is safe and secure, even well qualified and high profile woman can easily become the victims of eve teasing. "Eve-teasing" is an attitude, a mind-set, a set of behaviour that is construed as an insult and an act of humiliation of the females. Eve teasing is a mental torture and such incidence can happen to any women irrespective of their socioeconomic background. Eve teasing incidences are common to our society and women mostly ignore such incidence but they are becoming the reasons for many other serious crimes also making women life hell. Many women ended their life because they could not tolerate the harassment in the hands of eve teasers. Eve teasing is easy to commit but difficult to be booked. Vishakha and Others vs. State of Rajasthan and Others, Rupan Deol Bajaj vs. KPS Gill, Ruchika Girhotra, Priyadharshini Mattoo's are those cases which remain in headlines for years and shaking our inner consciousness and create a thunder blast in sleeping so called respectable cultured society, the verdict in these cases become a benchmark and resort everyone believe in justice that no accused can be escaped from punishment whatever their status in society, if they found guilty.

Key words: Sexual harassment, Molestation, Politics, Stalking.

Introduction

"Woman is the companion of man, gifted with equal mental capacities. She has the right to participate in the minute details in the activities of man, and she has an equal right of freedom and liberty with him. She is entitled to a supreme place in her own sphere of activity as a man is in his. This ought to be the natural condition of things and not as a result only of learning to read and write. By sheer force of a vicious custom, even the most ignorant and worthless men have been enjoying a superiority over women, which they do not deserve and ought not to have. Many of our movements stop half way because of the condition of our women."

–Mahatma Gandhi

Wherever I go, I never find justice. Someone said she crossed her limits so that she has to pay. Some people raise questions on my dressing. If I talk freely and interact with the opposite sex, does it mean an open invitation for others to harass me? Why every time I was questioned for crimes which I never did. Why society shows me my limits and restricts me from flying freely in my own world. Why male dominant society always tries to cut my wings so that i can badly crash down and never survive. These are the burning questions which this male dominated society has to answer. Why don't men have any limits and put themselves in restrictions. These are the questions raised by every woman on this earth. Why can't I take my own decisions and become independent? Why every time I feel someone is following me and I am not safe. Violence is becoming a part of every woman's life. No woman is safe from violence and as our civilisation grows, the forms of violence also change, but the victims still remaining the same. Why don't we put women on the same level why women get a secondary position in society, being the creator of the world?

Women get respect in fairy tales, but in reality she is standing alone and struggling for equality and respect. Women are more emotional and sensitive, it is treated as their weakness and not as strength. Men tease in such a ways and means by which they can physically and mentally harass her. Women irrespective of their socioeconomic background can become victims of eve teasing. Eve teasing becomes a social stigma, which target any women at any place, anytime, even if they are at their safest place. Everyday sexism', 'sexual terrorism', 'public harassment', 'stranger harassment', 'uncivil attention', 'sexual violence', 'offensive public speech', 'catcalls' have been commonly used as multiple ways of naming street harassment in west. "Eve-teasing" is an attitude, a mindset, a set of behaviour that is construed as an insult and an act of humiliation of the female sex. Eve teasing is an act of terror that violates a woman's body, space and self-respect. It is one of the many ways through which a woman is systematically made to feel inferior, weak and afraid. Whether it is an obscene word whispered into a woman's ear, offensive remarks on her appearance, an intrusive way of touching any part of a woman's body, a gesture which is perceived and intended to be vulgar. All these acts represent a violation of a woman's bodily integrity.

Eve teasing denies a woman's fundamental right to move freely and carry herself with dignity, solely on the basis of her sex (Hindu, August 2, 1998). Verbal, Physical, Psychological and Sexual harassment through some objects are the types of eve teasing which used by accused. Eve teasing is a form of sexual aggression toward women or girls in South Asian countries (India, Pakistan, Bangladesh, and Nepal). Eve teasing or sexual harassment is widely prevalent in India. Dhillon and Bakaya (2014) conducted a study to understand street harassment as experienced by young women in Delhi. Interviews were conducted with 20 women between the ages of 18 and 30 years to understand the nature of harassment they faced, its perceived consequences, their ways of coping with it, and the changes they felt were needed for them to feel safer. Findings revealed that harassment occurred most often in crowded spots and in daylight. High levels of harassment were attributed to factors like prevalent attitudes toward women and weak implementation of laws. Participants saw their lives as being restricted in several ways by the harassment. The police was seen as apathetic, and women took on themselves the responsibility for staying safe. Sometimes, women chose to defend themselves by moving away from harassers rather than confronting them due to fear of escalation. However, several participants felt that staying quiet allowed the perpetuation of harassment. The major change that women sought was more effective police functioning.

The highest crime rate in 1995 was reported from Tamil Nadu (22.7 per cent), followed by Maharashtra (17 per cent), Andhra Pradesh (16.2 per cent) and Madhya Pradesh (16.1 per cent). Ghosh (2011) found that more than 75 per cent of the boys feel that man and women are not equal. Rather, they remark that men are superior to the women. Such feelings are infused by their parents and society which motivate them to underestimate or disrespect the women. On the other hand media, be it internet or television plays a significant role in pervading eve teasing. Media present a woman as a substance of enjoyment and pleasure which pollute the human psyche and motivate the male to indulge in the act of eve teasing. Eve teasing, is an offense which is easy to commit, but too difficult to be booked. Under law the sections which deal with eve teasing are:

Section 354: Assault or criminal force to woman with intent to outrage her modesty

Section 509: Word, gesture or act intended to insult the modesty of a woman

Section 294: Obscene acts and songs whoever, to the annoyance of others

According to National Crime Records Bureau, 'Crime in India, 2010' report, incidents of molestation (sec 354 IPC) in the country have increased by 5.8 per cent over the previous year (36,617). Madhya Pradesh has reported the highest incidence (6,772) amounting to 17.5 per cent of total such cases as well as the highest rate (9.9) as compared to the National average of 3.4.The number of sexual harassment (Sec. 509 IPC) cases have increased by 9.9 per cent over the previous year (10,950). Andhra Pradesh has reported 30.3 per cent of cases (3,316) followed by Uttar Pradesh 26.3 per cent (2,882). Andhra Pradesh has reported the highest crime rate 4.1 as compared to the National average of 1.0

Number of Cases Booked Under Section. 354 and Section. 509 During 2006-2010.

Years	Molestation/Eve Teasing	Sexual Harassment
	(S.354)	(S.509)
2006	36617	9966
2007	38734	10950
2008	40413	12214
2009	38711	11009
2010	40613	9961

Data source: NCRB 'Crime in India, 2010' report

Many women are not interested in reporting eve teasing incidences as they don't want to come in the limelight or afraid to bear its consequences. Islam (2012) investigated on Causes and Consequences of Eve-teasing in Urban Bangladesh: An Empirical Study. Findings suggested that this problem is rooted in different cultural and social factors like patriarchal social system, male's common perceptions for women, conservative family norms, unemployment and illiteracy, cultural and economic globalisation, lack of awareness among women and girls, limitations in enforcing laws etc. After being teased girls and women experience serious social, cultural and psychological difficulties and the study realised it as one of the significant causes for social isolation and self-rejection among girls. If we see back in time we can remember countless eve teasing incidences in which many high profile personalities are involved, which owned a respectable position and status in society as well as in their professional life too. It is really surprising and shocking such incidences are occurring in parties, social gathering, and workplaces and even in houses and many times even abuser are not felt ashamed whatever they behave. It is worth sharing eve teasing experiences which not only rocking our news headlines, but also shaking our inner consciousness and create a thunder blast in sleeping so called respectable cultured society. If we are so well mannered and cultured society, then we have to think why such a shocking incidence occurs in our society?

Rupen Deol Bajaj vs KPS Gill Case

Rupan Deol Bajaj is a retired I.A.S officer. She came to limelight when, she lodged a complaint against KPS Gill, who was at that time Director General of Police, Punjab, that he had molested her modesty by 'patting' her 'posterior' in an intoxicated state, during a party hosted on 18 July 1988 at the Chandigarh residence of then Punjab Financial Commissioner (Home) S L Kapoor. KPS Gill was finally held guilty of the charges. The High court of Punjab and Haryana, Chandigarh on 20 August 1998 upheld Gill's conviction under Section 354 (outraging the modesty of a woman) and Section 509 (word, gesture or act intended to insult a lady) for his action against Deol. KPS Gill was sentenced to pay a fine of Rs 200,000, be imprisoned rigorously for Three months and simply for Two months, and finally to serve Three years of probation.

Ruchika Girhotra Case

The Ruchika Girhotra Case involves the molestation of 14-year-old Ruchika Girhotra in 1990 by the Inspector General of Police *Mr. Shambu (S.P.S. Rathore)* in Haryana, India. After she made a complaint, the victim, her family, and her friends were systematically harassed by the police leading to her eventual suicide. On 22 December 2009, after 19 years, 40 adjournments, and more than 400 hearings, the court finally pronounced Rathore guilty under Section 354 IPC (molestation) and sentenced him to six months imprisonment and a fine of Rs 1,000. The CBI had opposed Rathore's plea and had sought an enhancement of his sentence from six months to the maximum of two years after his conviction. Rejecting his appeal against his conviction by a Central Bureau of Investigation (CBI) special court, Chandigarh District Court on 25 May sentenced the disgraced former police official to one and a half years of rigorous imprisonment, enhancing his earlier six-month sentence and immediately taken into custody and taken to the Burail prison.

Teachers also Involved in Eve Teasing Incidence

Teachers, who are treated equal to God, are also involved in such shameful acts. The government has suspended two teachers from Government College of Physical Education - KS Gill and Kulwant Kaur Sandhu -on the basis of the report of the fact finding committee set up the DPI (colleges), which probed the incident of eve-teasing at the college. Two other teachers, Parabh Sharan Kaur and her husband Jagroop Singh, have been transferred.

Interestingly, Rajni Thakur, a girl student of the college, had charged KS Gill with making "an indecent proposal" to her. When she brought the matter to the notice of Kulwant Kaur Sandhu, a woman teacher, she allegedly supported Gill. Following this, the girl reported the matter to DPI (colleges).

Priyadharshini Mattoo's Case

There is no Indian definition of stalking, as only after the Matoo's case stalking has gained significance. On January 23, 1996, the law student (Priyadharshini Matoo) was found dead in the bedroom of her parents' South Delhi apartment. A year before her death, Mattoo had lodged a complaint with the police about a Delhi University law student who had been stalking her. The stalker was later charged with raping and murdering her and sentenced him to death. On October 6, 2010, the Supreme Court of India commuted the death sentence to life imprisonment. Stalking refers to repeated harassing or threatening behaviour by an individual, such as following a person, appearing at a person's home or place of business, making harassing phone calls, leaving written messages or objects, or vandalising a person's property. Any unwanted contact between two people that directly or indirectly communicate a threat or place the victim in fear can be considered stalking.

Gwalior Woman Judge a Sexual Harassment Case

The Supreme Court issued a notice to a judge of the Madhya Pradesh High Court in connection with a sexual harassment complaint lodged against him by a Gwalior woman judge. In its ruling, the apex court stayed a committee appointed to probe the allegations of a judge in Gwalior who has claimed that she was sexually harassed by a senior judge of the Madhya Pradesh High Court. The woman judge had moved the Supreme Court asking the Chief Justice of India to appoint a committee with three members to explore her allegations. When she resigned, she said that a judge at the Madhya Pradesh High Court had repeatedly harassed her, asked her to dance to a Bollywood song at his home, and transferred her to a remote court when she refused his advances.

Aaj Tak Reporter Becomes Victim of Eve Teasing

Aaj Tak reporter Anjana Kashyap who was reporting on Delhi gang rape case from the outside Safdarjung Hospital where the gang rape victims was admitted and critical. Around 11.30 pm while Kashyap was speaking live three men arrived there in car and stopped their car one of the men who was sitting behind, said something and smiled soon they realised she was reporter with camera and cameraman. So they run away from the scene.

Rinku Das Eve Teasing Case

Rinku Das, a 23-year-old call centre employee in Kolkata, was returning by local train to her home in Barasat on the outskirts of the city. It was after dark and her 16-year-old brother, Rajib, was waiting with his bicycle to escort her home. A group of drunken men started making lewd comments. Rinku asked her brother to pedal faster. But they were not quick enough. One of the men caught up with her and grabbed the handlebars of the bicycle. He pulled her off the bike and sprinkled alcohol all over her. The brother tried to stop them, and they started beating him. Rajib died the next morning.

Statements given by well-known personalities which became headlines show their sensitivity toward victims and civilised society:

Samajwadi Party Leaders

Abu Azmi, the Maharashtra Chief of Samajwadi Party. According to him unmarried women should not be allowed to have sex at all, consensual or otherwise. And if that happens, they should be hanged. This is the same guy who had said that wearing short clothes around boys who are not the girl's relatives should be banned. Samajwadi Party chief Mulayam Singh Yadav is not left behind, who brought joy to all the rapists of the nation when he said in a rally in Uttar Pradesh that boys make mistakes and that does not mean that you hang them.

BJP leaders

BJP MLA from Alwar, Rajasthan said that sexual harassment arises from the fact that schoolgirls wearing skirts inevitably draw attention from mischievous elements while on the way to and from school. They even don't hesitate in making such statement as Madhya Pradesh BJP leader Vijayvargese gave the example of 'Sita-Haran' in the Ramayana - how women who step out of their boundaries are bound to get into trouble.

Former Haryana Chief Minister Om Prakash Chautala

When a Haryana Khaap Panchayat said that lowering the marriageable age for girls will prevent the rise of rapes in Haryana. Former Haryana chief minister Om Prakash Chautala supported khaap decision and said girls should be married at the age of 16, so that they have their husbands for their sexual needs, and they don't need to go elsewhere. This way rapes will not occur.

Pondicherry Education Minister

Pondicherry Education Minister T. Thiagarajan suggested that girl students should be made to wear overcoats to prevent men from lusting after them.

Trinamool Congress Leaders

MP Tapas Pal threatened to rape women members of the opposition in open. The FIR was filed under IPC Sections 504 (intentional insult with intent to provoke breach of the peace), 505 (statements conducing to public mischief), 506 (criminal intimidation) and 509 (word, gesture or act intended to insult the modesty of a woman). Trinamool Congress legislator

Chiranjeet Chakraborty said one of the reasons behind the increase in incidents of eve-teasing is short dresses and short skirts worn by women. This in turn instigates young men. Mamata Banerjee, CM, West Bengal is not left behind. She said Rape cases are on a rise in the country because men and women interact with each other more freely now.

Most Shocking Statement

Ranjit Sinha, head of the Central Bureau of Investigation said "if you can't prevent rape, enjoy it."

We can judge the condition of our country on the basis of statements which are given by the people who are holding respectable, high positions and responsible for the efficient working of administrative machinery. If our political leaders who run our country and also representatives of common man make such stupid and irresponsible statements, then how we can punish the culprits to make our rules, regulations and law machinery so effective that they will able deliver justice to the victims. But when justice came as in the cases of Rupan Deol Bajaj vs. KPS Gill, Ruchika Girhotra Case, Priyadharshini Mattoo's Case gives hope to the victims and gave a slap on the faces of those who think they can do anything with the women and manage to get out of these safely. The political party always used to play such dirty games just to secure their vote bank, but they have to understand their moral duty to think before what they are going to speak as they are the role model of many. No need to follow such kind of people whose thinking is so narrow minded that they always ready to put the blame on women without considering the real picture.

I want to share my friend's eve teasing experience that is really interesting and I salute her for her courageous step. One day she came from, her workplace on her vehicle and she went to petrol pump for filling the fuel in her vehicle. One boy was stalking her, but she thought maybe her doubt, but soon she realised he was following her, but to confirm this she changed her route and didn't take her usual route for going home. She selected crowded market route. She went to a shop and she saw that boy who following her stopped at a distance and waited for her as she came out from the shop he still waited for her. Now she was confirmed he was following her. Then she took her vehicle and drives directly to the same direction where he was waiting for her and she came closer and stopped her vehicle and directly asked him what was the matter why he was following her? He never expected such a bold step from a girl. He was confused and ashamed. He was not able to speak and he just ran away from the site. This is really an inspiring incidence which teaches us how to face such situations bravely and took such a bold step to bring a change in the thinking of those who are not aware of women power.

Now the time has come to make realise this male dominated society, why women called Durga, Chandi, and Kali so men never make a mistake in underestimating a woman and her will power. A woman has to raise her voice against injustice. It is the cruel reality of our society that eve teasing incidence is becoming the reason for serious crimes as in many cases when girls raise their voices against eve teasing, the culprits try to take revenge from the girls and attack the girls as in the recent case a boy did acid attack on the girl as she raised objection on the boy's actions who used to harass her daily. Many times when someone tries to help the victim, they also become the target and face fatal results as happened in the case of Manoj Kumar Sharma, who worked as a technician for Indigo airlines, was returning home at around 10 pm at night. He saw some miscreants teasing a girl, he stopped, intervene and try to protect the girl. One of them took out a knife, stabbed him in his abdomen and fled from the spot. Manoj was carried to Deen Dayal Upadhyay Hospital where he was declared brought dead. Manoj was a real hero who sacrifices his life in protecting a girl and we have to think what reward he gets in return.

Kaur (2014) conducted a study on the effects of eve teasing: a case study of women in Chandigarh. The results revealed that every woman becomes victim of eve teasing irrespective of her age, education, occupation, race, caste, etc. Majority of the women victims were between the age group of 12-25. Most of the women were educated and working in different fields of their interest.

It was found that place doesn't matter for an abuser to tease women. They do eve-teasing wherever they get a chance for this shameful act. Eve teasing also leaves its effect on victims' psychology by making their mood irritable and filled their minds with fearful thoughts and fear of strangers. Many of the victims felt sadness after eve-teasing which also disturbs their sleep. In a few cases, victims were surfacing nightmares at night and found difficulty in concentration while working. In physical effects major complaints of women due to eve-teasing were probed and it was coming to the fore these women victims were facing problems like backache, headache, irregular periods, injury during harassment and injury during self-defence, etc. Devi and Jasrotia (2013) investigated eve teasing in the Punjab University Campus: a study of girl's hostel students. Results revealed that eve teasing was a common phenomenon of the university.

The majority of respondents agreed that eve teasing was irritating and they were fed up with the eve teasing in the campus. The study also highlighted that the respondents agreed that they did avoid going to the market during odd hours. Respondents stated that university campus should be free of eve teasing.

Conclusion

Today women are in the danger zone. Every girl face eve teasing incidence in her life and most of the times remains silent on such shameful acts just for the sake of their family respectable status in society or don't want to become a topic of talks. Eve teasing incidence will not stop until and unless the culprit have a fear in his mind. They should be realised that he must be punished immediately if he found indulging in such activities. Law machinery has to make more clarity in defining eve teasing laws and its related punishments. The political leaders always make such statements which secure their vote bank but they have to understand their moral responsibility and concentrate on what they are going to reflect by their speech as in many cases they directly or indirectly make such statements which encourage the bad culture in society. This is really irresponsible behaviour of civilised person, by doing so how we can expect justice for the victims. In Vishakha and Others vs State of Rajasthan and Others, the Supreme Court has in exercise of powers under Article 32 of the Constitution laid down guidelines and norms with regard to sexual harassment in workplaces which is to be treated as 'law declared', under Article 141. Vishakha Case guidelines now help in dealing with such shameful act and punish the culprits. Eve teasing is a shameful act and socioeconomic background doesn't matter even in the case of victims as well as in the case of accused. Eve teaser has no religion and they don't believe in humanity. They just mentally torture women by their act and making her life hell. They do such acts for fun and by doing such shameful act they show their dominance over women. But now time has changed, women are no longer just victims they know how to win the lost battle and they are just set ready to fight such hard battles.

References

- Ghosh, D. (2011). Eve Teasing: Role of the Patriarchal System of the Society. Journal of Indian Academy of Applied Psychology, 37, Special Issue, 100-107
- http://epao.net/epSubPageExtractor.asp?src=features. Spotlight_

On_Women.Supreme_court_on_ve-teasing_of_ woman_And_Its_guidelines

- http://www.mensxp.com/special-features/today/22414-10-most-controversial-statements-by-politicians-on-rape.html
- http://www.undp.org/content/dam/india/docs/sexual_harassment.pdf
- http://www.youngisthan.in/india/16-most-stupid-statements-given-by-our-leaders-on-rape/6275
- Islam, T. (2012). Study on Causes and Consequences of Eve-teasing in Urban Bangladesh: An Empirical Study. SUST Studies, 15 (1), 10-20
- Kahol, Y. (2003). Violence against women. Reference Press. New Delhi.
- Veer, U. (2004). Crime against women. Anmol Publications Pvt. Ltd.
- Dhillon, M., and Bakaya, S. (2014). Street harassment: A qualitative study of the experiences of young women in Delhi. Sage, 1-14.
- Kaur, S., and Babalpreet. (2014). Effects of eve teasing: A case study of women in Chandigarh. The International Journal of Humanities and Social Studies, 2 (7), 97-102.
- http://zeenews.india.com/news/delhi/airlines-employee-objects-to-eve-teasing-stabbed-to death_896361.html
- Devi, R., and Jasrotia, A. (2013). Eve -teasing in the Panjab University Campus: A study of girls hostels students. Asian Journal of Multidimensional Research, 2(8), 81-94.
- http://www.keralapolice.org/newsite/pdfs/study_report_women/crime_against_women_report.pdf
- www.streetharassment.org
- National Crime Records Bureau: Home Ministry of India 2010.

8

Nature, Type and Effects of Eve Teasing

Manglika Tripathi

Abstract

Eve teasing is the word used in India for misbehaviour with girls and women in public, which includes passing lewd comments, whistling, groping, physical abuse and rape. It is commonly known as street harassment of women by men. Eve was the first woman according to bible so a woman or a girl is denoted as eve and any kind of misbehaviour with her is considered as teasing. It starts with simple teasing and passing comments which are considered fun among the teen age boys and most of the times it is avoided considering it 'nature of boys'. As a result of ignorance of such attitude of boys in family and society they are unknowingly encouraged to commit crimes like rape. In societies like India which is basically a patriarchal society boys are given more preference and their inappropriate behaviour with girls is considered normal or the fault of the girl. Social menace like eve teasing is very common in a patriarchal society as the society is male dominating and male is considered superior in such kind of set up. Inappropriate behaviour of men is considered a masculine trait and it is quite normal in male dominating societies. Men usually tease or misbehave with girls to impress their peer group. This is a show off of power in male world. This is also the side effect of media and movies which portray these as attributes of men and encourage the youth to behave in this way in order to attract girls.

Key words: Harassment, Patriarchal, Preference, Fun, Peer group.

History and Tradition of Eve Teasing

This is the problem women are facing for many years but it is only recently women started talking about it. Whenever any invasion is done in any land the easiest target for the invaders were the women, if they kill the husband they use to keep their women. Traditions like Parda system, Sati Pratha started to avoid eve teasing. People thought it is better to keep women in parda then to stop men from harassing her, it was better for her to die with her husband then to have been raped by the invaders. A different lifestyle was given to widows to avoid their harassment within the family, they were told to live separately and to shave their head, considered untouchable so that no man should go near her. This is not a problem of one particular land it was there throughout the world, it is only that some of us realised the problem before and took measures for it and started talking about it very recently.

It was not very long ago when media and society gave attention to this topic, it was in the 1970s in India when more and more people started talking about the issue. It was the time when women started to open up and more and more families considered sending their daughters to schools and colleges. Some of the women also came out to do job and live on their own. As it was a new beginning of women empowerment in India it also brought along the problem of harassment in public places. This problem grew in such strength that Indian government had to take necessary measures. Police officers were sensitised about the issue; plain clothed female police officers were deployed to arrest the eve teasers and some of the states started setting up dedicated women helpline in police stations and special police cells. After this more and more women came out to report cases of harassment because of the change in the attitude of the society. Women started to speak about misbehaviour with them and men found a new way of harassing her, cases of throwing acid on the face of women who spoke about Eve teasing were distorted. Many women even lost their life. As a result of this women got scared and avoided complaints of eve teasing. Some Non Governmental Organisations took up this issue and started helping the victims in terms of registering their case and getting them justice. It is the effort of these NGOs that 'The Delhi Prohibition of Eve Teasing Bill 1984 was passed it also legalised the term Eve Teasing.

Nature, Type and Psychology of Eve Teasing

Eve Teasing can be a whistle made at a girl, or a lewd comment passed on a girl, or touching her inappropriately in public place or any kind of misbehaviour or harassment done to a girl. If a girl is feeling uncomfortable with a comment or a gesture then it is considered misbehaviour with her. Boys do it for time pass and for their fun, not realising its effect on the girl. They do it to take out their sexual frustration. With young boys following a girl and passing comments on her is kind of a hangout thing to do with friends and they don't realise the serious outcomes of their behaviour. On the other hand they grope or touch women women inappropriately or harass them to satisfy their sexual needs. The case may be vice versa as well but this is the common trend.

In men's world passing comment on a girl or following her and teasing her are considered masculine trait and a show off amongst their friends. Men feel proud to put their claim on women they like and they can go to any limit to get her. Eve teasing is considered a trait of a hero as shown by our movies, over the years our movies have shown that the hero teases heroine and she fall in love with him. He misbehaves with her in various occasions and she gradually find it his machismo, some movies even show forceful kiss by a hero to heroine and she forgives him and falls for him.

The youth and teenagers are fond of movies and this is the message they take home when they go for entertainment. Boys feel it is normal as all his ideal heroes do this and they get the girl so it is the way for him to get the girl. What they fail to understand is the difference between reality and fiction. They adopt the same formula in real life and the girl resists which result into his aggression which causes Rape and Acid Attack. This is not the only reason behind such cases but it plays an important role in eve teasing. This kind of behaviour of boys also depends upon their family upbringing and their friend circle these things also shape the psychology of an individual.

Immediate and Long lasting Effects of Eve Teasing

When a women is harassed in public for the first time she feels helpless and regrets being a women and someone who can be easily used or misbehaved with. "She is at a public place and suddenly she feels an inappropriate touch and she turned behind to see so many people, she has no idea who was it and why he did it but that touch makes her want to wash herself immediately, makes her feel vulnerable and she hates her body for that moment she tries to take her mind of that, but that feeling of an unwanted touch remains with her for long time." It effects the growth of an individual they are scared of everyone, it gives you the feeling of helplessness as most of the times you don't know who the real culprit is and this urge of punishing the person who did wrong to you kind of kills you from inside. Many times women don't say anything because of social pressure and fear of rape or acid attack due to which they go into depression for not standing for themselves.

A boy follows a girl she made it clear to him that she is not interested, he doesn't stop doing so she either complains about it or tolerates it silently. The problem with tolerating silently is that the boy is encouraged to do anything he wants with her in order to put a claim on her and problem with speaking out is that if no strict action is taken against him he can do more harm to her. Now the girl is confused what course of action she should take, most girls take the silent path, they tolerate it for a long time then either change the school or college sometimes even the city to keep themselves safe. Their families also put restrictions on the girls. Some of them even stop sending the girl out rather than raising a voice against the culprit. This is one offence where mostly the victim suffers and the accused is set free to commit more crimes.

What Women can do Against Eve Teasing

It is very important to raise a voice against an evil in the society. If we will remain silent these cases are going to increase day by day. If a women faces a situation where she has been harassed she should complaint about it in the police station. It is also important to carry things like pepper spray or electric gun with them. Self defence class is also must for every women and girl. Schools should give free self defence classes to girls so that she can helps herself. This often happens in a crowded place where no one could know who did it and it is very difficult to catch the culprit in such cases one can be careful and quick. If a woman is able to grab the hand of the person who is trying to touch her or try to kick that person, it may help them. The safety measures are for women to be safe and to react if such thing happens. Our main motto should be to stop such things from happening at all.

To stop this evil from the society measures should be taken to sensitise people, society needs to change. This change will take decades but we should start doing it within our families, a boy should be taught from his childhood how to behave with girls, parents need to check the environment of their boys and girls, their friend circle and their surroundings. Family plays a major role in shaping the attitude and behaviour of a person so it is important to first bring change within the family which would bring change in the society.

Relief Available to Victims of eve Teasing and Law of Land

Many of the states have launched a female cell for safety of women and a dedicated number for filling complaints of eve teasing cases. It is a good way to help a women in need, and one of the best initiative by the government. Law related to eve teasing were not very strong, the offenders were taken under section 354 (for molestation) or under section 509 (of words, gestures or acts intended to insult the women) under Indian Penal Code, both these were bailable. After the Nirbhaya Delhi Rape Case in 2012 the law makers have brought some changes in it and brought some strict punishments under Section 354 A B C and D for sexual harassment act the offence under these sections contain- intent to disrobe a women, voyeurism and stalking, punishment given under these sections includes up to Seven years of imprisonment in some of the cases.

Comparison of Eve Teasing Cases Between Different Countries

India was said to be the fourth most dangerous place for women in the world according to a survey conducted by Thomson Reuters' Trustlaw Women in 2011. With Afghanistan being the first, Democratic republic of Congo second and Pakistan was ranked third among the countries reporting highest number of cases of crime against women. The 2013 report of National Crime Records Bureau on Crime Against Women indicates that India is still not a safe place for women, around 30954 incidents were recorded throughout India with Uttar Pradesh, Andra Pradesh and West Bengal recording the highest number of cases of crime against women, less cases were recorded in the north east and south of India.

Self Experience of such incidence and attitude of family and society towards such incidences:

Almost every girl in India has experienced incidence of eve teasing. Being a girl I have also experienced it many a times during travelling, in a movie hall, in crowded market, at railway station, in school and college at every level of my life. I would like to tell one incidence when I was going to college in an auto rickshaw and the man sitting next to me (who was around 50 year old) tried to touch me, at first I thought it was by mistake then he repeated it again, by that time I was sure that it was purposive so I hit him hard with my elbow and said that behave yourself and sit properly and also told the auto driver to stop the auto. The auto driver stopped the vehicle and asked that man to sit at seat with him. This was one of the many incidences happened over the time, I made it a point to raise my voice most of the time but it was difficult to say anything when this happens in a crowded place and you don't know who has done it with you. A feeling of anger and frustration is there when you are not able to say anything and not able to punish the person who did wrong to you. The sad part is that when you tell such incidence to your friends or family members they will tell you to behave properly or wear decent clothes or not to go to such places or not to travel by public mode rather than complaining about the incidence.

Our country has become so unsafe for women that women are not able to walk outside freely. My friend use to live in Delhi and one day she just came out of her building and a drunken man came from back and grabbed her, she shouted and tried to kick him so people came to her rescue and took the man to police station. Sadly that man got free on bail and her case is still pending in court.

Even today if a girl is humiliated and misbehaved in public people will say it must be her fault she must be wearing short dress or must be encouraging the boys. It is the time when we should start teaching discipline to our boys; boys need to be taught not to misbehave with girls. Feminism and equality of gender is the need of the society today and parents need to teach their children what is wrong. They have to treat both son and daughter equally.

Suggestions for Eradication of the Problem

It is not easy to eradicate a social evil like this in days or months. Eradication of such problem will take years and it will only happen when thinking of society will change and equality is maintained in the society. I see in many families even today it is ok for boys to wear shorts and boxers and if the girl wears it, she is asked to wear full clothes, a boy is allowed to attend late night parties with friends and girls are restricted to party only till a specific time and be inside the house by evening. It is normal for a boy to have a girl friend but it is a crime for a girl to have a boy friend.

In conclusion I would like to say that the double standard of society needs a change and it has to start from the family itself. Schools should take classes on gender sensitivity and it should be a compulsory topic for all the students. Strict punishment should be given to the accused so that he is not able to repeat it again. A person's character certificate and a background check should be done before giving him any job. Laws should be strict for the accused and the case should not be stretched for long. Decision should be in appropriate time to avoid another incidence of misbehaviour by the same person. Recently because of ignorance of the above mentioned things a driver was given job by Uber Cab who was already a rape accused and so he dared to commit a rape again with customer. Elongated justice is no justice, justice should be timely and strict to make the person regret his doings and scare the hell out of others who are thinking of committing similar kind of crimes.

References

- Wikipedia links for eve teasing and Nirbhaya law.
- National Crime Records Bureau India website

9

Why Do They Do It ?

Amit Kumar Dutta

Abstract

Eve teasing is a social crime perpetrated against women. It is an expression of a man's desire to subdue and inflict humiliation on women through different indecent and un - acceptable activities. This paper attempts to understand the psychology of the eve teasers especially in the Indian context and identifies different reasons which are responsible for the development of such a negative attitude. The paper also discusses the psychological impact of eve teasing on the victim and the legal remedies available to the affected. Even though eve teasing cannot be completely eradicated from society, the paper concludes that proper education and counselling in addition to strict laws are important measures that can help us address this unhealthy social problem.

Key Words: Eve teasing, Perpetrate, Women, Psychology, Education, Counselling

Introduction

Can anything be more shameful than eve teasing? The answer definitely has to be no. Nature has created woman to nurture human civilisation and provide companionship and emotional support to man. Women during the ancient period were respected and occupied an important position in society. However, their position declined with the passage of time as they were made an object of exploitation, subjugation, humiliation and other forms of deprivation by men.

Eve teasing is a social crime and a blot on human civilisation. According to the views of the UN Special Rapporteur on Violence against Women, Eve Teasing is :

"A personal attack on women's minds and bodies, instilling fear and violating a woman's right to bodily integrity, education and freedom of movement. It is utilised as a powerful mechanism of control and intimidation, through which women's subordinate social status is maintained. The immeasurable damage to a woman's self esteem and the subsequent avoidance of public places by single women could hardly take us on the way to addressing gender equality."

There are many ways through which this shameful act is perpetrated such as whistling, hooting, passing lewd comments, singing derogatory songs, etc. The objective behind these activities is to lower the dignity of women by making them feel inferior. Eve teasing is a reflection of a sick society because such a shameful and un-dignified act can never be acceptable to any civilised society or state. It is a complex social problem because there are myriad reasons why the perpetrators of eve teasing indulge in such an act. However, it should be the endeveour of every enlightened and progressive society to find a solution for this complex social problem.

Literature Study

In a Study Done by :

1. Deepa Ghosh to understand the attitude towards eve teasing among under graduate students, the author found out that there were some social factors such as patriarchal mindset of the boys, improper socialisation, media's role, lack of consciousness about the legal provisions, which are responsible for eve teasing behaviour among the youth.
2. Reena Devi and Anu Jasrotia have studied violence against women among the girl's hostel students of Punjab University, Chandigarh with special reference to eve teasing. The authors concluded that eve teasing was a common phenomenon in the university.

3. Eve teasing as a form of violence against women in the district of Srinagar by Chesfeeda Akhtar, the author has concluded that there is a correlation between eve teasing and the profile of its perpetrators, and, certain psychological factors are responsible for this kind of violence.
4. Kuruvilla and Suhara to find out the response patterns of girl students to eve teasing in the campus of University of Calicut, Kerala, the authors found that the respondents encountered many attempts of eve teasing in their life. Lack of respect for women and non existence of strict laws for offenders were the reasons that contributed to eve teasing.
5. Katherine Anne Montano Good, the author has made a study on eve teasing and gender equality in the post colonial framework of India and traces the origin of the present problem of eve teasing in Indian society to political and cultural perception of women and their role during colonialism, nationalism, partition and the modern time.
6. Eve teasing is just not a social problem in our country but also in our neighbouring country Bangladesh. Dr Z Akhtar has discussed the role of open and distance education in empowering Bangladeshi women, who are silent victims of eve teasing.
7. On violence against women, the author Manju has concluded that the impact of psychological violence can destabilise a woman mentally and restrict her social mobility.
8. In an article titled SC on Eve Teasing: Human Rights of women in India, the author Dr Mukesh Yadav has discussed some legal issues concerning eve teasing and voiced concern for protecting the dignity of women.

Research Methodology

This paper has been prepared by referring to secondary sources of information such as journals, articles, etc.

The Psychology of Eve Teasers

Eve teasing is a complex social problem and a challenge to civilised human society. It begins with unwanted glares and attention of males towards the opposite sex. Sometimes females ignore the so called unwanted attention and glares but things take an ugly turn when such a thing is repeated continuously. The motive behind the unwanted attention is to outrage the modesty of women and make them feel as objects of sex. No women are safe from the glares of perverted men. Therefore, what might begin as an innocent look may take the form of sexual harassment or eve teasing?

The reasons why eve teasers perpetrate such a shameful act are not always easy to understand. Peeping into an eve teasers mind can lead us to grey areas not black and white. Therefore, in order to understand the psychology that motivates eve teasers to inflict humiliation on our mother's and sister's, we need to understand the equation of man and woman relation and the social dynamics that is built around it.

Nature has created woman to complement man, not to compete against him. The secret to achieving social harmony lies in a balance in man woman relationship. This is possible when each gender have respect and admiration for each other. Even though society have accepted the inherent limitations which a woman has for her biological differences with man, a man's attitude towards a woman is also dictated by the norms and ethos of the society to which he belongs. Therefore, even though the problem of eve teasing exists by and large in every society, its magnitude differs from one society to another.

The position of women is deplorable in many Asian and African countries. There are frequent incidents of crime against women in many South Asian countries. In the Indian context, eve teasing is certainly a matter of great concern. Even though there are laws to punish those who outrage the modesty of women, the victims of eve teasing prefer to remain silent without complaining it to the law enforcing authorities. The Supreme Court has laid down certain guidelines in the Vishaka case to prevent sexual harassment of women at workplace. There are legal provisions to punish eve teasing such as Section 294,509 and 354 of Indian Penal Code.

To understand the problem of eve teasing and the psychology of the eve teasers in the Indian context, a proper understanding of the Indian society in the pre and post colonisation period is required. The Indian society since ancient period and before colonisation by the British was village centric. In villages, due to several orthodox practices and customs, women were not allowed to step out from the corridors of their household. They were denied freedom of movement and would have to surrender to the diktats of men. Several primitive customs such as sati, child marriage, pardah, etc which was detrimental to the dignity and self esteem of women existed. The social structure in India changed after the advent of the English. The English tried to create a feeling of inferiority of Indian culture in the minds of the Indians. Moreover, many social customs and taboos were challenged. Therefore, the Indian men found themselves in a situation, where they could not freely express their stereo–typed mentality against women. This created much social tension leading to violence and increase in crime against women. Moreover, due to the patriarchal nature of Indian society, family and social customs create a feeling of inferiority complex among women. In Indian society, unfortunately, even today, men get undue preferences for their gender.

The patriarchal system is responsible to a large extent in encouraging eve teasing or sexual harassment in the Indian context. Undeniably, the Indian society is biased in favour of men. Right from the moment a woman is conceived till her death, a woman in our country have to face many humiliation and myriad forms of exploitation. The birth of a daughter is not considered auspicious because an average Indian family would like to see the birth of a male child. After birth, a woman is made to feel inferior and dependent. She has to depend on her father, brother, husband and son at different stages of her life. This is why, female infanticide is still practiced in certain parts of the country. Even the woman who gives birth to a baby child is neglected. She is not provided with nutritious food and proper care and as a result, the child born suffers from many ailments. Moreover, different types of crime such as torture, domestic violence, murder, abduction, rape, trafficking, etc are being perpetrated against women and the perpetrators of such criminal acts manage to escape and continue with their shameful acts with relative impunity.

The average women in India still do not enjoy the freedom of choice. Except for a few em–powered women in the upper echelons of the society, women in general in the Indian society are compelled to be dependent on men. Everything that a woman does, what kind of clothes she should wear, where she should go, whom she should and should not talk to, etc are dependent on a male's wish. This attitude is responsible in developing a mindset among Indian men that a woman should always be under his thumb and her duty is to satisfy his carnal pleasures whenever he wants. Sometimes, poor upbringing of children in a family and lack of socialisation is responsible in encouraging eve teasing. Young men who are not taught about the ways of behaving with a woman, grow up with a distorted mindset about women.

Unfortunately, despite sixty seven years of independence, we have not been able to create a just and equal society. The fruits of economic development have not reached to every segment of the society and, therefore, despite all tall claims of our progress and development since independence, we live in a skewed society, where the gulf between the rich and the poor is enormous. One of the demerits of India's current dogged pursuit of neo-liberal economic policies is the neglect of the rural and backward areas. The consequence of this is migration of people from villages and backward areas to cities and urban areas. Even though urbanisation is an in – evitable consequence of a country's economic development, it has its own share of problems. More often than not, people who migrate to urban cities are unable to settle themselves for want of land, housing facilities, etc. Therefore, the only destination for them is slums where the living conditions are unsuitable for a civilised life. The migrants who have to negotiate cramped spaces for shelter are not able to adjust to the ways of modern city life. Unable to find proper employment and frustrated with their existence, they easily take to crime. The rural migrants, who are not always comfortable with what they see of modern city women, develop wrong perceptions about them and end up teasing or molesting them.

Indian society is developing and we are trying hard to embrace the western lifestyle in our everyday practices. Since the income of an average Indian has increased compared to what it was sixty seven years back, consumerism is gaining ground in Indian society. Consumerism, which is an outcome of globalisation, is a western philosophy where individuals spend lavishly behind consumer items even though such expenses may be beyond their means. Unfortunately, due to commerce driven consumerism, women have been converted into commodities. Indian society traditionally has never been a materialistic society because India is a land of spiritualism. In order to gain cheap publicity, improve bottom line and better market share, companies do not hesitate in portraying women as objects of sex and lust. Sometimes, in order to sell certain products companies depict women in such a manner that titillates the fantasies of men. The impact of consumerism has been the deterioration of the dignity of women. Women traditionally are worshipped in India as mother goddesses. An average Indian male is not used to seeing women in miniskirts or bikini and such depiction of women through commercials and films have perverted their mind. The consequence is increase in cases of eve teasing and sexual molestation.

Films and the media, especially Hindi movies have a profound impact on the socio-cultural life of an Indian. Hindi movies, which are considered to be opium of the masses, have a strong effect on the youth. Unfortunately, today Hindi movies have become one of the sources for the development of wrong notions and perverted ideas about women in the youth's mind. The portrayal of women in the movies of the 1950's, 60's and 70's would focus on strong character roles. It is very difficult for a movie lover to forget the role of the late Nargis Dutt in Mother India, where she is shown playing the role of a charming and principled mother, even going to the extent of killing her son to save the dignity of a woman. Heroines of that generation such as Asha Parekh, Hema Malini, Waheeda Rahaman, Vyjantimala besides Nargis Dutt potrayed powerful women characters depicting the true nature of an Indian woman. However, with the passage of time, specially the middle and late 1990's and 2000's, the role of women in Hindi movies became confined to objects of sex and lust, meant to titillate the fantasies of young minds. Madhuri Dixit's famous ek,do teen number in Tezab, Kimi Katkar's dance in Jhuma, Chuma de de in Hum, Raveena Tandon's seductive dance in a wet saree in Mohra, a drunk Kajol dancing in rain to seduce Shah Rukh Khan in Dilwale Dulhaniya Le Jayenge, Katrina Kaif's dance numbers in Chikni Chameli and Sheila ki Jawani, etc are some examples from Hindi movies whose ultimate objective is to whet the fantasies of young minds and create in them a distorted idea about women.

A shameful and worrying trend noticeable in Hindi movies since middle of the First Decade of 21st Century is blatant depiction of women's flesh. It seems the censor board is not concerned about the impact of such movies on the society, specially the youth, and therefore, movies with erotic and objectionable contents are released with A or U/A certificate. As for example, certain scene from the movie Murder, where Mallika Sherawat is shown in certain adult scenes is enough to explode the erotic fantasies of a young mind. The movie Murder seems to have set a trend for such adult content movies and many such movies like Hate Story, Murder Two, Khwaish, Ab Bas, etc have been released where there is blatant portrayal of sex and women skin. Moreover, actors like Sunny Leone have gone a step ahead in encouraging the erotic fantasies of the youth through her skin shows in Jism 2, Ragini MMS 2, JackPot, etc.

Today, due to the rapid proliferation of the information and communication technology, pornography and blue films are easily available to the common man and the sad part of the story is despite legal restrictions, a large majority of the viewers are men who are below eighteen years of age. Advancements in mobile technology has made it possible to download pornography with relative ease and there are many internet sites where blue films are easily available. The impact of pornography on young, immature minds is disastrous and such things definitely motivate today's youth to commit many heinous crimes against women.

Even the media is competing to capture youth attention through the depiction of women in skimpily clad clothes in the advertisements of condoms and alcohol. There are certain advertisements which are aired on television having erotic or adult contents. For example, Sunny Leone's endorsement of Mankind condoms, the use of Axe deodorants to seduce women, etc are some advertisements which can easily pervert a man's mind. Practically, all of us are surrounded by the media and therefore the media's projection of certain things about women which the Indian society is still uncomfortable with can definitely have negative consequences.

The cumulative effect of the impact of movies and the media is the degeneration of the youth's character beyond imagination which is blatantly expressed through sexual molestation of girls and women.

Impact of Eve Teasing on the Victim

Eve teasing like any other crime leaves behind a serious impact on the psychology of the victim. Eve teasing is an attack on a women's human right to lead a life of dignity without any kind of fear or provocation and challenges gender equality in society. Different scholars have conducted research on the impact of eve teasing on the psychology of women and have concluded that it has disastrous long term consequences. Unfortunately, like other crimes eve teasing is difficult to prove because it does not leave behind any physical scars. However, the impact of eve teasing depends on the period of time. It means eve teasing has both short term and long term effect on the victim. In the short term, the victim develops a feeling of guilt, avoids places and people, feels afraid of going out of home, develops a fear psychosis, etc. In the long term, the victim develops many psychological problems like loss of mental balance, becomes dumb, depressed, retires from public life, develops suicidal instincts and other forms of psychological ailments. If the victim is unable to recover from the long term consequences, she might make an attempt to end her life. Therefore, the impact of eve teasing, whether short term or long term, has serious psychological impact on the victim which may even cost her life.

Legal Remedy

Eve teasing is a shameful social crime. An important reason why the perpetrators of eve teasing get away and repeat their act of cowardice is that the victim in most cases do not complain to the police or seek legal remedy.

This definitely encourages the eve teasers to continue molesting women without any fear of consequences. Even though eve teasing is difficult to prove, every victim of this shameful crime should come forward and report their complain to the police in order to get the guilty punished. Article 21 of the Constitution of India guarantees every citizen the fundamental right to lead a life of dignity and honour and therefore, it is the responsibility of the state and the law enforcing authorities to bring the guilty to book and punish the eve teasers.

Even though eve teasing is not defined by the Indian Penal Code (IPC), there are three sections which deal with the crime of eve teasing. They are Sections 509, 294 and 354.

According to Section 509 of IPC, word, gesture or act intended to insult the modesty of any woman, utters any word, makes any sound or gesture, or exhibits any object, intending that such word or sound shall be heard, or that such gesture or objects shall be seen, by such woman, or intrudes upon the privacy of such woman, shall be punished with simple imprisonment for a term which may extend to one year, or with fine, or with both.

Section 294 of IPC, deals with obscene acts and songs. Whoever to the annoyance of others :

1. Does any obscene act in any public place, or
2. Sings, recites or utters any obscene song, balled or words, in or near any public place, shall be punished with imprisonment of either description for a term which may extend to three months, with fine, or with both.

Section 354 of IPC, deals with the assault or criminal force to woman with intent to outrage her modesty. Whoever assaults or uses criminal force to any woman, intending to outrage or knowing it to be likely that he will thereby outrage her modesty, shall be punished with imprisonment of either description for a term which may extend to two years, or with fine or with both.

Even though there are no uniform laws in India to punish eve teasing, Tamil Nadu is the first state in the country to bring an ordinance, namely, the Tamil Nadu Prohibition of Eve Teasing Ordinance, 1998, which later became an Act, namely, the Tamil Nadu Prohibition of Eve Teasing Act, 1998. Moreover, the Supreme Court has laid down certain guidelines on sexual harassments in Vishaka and Others v State of Rajasthan, (1977) 6 SCC 241. Moreover, it has explained the meaning of 'modesty' in relation to woman in Rupan Deol Bajaj and Another v K.P.S. Gill; (1995) 6 SCC 194. The Parliament is currently considering the Protection of Women against

Sexual Harassment at Workplace Bill, 2010, which is intended to protect female workers in most work places.

Conclusion

Eve teasing is a complex social problem without any quick fix solution. It is not realistic to think that eve teasing can be completely eradicated from society. The ingenious mind of men will find some new form of mischief. Eve teasing is a disgrace to civil society. Law can punish the eve teasers but cannot cure their perverted psychology. Before finding a solution, we need to go to the root of the problem of eve teasing. The perpetrators of eve teasing are perverted men suffering from some kind of negative psychology about women. Treating eve teasers as mere criminals and putting them behind bars will not help us in achieving a solution. Society should take responsibility for the behaviour of the so called 'Road Romeos' and come forward to root out this social malice. The foundation of eve teasing lies in the unequal treatment of men and women since childhood. The patriarchal Indian system can also be held responsible.

It is through proper education, guidance and counselling that we can bring on track our misguided brothers and friends. There is a serious need to revamp our present education system because it does not stress on developing a holistic human personality. More emphasis needs to be put on value based education, inculcating respect for women, the ability to think beyond text books, syllabus and examinations and relating one's knowledge with the happenings in society. Moreover, time has come for our existing family system to shed certain conservative practices concerning women and allow space for socialisation between boys and girls. Besides, parents need to be particular about giving proper guidance to boys during their formative years regarding their behaviour with girls. Boys should be taught to respect their opposite gender and that they are not creatures from an alien planet.

The laws relating to punishment for eve teasing should be made stricter and should be given more teeth. Even though there are specific provisions in the Indian Penal Code for punishing eve teasing, unfortunately they are like toothless tigers. Punishment of the guilty is subject to availability of proof, which is not always easy to establish. Moreover, the legal framework in our country is not adequate to punish eve teasers as there is no uniformity in the laws. So far, only the state of Tamil Nadu has put in place an Act to punish eve teasing without the other states following suit. Only through strict laws and their speedy enforcement we can deter the eve teasers from perpetrating such shameful crime.

The policing system should be made more sensitive to the problem of eve teasing. More female police should be deployed in civil dress in public places, parks, shopping malls, near cinema halls and restaurants, busy markets, railway stations, bus stands, schools, colleges, universities, etc. to nab the eve teasers. A vigilant eye should also be kept on different cyber activities which are responsible for corrupting the youth. Moreover, the police should also coordinate with the civil society and NGOs to create awareness about eve teasing through road shows, seminars and discussions.

The entire civil society should rise up to launch a movement to liberate the society from the stigma of eve teasing.

References

- Ghosh, Deepa. (2011). Eve Teasing: Role of the Patriarchal System of the Society. *Journal of the Indian Academy of Applied Psychology,* 2011, 100 - 107
- Devi, Reena, Jasrotia, Anu. (2013). Eve Teasing in the Punjab University Campus: A study of Girls Hostel students. Asian *Journal of Multidimensional Research,* 2013
- Akhtar, Chesfeeda. (2013). Eve teasing as a form of violence against women: A case study of District Srinagar, Kashmir. *International Journal of Sociology and Anthropology,* 2013, 168 - 178
- Kuruvilla, Molly, Suhara, Fatimath. (2014). Response Patterns of Girl Students to Eve Teasing : An Empirical Study in a University Setting. *International Journal of Education and Psychological Research,* 2014
- Good, Montano, Anne, Katherine. Eve Teasing And Gender Equality in the Post Colonial Framework of India.
- Akhter, Zobaida. (2013). Eve Teasing, Tears Of The Girls : Bangladesh Open University towards Women Empowerment. *International Women Online Journal of Distance Education, 2013*
- Manju. (2014). Violence against Women in India. *Research Journal of English Language and Literature (RJELAL),* Vol.2, Issue 1; 2014
- SC on Eve - Teasing: Human Rights of Woman in India. J Indian *Acad Forensic Med.,* April - June 2013, Vol. 35, No. 2

10

Eve-Teasing : Psychology of a Sick Mind

Vishakha Shukla

Abstract

Eve teasing is a ridiculous form of enjoyment for men and a physical as well as mental trauma for women. This is one of the routine problems women faces in Indian society. Of all the forms of violence against women that can be assumed, eve teasing is the most ubiquitous and insidious because it is considered normal behaviour and not an assault to females. Psychology working behind this type of male behaviour has roots in social and criminal psychology. Eve teasing is visible in various forms in our society. Many psychological theories define and elaborate eve teasing differently. Here we are discussing the psychology behind eve-teasing that is the psychology of a sick mind.

Key Words: Trauma, Criminal, Behaviour, Ubiquitous, Insidious

Introduction

According to the article 1 of the United Nation Declaration on Violence against Women, violence against women is to be understood as-any act of gender based violence that results in, or is likely to result in, physical, sexual or psychological harm or suffering to women, including threats of such acts, coercion or arbitrary deprivations of liberty, whether occurring in public or private life. Eve teasing is the form of violence which comes within the range of the above definition of United Nation Declaration on Violence against women. It harms the dignity, freedom and psychology of a woman.

Eve-teasing today has become pernicious, horrid and disgusting practice. The Indian Journal of Criminology and Criminalities (January-June 1995 Edn.) has categorised eve teasing into five heads viz.:

(1) Verbal eve teasing;
(2) Physical eve teasing;
(3) Psychological harassment;
(4) Sexual harassment; and
(5) Harassment through some objects.

There is hopelessness in the environment regarding public psyche because in spite of so many incidents of eve-teasing, there is no change in the mindset of people. There are a lot of evidences like two youngsters were killed by some eve-teasers when they tried to save a girl from them. It is also worrisome that public who witnesses such incidents always remain mute spectators. We used to listen news in media like people who dared to oppose the eve-teasers were killed by them brutally and the public watching the whole episode never come forward to help them. The situation is really worrisome as well as shameful. Drained public sympathy for the victims on the spot has emboldened many hood looms roaming in teasing spree in recent times. All human behaviour, criminal or otherwise, is a product of psychological mechanisms (instantiated in the brain) combined with environmental input that activates them or inhibits their activation. Since criminal behaviour forms a predictable subset of human behaviour; and all human behaviour requires psychological mechanisms for its production; and all psychological mechanisms, at some level of description, owe their existence to evolution by selection; then evolved psychological mechanisms necessarily plays a key causal role in the production of criminal behaviour.

Eve teasers are supposed to have a criminal psyche but a criminal mind is not born it is constructed by various socio-economic factors. The crimes having their roots in two important spheres of life that can be classified into –First the crimes committed out of hunger and another one committed out of sexual frustration. The legal system in India believes that the former one can be dealt with iron fist but at the same time are afraid to register cases on the latter as it might accelerate plethora of complaints that our legal system is incapable of sorting them out. This is shameful. Does our system consider the man who molests women out of uncontrollable sexual urge less dangerous than a robber? The robbery is the result of incoherent socio-economic equations of the society but the other one is the result of criminal mind which is not necessarily driven by socio-economic factors. It is sick mind nothing else.

Psychology Working Behind Men

A gender role is a set of attitudes, behaviours, and self-presentation methods ascribed to members of a certain biological sex. All cultures across all times have had what I call a "culturally preferred gender role" (CPGR; what a man is supposed to be like) that males are encouraged (or forced) to adopt. Men usually grow up learning these things and other "rules of masculinity" from their fathers, media, and peer groups. The three major themes of these are :

Strength: Emotional toughness, courage, self-reliance, aggression, rationality.

Honour: Duty, loyalty, responsibility, integrity, selflessness, compassion, generatively.

Action: Competitiveness, ambition, dominance, risk-taking.

When men meet the expectations of a CPGR, there are benefits that usually include acceptance from other men, success in occupations traditionally held by men, increased social status, self-esteem, access to resources, and opportunities with potential mates. Basically, if a man thinks, feels, looks, and acts "like a man should" according to his culture, there are benefits, and these benefits reinforce men to continue with this type of masculinity. This process is called gender role compliance advantage.

However, conforming to a CPGR also brings serious negative consequences that include physical, mental, and relational health problems due to how restrictive or harmful the style of masculinity is for the individual. These problems are referred to as gender role strain and gender role conflict.

Men that do not conform to a CPGR do not receive the previously mentioned benefits, and instead usually experience negative consequences such as social rejection, loss of status, and fewer opportunities for work and potential mates. Therefore, many men who don't meet the expectations of a CPGR usually either a) try to change in ways that will be more in line with a CPGR, b) reject the idea of the CPGR and find the benefits through other means, or c) make efforts to create change in what the CPGR is.

Basically what this means is that in most cultures, men have few options related to gender expression. Thus, most men learn and make efforts to embody a CPGR to get the benefits, and then find ways to deal with the other problems that come with it. Unfortunately, a lot of the ways men cope with these problems are unhealthy (substance abuse, escapism, violence, etc) and often lead to depression, relationship destruction, and physical illness that need professional treatment. Even worse, since self-reliance is usually part of a CPGR, men often do not seek help that they need. The integrative model of masculinity (Meek, 2011) incorporates all of these threads to understand an individual male's masculinity, and the thing that influence it.

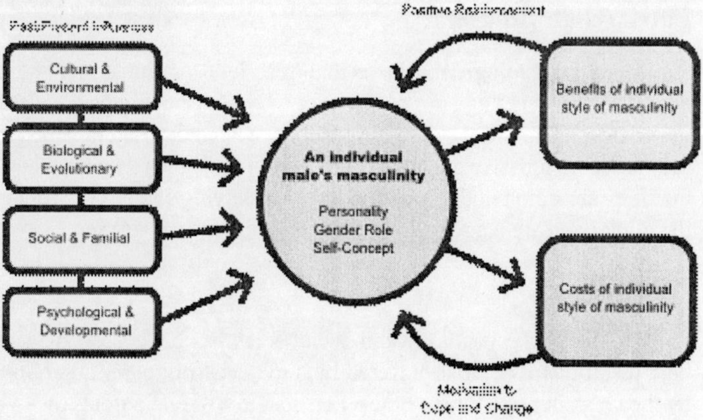

Psychology of Eve-Teaser

Invading One's Privacy

Reasons not easily comprehensible, offences committed to invade other's privacy are not at all considered crimes in India. Neither law nor any law enforcing agency do accept the concept of invading personal sphere. Anyone can smoke in public and puff it on others face, if you oppose that you do not like to be suffocated by nicotine, the smoker would not stop smoking on your face, rather he would ask you to mind your business. Similarly if your neighbour in a train listens to movie songs from his loudspeaker of Chinese mobile with full volume on you are supposed to bear that excessive behaviour to avoid unnecessary scuffle.

This mindset is example of an under developed sick mind, a mind with indifferent attitude towards others comfortableness, is actually graduated into the phenomenon of eve-teasing and when it is reflected along with their sexual perversion, it is taken as a substance having no appeal for serious consideration.

Disoriented Broken Personalities

Though movies and television play a latent role in promoting road side romeotype of heroism, it is difficult to say that all persons involved in eve-teasing are influenced by them. Basically these people are disoriented broken personalities to be treated psychologically preferably in mental asylums.

Patriarchal Mindset

Many psychologists believe that sex, love or fun is not the only motive that men indulge in this behaviour. Eve-teasing is closely related to the patriarchal mindset of the Indian male. Men are raised to believe that they are more powerful physically and emotionally than women. They feel that they are doing nothing wrong only just having some fun. Women on the other hand are made to feel vulnerable and the weaker sex.

Frustration

Teachers of psychology and social scientists believe eve-teasing to be a result of frustrations suffered by a majority of youth. Disappointed by the unbecoming attitude of teachers and indifferent parents they yearn for an outlet to vent their aggression and depression. Besides these many who do not inherit good values also tend to indulge in acts of sexual harassment.

Adulthood

Eve-teasing can be seen as a rite of passage for boys on their way to become men. Considering that sex is not the only motive it would be reasonable to conclude that the psychodynamics of eve-teasing are closely linked to the issue of masculinity and the masculine agenda.

Hierarchical Domination

At the risk of over simplifying a complex phenomenon it would not be imprudent to say that in our country, the construct of masculinity is usually equated with patriarchy. In other words masculinity is experienced not so much as a set of emotional gender, but more in terms of hierarchical domination over the feminine gender, so that the most man gets a socially dominant position over his female counterpart.

Gender segregation from childhood, lopsided parental relationship as well as the representation of man woman relationship in literature and popular cinema all serve to reinforce the patriarchal model of masculinity in the mind of the growing male child.

Social Status of Women

It may appear paradoxical that in a country like India where the mother is generally deified the growing male child does not learn to respect the members of his mother's gender. But it is because of this deification that the boy finds it easy to slip into the patriarchal mode for he does not relate to his mother as a woman but as a helpless and martyred dependent who needs to be pitied and cared for.

Expression of Valour

The vocal emergence of feminism has also pushed the contemporary male a little on the back foot, not only the women are threatening to encroach on his male dominion but also because he does not have any idea about how he can counter encroach on her, so he moves squarely into the adversarial position, something he is instinctively comfortable with and during adolescence, focuses not just on how he can express himself sexually, but also on how he can claim his patriarchal right. As part of his evolution into the patriarchal role an arena is required in which his valour can be expressed. Organised sport and cultural activities are examples of these but require some talent and application, whereas standing with a group of peers at a bus stop or in a Cineplex, passing lewd remarks, gesticulating lasciviously and generally behaving obnoxiously requires more numbers, and when the helpless girl is in no position to defend herself despite visible evidence of distress, domination gets established.

Neurochemicals in Criminal and Anti-Social Behaviour

Neurochemicals are responsible for the activation of behavioural patterns and tendencies in specific areas of the brain (Elliot, 2000). As seen in the Brunner et al. study, there have been attempts to determine the role of neurochemicals in influencing criminal or antisocial behaviour.

Included in the list of neurochemicals already cited by researchers are monoamine oxidase (MOA), epinephrine, norepinephrine, serotonin, and dopamine.

Monoamine oxidase (MAO) is an enzyme that has been shown to be related to antisocial behaviour. Specifically, low MAO activity results in disinhibition which can lead to impulsivity and aggression (Elliot, 2000). The Brunner et al. study is the only one to report findings of a relationship between a point mutation in the structural gene for MAOA and aggression, which makes the findings rare. However, there has been other evidence that points to the conclusion that deficiencies in MAOA activity may be more common and as a result may predispose individuals to antisocial or aggressive behaviour (Brunner et al., 1993). MAO is associated with many of the neurochemicals that already have a link to antisocial or criminal behaviour. Norepinephrine, serotonin, and dopamine are metabolised by both MAOA and MAOB (Elliot, 2000). While, according to Eysenck (1996), MAO is related to norepinephrine, epinephrine, and dopamine, which are all related to the personality factor of psychosis.

Serotonin is a neurochemical that plays an important role in the personality traits of depression, anxiety, and bipolar disorder (Larsen and Buss, 2005). It is also involved with brain development and a disorder in this system could lead to an increase in aggressiveness and impulsivity (Morley and Hall, 2003). Lowenstein (2003) states, studies point to serotonin as one of the most important central Neuro-transmitters underlying the modulation of impulsive aggression". Low levels of serotonin have been found to be associated with impulsive behaviour and emotional aggression. In addition, children who suffer from conduct disorder have also been shown to have low blood serotonin (Elliot, 2000). Needless to say, there is a great deal of evidence that shows serotonin is related to aggression, which can be further associated with antisocial or criminal behaviour.

Psychological aspects of the Eve Teasers

The first question to be addressed is: "What is the psychological nature of eve teasing?" Can it be characterised as youthful exuberance, over-active sexual attraction, and enthusiastic expressions of love; or is it, in fact, a sexual deviation? Groth and Burgess of Boston College wrote that the medical evidence justifies their position that eve teasing should be considered a sexual deviation. Their research suggested that the eve teaser is driven by psychological deviations, which express themselves in sexual aggression.

They argued, in their study, that there are four definitions of sexual deviancy, which cannot fully explain the data on eve teasers. These are often the ones the average person thinks of when thinking of eve teasing, but which are, in fact, inadequate explanations. They include measuring deviancy by determining:

- The sexual object
- The mode of gratification
- The intensity and/or frequency of sexual activity , and
- The context of the act.

They recommend, instead, that sexual deviancy should be seen as caused by the psychological dynamic of the sexual perpetrator. It is "sexual behaviour in the service of non-sexual needs." They argue that eve teasing should be defined as a pseudo sexual act that is not about sex but occurs to gratify other needs.

They studied both eve teasing perpetrators and their victims and found that eve teasing is always characterised by force (including verbal and physical force). In the majority of cases, the eve teaser simply overpowers his victim.

The eve teasing motivated by power is, instead, a planned attack in which the eve teaser fantasises about the way his victim will appreciate and enjoy the power he uses. It is about seeing his victim completely powerless and gaining pleasure from the feeling of having power and control over her.

Eve teaser often has diagnosable personality disorders, but they can also suffer from developmental disorders. A developmental disorder represents, "a failure to achieve an adequate sense of self-identity and self-worth." The disorder occurs because the eve teaser is "inhibited in forming an adequate masculine self-image and cannot gain mastery over his life." teasing provides him with the false feeling of having power and control. Thus, the eve teasing defined as the violent misuse of the sexual act to fulfil deviant psychological, developmental and personal needs.

Thus it is clear from the above discussion that eve teasing is nowadays a serious problem in our society and effect of various social, environmental and genetic factors. The after affect on women's psychology and physique is gruesome. Now it's time to think over this issue seriously and work together towards it positively.

References

- Buss, D. M. (2003). *The evolution of desire: Strategies of human mating (Rev. Ed.)*. New York: Free Press.
- Buss, D. M. (2012). *Evolutionary psychology: The new science of the mind* (4th ed.). Boston: Allyn and Bacon.
- Buss, D. M. , and Duntley, J.D. (2008). Adaptations for exploitation. *Group Dynamics: Theory, Research, and Practice,* 12, 53-62.
- Buss, D.M. and Duntley, J.D. (2011).The evolution of intimate partner violence. *Aggression and Violent Behaviour,* 16, 411-419
- *Buss,* D. M. , and Shackelford, T. K. (1997). From vigilance to violence: Mate retention tactics in married couples. *Journal of Personality and Social Psychology, 72,* 346-361.
- Duntley, J. D. , and Shackelford, T. K. (2012). Adaptations to avoid victimisation. *Aggression and Violent Behaviour,* 17, 59-71.
- www.psychologyofmen.org (retrieved on 12.11.14)
- www.gettheguy.co.uk/male-psychology (retrieved on 14.11.14)
- en.m.wikipedia.org (retrieved on 14.11.14)

11

Eve Teasing: A Psychoanalytic Explication

Zeba Aqil

Abstract

Today eve Teasing has become pernicious, horrid and disgusting practice. Violence against women is the fastest growing crime in India. There are various laws to curb-this problem of eve teasing which is spreading like an epidemic. In this chapter an attempt is made to offer psychological solution to this problem. Author has tried to conceptualise Freud's psychoanalytic constructs, Eros (life instincts) and Thanatos (death instincts), Oedipus complex and super ego function in this regard. Eve Teasing is a mental disorder which can only be resolved from early child practices of proper role modelling and parental identification. Parents especially the father figure has to play a major role from childhood to set proper moral standards for their children especially male child to idealise in the ethical transformation of his animal self to morally upright human being.

Key Words: Eros and Thanatos, Oedipus complex, Super Ego Function.

Eve Teasing is a euphemistic expression that lives in post colonial India and refers largely to sexual harassment of women in public spaces, thereby constituting women as 'eves' temptress who provokes men into states of sexual titillation. This popular perception of sexual harassment posts the phenomenon as a joke where women are both a tease and deserve to be teased considered a growing problem throughout the sub continent, eve teasing ranges in severity from sexually coloured remarks to outright groping".

–Pratikha Baxi

The term Eve teasing is used to refer to sexual harassment of women in public places such as the streets, public transportation, parks, beaches and cinema halls. This type of a public harassment by a lone man or gangs of men includes such as verbal whistling and staring and physical assaults such as fondling and rubbing against women in public places. In addition several instances of eve teasing have been followed by more violent assaults such as rape and murder. Eve teasing is very common in India. Almost every young girl is a victim of teasing especially by the local boys. Most people avoid it as a common matter. Opposite sex attraction is an innate motive, with which every boy and girl is born, but not every time. It can't be tolerated when it crosses limit, it becomes a serious problem. This is against the women rights without any doubt.

Psychoanalytic Explication

Psychoanalytic theory of human development developed by Sigmund Freud gives an important insight into the problem of eve-teasing. Freud gave two important concepts of Eros and Thanatos. Eros (Life Instinct) and Thanatos (Death Instinct)–Eros drives human to procreate, have survival skills and maintain order. The death instinct (Thanatos) comprises of all the negative tendencies including teasing or invading other persons privacy. Thanatos exists in all the sins a person commit every day. Therefore it can be said it is present in that person also who teases a woman first for his pleasure. When a person is high on this death instinct will do destructive acts against anybody. Both of these instincts are present in every person. Point of consideration here is that one should resolve the death instinct by the life instinct as much as possible.

In this area counselling from early childhood will be very helpful in directing children's mind towards more of Eros i.e., creating, life and love from Thanatos i.e. hurting, teasing and inflicting negativity on others.

Oedipus Complex

In psychoanalytic theory, a desire for sexual involvement with the parent of the opposite sex and a concomitant sense of rivalry with the parent of the same sex is a crucial stage in the normal development process. Sigmund Freud introduced the concept in his book "Interpretation of Dreams" (1899). The term derives from the Theban hero Oedipus of Greek legend, who unknowingly slew his father and married his mother, its female analogue, the Electra complex, is named for another mythological figure, who helped stay her mother.

Freud attributed the Oedipus complex to children of about the ages three to five. He said the stage usually ended when the child identified with the parent of the same sex and repressed its sexual instincts. If previous relationships with the parents were relatively loving and not traumatic, and if parental attitudes were neither excessively prohibitive nor excessively stimulating, the stage is passed through harmoniously. In the presence of trauma, however, there occurs an "infantile neurosis" that is an important forerunner of similar reactions during the child's adult life. The superego, the moral factor that dominates the conscious adult mind, also has its origin in the process of overcoming the Oedipus complex. Freud considered the reactions against the Oedipus complex the most important social achievement of the human mind.

Super Ego = Moral conscience, self-disciplining mechanism; it operates by producing a sense of guilt.

This Oedipus complex is resolved successfully, when boy child identifies his father. During this identification father figure should posses high moral and ethical principles which would be later on followed by the son. If high level of super ego and moral reasoning is developed in the child he will not become an eve teaser in his adult life.

Super Ego Function

The super ego is the ethical component of the personality and provides the moral standards by which the ego operates. The super ego develops during the first five years of life in response to parental punishment and approval. The developing superego absorbs the traditions of the family and the surrounding.

Society serves to control aggressive or other socially unacceptable impulses. It tries to force the ego to act morally rather than realistically. Nowadays if parents and teachers go through Freudian analysis thoroughly they would realise that of high level of super ego is developed from very beginning in children they would not develop as teasers in the society. Superego adds morality to the action which is taken. There are two parts of the superego.

1. The ego ideal includes the rules and standards for good behaviours. These behaviours include those which are approved of by parental and other authority figures obeying these rules leads to feelings of pride, value and accomplishment.
2. The conscience includes information about-things that are viewed as bad by parents and society. These behaviours are often forbidden and lead to bad consequences punishments or feelings of guilt and remorse.

The superego acts to perfect and civilise our behaviour. So development of superego becomes an important constituent in overcoming teasing behaviour.

If all the concepts of Freuds like thanatos, Oedipus complex and superego functions are incorporated into one then a lot of insight can be developed towards solution of the eve teasing problem.

Eve teasing is an epidemic which cannot be resolved merely by the law. We have to reach the root cause of the problem which lies far in the childhood of eve teaser. Eve Teasing is closely related to the patriarchal mindset of the Indian male. Men are raised to believe that they are more powerful physically and emotionally than women. They feel that they are doing nothing wrong just having some fun. Women on the other hand are made to feel vulnerable and the weaker sex.

This problem of eve teasing can be only resolved when Oedipus complex is waned easily with identification of a father who himself is morally and ethically a benchmarks for his son. When a child idealises a father figure who respects the modesty of female especially his wife, mother and other ladies, child will himself develop these qualities. If father has dominating death instinct (Thanatos), son would easily idealise this and would move towards this negative tendency of teasing others and hurting one self. Violence against women is a social evil and must be faced socially and psychologically.

The superego or the ethical branch of personality retains the character of the father, while the more powerful the Oedipus complex was and the more rapidly it succumbed to repression (under the influence of authority, religious teaching, schooling and reading) the stricter will be the domination of the super ego over the ego later on–in the form of conscience or perhaps of a unconscious sense of guilt".

Conclusion

Teachers of psychology and social scientists believe eve-teasing to be a result of the frustrations suffered by a majority of youth. Psycho analytic theory of Sigmund Freud offers a valuable suggestion to solve the problem of eve testing. This kind of deviant behaviour results from abnormal, dysfunctional, or inappropriate mental process within the personality of the individual. This defective mental process could be caused from a variety of things, including a diseased mind, inappropriate learning, improper conditioning, and the absence of appropriate role models or the strong presence of in appropriate role models.

To eradicate this menace of eve teasing, it has become the need of the hour to raise proper role models in the society who would inspire little children by their moral and ethical values. A high quality of super ego should be developed in children's from early childhood and this is only possible when it is modelled properly by the parents. The concept of patriarchal society should be completely finished from the society. Parental supervision plays an important role in the development of super ego and eradication of eve teasing.

References

- Breuer, J. and Freud, S. (1893-1895). Studies on hysteria, in The Standard Edition of the Complete Psychological Works of Sigmund Freud, translated and edited by Strachey J (24 vol). London, Hogarth Press, 1953-1974, pp 2-3
- Fenichel, O. (1945). The Psychoanalytic Theory of Neurosis, New York, Norton.
- Freud, S. (1921). Group psychology and the analysis of the ego, Standard Edition, 18, pp. 67-143.
- Freud, S. (1923). The ego and the id, Standard Edition 19, pp 3-66.
- Freud, S. (1924). The dissolution of the Oedipus complex, Standard Edition 19, pp 172-179.
- Freud, S. (1925). Some psychical consequences of the anatomical distinction between the sexes. Standard Edition 19, pp 243-258.
- Freud, S. (1928). Dostoevski and parricide. Standard Edition 21,pp 175-194.
- Jones, E. (1957). The Life and Work of Sigmund Freud, Vol 3. New York, Basic Books.

12

India Strict against Eve Teasing and Sexual Harassment at Work Place

Saurabh Mishra and Deepti Mishra

Abstract

In last few decades due to degrading moral values eve teasing has emerged as one of the most challenging social problem in India. Not a single place, not a single moment women is left without fear of being sexually harassed or teased by stranger on road, bus, train, shopping mall irrespective of their caste, creed, religion, age and economic status. In 21st century women in India have recognised their abilities and came out breaking the fourwalls of home to participate in economic activities similar or even better than any other men. Just like any other place on this earth women became a soft target for exploitation at work place also. In recent year number of cases of eve teasing and sexual harassment at work place were exposed to public through news papers and news channels about chances of women being exploited by their colleague, seniors, employers and some time by juniors also. To protect the modesty and dignity of women at work place Government of India have legislated sexual harassment of women at work place (Prevention, Prohibition and Redressal) act 2013 and Criminal amendment act 2013 on 19 March, 2013. Although this act is comparatively strong and mandatory for implementation by all offices, organisation, institutions, enterprise, or any branch of it but still have some loop holes. Although this act is new one and it has to go through a number of developments and reforms to make it more effective and accountable. This chapter will discuss the important provisions of sexual harassment of women at work place (Prevention, Prohibition and Redressal) act 2013 and Criminal amendment act 2013 and point of criticisms. At last some important suggestions are included which may give a upper hand to victims and society to fight against peculiar problem of eve teasing and sexual harassment at work place.

Key Words: Values, Harassment, Colleagues, seniors, Employers, Mandatory

Introduction

Eve teasing and Sexual harassment at work place is a serious irritating factor that renders women involvement in works affects her right to work with dignity which is otherwise available to all the citizens of India. It is an unwelcome verbal visual or physical conduct of sexual nature that affects the working condition or creates a hostile work environment. It not only affects victim's job performance negatively but it may endanger victim's job. It may leave physical or psychological marks for whole life. Its milder and subtle form may include verbal expression, inappropriate gestures, proposition for dates and sexual favours. It may also include blatant and ugly forms like leering, physical grabbing, sexual assault or sexual molestation.

A survey jointly conducted by Oxfam India and the Social and Rural Research Institute, a wing of IMRB International. In Delhi, Mumbai, Bangalore, Chennai, Kolkata, Ahmadabad, Lucknow and Durgapur and covered 400 working women about sexual harassment at work place reported that 17 per cent of women accept that they have experienced act of sexual harassment at work place. Maximum numbers of cases were reported in labourers (29 per cent), domestic workers (23 per cent), and small scale manufacturing units (16 per cent). It was also found that out of above victims 20 per cent of women were the sole earning members of their family indicating that their economic vulnerability makes them a soft target for sexual harassment at work place. Survey also reported that main reason for not reporting about such incidence is fear of losing job and social insult.

Another survey conducted by reputed newspaper The Hindu demonstrated the helpless condition of women in country against sexual harassment at work place. It reported that-

- 91 per cent of women do not report such incidence due to fear of victimisation.
- In 72 per cent cases harasser was employer or superior.
- 88 per cent female workforce in IT sector especially in BPO sector suffered from work place sexual harassment situation.
- 50 per cent working women accept that they have been subjected to abusive language, physical contacts or sought for sexual favours.
- 47 per cent women don't know where to report such type of incidence.

The situation becomes even worse when victim has to stand against business tycoons like Tarun Tejpal of Tehelka, Murthy of Infosys, David Davidar of Penguin, Gopal Kanda of MDLR Airlines because they have power of money and political connections, by utilising these instruments they can easily come out through the loop holes of Indian Law System. If victim files a complaint then she has to face threat of life to herself and her family members. Even relatives, friends society members do not dare to come with the victim due to fear of their life.

According to human rights act 1993, human rights means the right related to life, liberty, equality and dignity of individual guaranteed by constitution enforceable by courts in India. These rights are equally available to all the citizens of India without any gender bias. Due to the social, educational and political upliftment Indian women are no more restricted within the boundaries of family. Now they are working equally or better as compared to men in all the fields of life so it becomes necessary that they should get safe and secure environment at work place. Without safety and security at work place they will not be able to contribute maximum to their job and finally to development of country. It is true that in recent years the number of cases related to the issue of sexual harassment has been increased in India and prime reason for it is more and more participation of women in economic activities. This type of menace was already embedded in male dominated Indian society but remain unnoticed due to unwillingness of aggrieved women and their family to report it. But the situation has changed in recent years due to increase in literacy rate and involvement of media for social causes.

Discussion

Before discussing rights of women on the issue of eve teasing and Sexual Harassment at work place, it is important to make clear that what does eve teasing and sexual harassment means to a working female. As defined under the sexual harassment of women at work place (Prevention, Prohibition and Redressal) act 2013 and Criminal amendment act 2013 passed by Lok Sabha on 19 march, 2013 includes such unwelcome sexually determined behaviour (whether directly or by implication) as :

1. Physical contacts and advances involving unwelcome and sexual overtures; or
2. A demand or request for sexual favours; or
3. Making sexually coloured remarks; or
4. Forcibly showing pornography; or
5. Any other unwelcome physical, verbal or non verbal conduct of sexual nature

Sexual harassment result in violation of fundamental rights of women to equality under article 14 and 15 of Constitution of India, her right to life and living with dignity under article 21 of constitution of India and right to practice any profession or carry any occupation, trade or business which include right to safe environment free from sexual harassment. Although a burning issue but like the other women related issues it was unable to become a part of national debate till 64th year of independence. Understanding the absence of any legislation covering issues of sexual harassment at work place, Supreme Court of India has laid down few necessary guidelines and norms in VISHAKHA VS STATE OF RAJASTHAN for protection of fundamental rights of women. These rules were applicable to all women including students, part time or full time worker. It put a lot of emphasis on part of employer to take appropriate preventive and curative measures. The apex court also emphasised that these guidelines had to be duly observed by all work places or other institutions until legislation is enacted for the same purpose and that these should be treated as law under article 141 of constitution. These guidelines and norms recommended by apex court were in accordance with the recommendations and conventions of various international organisations like ILO and European committee etc. Its recommendations included complaint mechanism, inquiry setup, criminal proceedings conciliation process, preventive actions to be taken by employer.

Just like legislation of any act, enactment of the sexual harassment of women at work place (prevention, prohibition and Redressal) act 2013 took a long time for coming in to existence. The bill was first introduced by women and child minister in 2007 and approved by union cabinet in January 2010. It was tabled in Lok Sabha in December 2010 and referred to parliamentary standing committee. Committee report was published on 30 November 2011. In May 2012 union cabinet approved an amendment to include domestic workers. The amended bill was finally passed by Lok Sabha on 26 February 2013. It received assent of President of India on 23 April 2013as Act No. 14 of 2013.

Important Features of the Act

The important provisions of the act are as follows :

- It extends to whole of India. It means that rights are available to all women with in the territory of country whether citizen or not.
- Definition of aggrieved women not only include employee of office or organisations but also household workers. Employment could be of permanent or temporary nature, employed directly or through agency, remunerated in cash, kind or on voluntary basis. Under this provision Probationer, trainee, apprentice or called by any other such names are also included.
- Under definition of employer it covers all government, non government departments, organisations, institutions, establishment, enterprises or any other branch or unit of appropriate government or local authority or a person responsible for management, supervision and control of work place.
- Definition of sexual harassment as covered under the act is very wide and covers all type of direct and indirect acts when safety, security and dignity of women is at ruin.
- It provides that not less than half of the total number of members of internal committee shall be women including presiding officer of committee must be a woman employed at senior level at work place among employees.
- A district level committee must be constituted by appropriate government officer to receive complaint of sexual harassment from organisation where internal committee is not constituted by employer deliberately or the number of employees working in the organisation is less than ten.
- It is also provided that any aggrieved woman can make complaint in writing to internal committee or local committee. In case woman is not literate enough, presiding officer or member of internal committee or chairperson or member of local committee shall render all reasonable assistance to woman for making complaint in written.

- Although time specified for filing a complaint is maximum three months from the date of incidence took place. Internal committee or local committee can allow another three months for period of filing complaint if it is satisfied that circumstances prevented the aggrieved woman from filing complaint with in prescribed time period.
- In case woman cannot make complaint by herself due to physical or mental incapacity or death or otherwise her legal heir or such other person is provided with the same right for filing complaint.
- Before initiating a inquiry committee should take step to settle the matter between parties at request of aggrieved woman, but no monetary settlement shall be made as basis of conciliation.
- It is responsibility of internal committee or local committee as the case may be if prima facia case exists; they can forward the complaint to police with in a period of seven days for registering case under section 509 of Indian Penal Code.
- This act provides that aggrieved woman has right to demand transfer of complainant or respondent, and demand for a special leave for a period of three month or any other relief as prescribed.
- After completion of inquiry if committee comes to conclusion that allegations made against respondent are true then it can recommend the employer to take the action for misconduct as per service rules applicable to respondent.
- It makes the provision of compensating the aggrieved woman or her legal heirs by respondent or by employer after deducting the same amount from salary and wages of respondent. If respondent fails to make such payment to aggrieved party local committee may forward for recovery of sums as an arrear of land revenue to concerned District officer. All such actions by employer or District officer must be completed within sixty days from the day of receipt of recommendations.
- There is a provision that after filing complaint by aggrieved woman identity of woman respondent or witness and any information related to conciliation, inquiry proceeding, recommendations and action taken shall not be published or communicated or made known to public press or media in any manner, but it does not prevent in dissemination regarding justice secured by any victim of sexual harassment under this act without disclosing the name, address, identity or any other particulars.

- This act also provides that if any employer fails in compliance of provisions of this act then employer can be penalised which may extends up to fifty thousand rupees for first time. If employer fails second times penalty can be raised twice or his licence or registration to carry out business can be withdrawn or cancelled by government or appropriate local authority.
- It is advantageous that this act shall not in derogation of provisions of any other law for time being in force.
- The central government has been vested vast powers to make appropriate amendment in rules and regulations of this act, which are beneficial to aggrieved woman by notification in official gazette.

Criticism

Although the law enacted for protecting women from sexual harassment covers a wide area but few provisions of the law does not seems sensitive enough to strengthen the hands of victimised women these are mentioned here :

- In case internal committee or District level committee find that complaint made is malicious or false in nature, it may recommend penalty on complainant in accordance with the service rule applicable. This provision can be criticised on the basis that if employer or person sitting on higher post in organisation can pressurise the members of internal committee to take the decision in their favour. Similarly when case is reported against reputed personality who have economic and political powers, with the help of team of lawyers they will be able handle the case easily like any other case. By this way complaint made by victim can easily be probed as false and malicious.
- State machinery who has to implement the law do not carry sympathetic behaviour towards women which makes the condition even worse with a new type of sexual harassment where she has to describe the whole process of sexual harassment several times, such as when did it started, what happened, how many times it happened, you unwelcomed it or not, why you are so late in filing a complaint and many more questions which are asked during the period of inquiry. Thus instead of going for justice women decide to go other way and remain quiet or resigns from job.
- Due to media pressure when machinery tries to implement the laws strictly many private organisations are applying a secret

policy of not employing women for core jobs. They want the women employs to work as show piece or on less important post such as Receptionist or Telephone operator where they work in public view and chance of sexual harassment are least. Obviously this type of strategy effect the carrier building of women because any employer can make discrimination in recruiting women avoiding any case of sexual harassment of work place.

- Mechanism of conciliation is another very important issue of criticism because through the conciliation process respondent may bribe the aggrieved party. Similarly any women can blackmail or torture any superior employee or employer showing him the fear and ill consequences of filing complaint subjected to sexual harassment at work place. This provision does not promote the justice but seems as an instrument for just solving the issue. It shows that in the eyes of government and law sexual harassment at work place is not a serious crime.

Suggestions

Sexual harassment at work place is a serious crime which is spreading very widely as women are entering in to new areas for employment. Its true picture always remains unrevealed because victims always prefer to remain quite. Maximum numbers of cases remain unreported. Few years prior it was reported in unorganised sectors only but now days it is becoming more common in civilised and literate fields and professions such as Education, banks, Medical profession, IT sector etc. Here are few suggestion if implemented with Commitment will certainly be able bring change in social status of women –

- Women reservation bill which is pending due to negligence of our law makers should be passed immediately with the compulsory provision of reservation of women in employment in public as well private sector, so that any employer will not be able to discriminate on the basis of gender by not recruiting the women.
- State machinery especially Police, Lawyers, Judges should be specially trained to deal with the sensitive cases related to women such as sexual harassment or rape, so that their self respect should not be hurt during inquiry.
- Provision of conciliation should not be effective once complained is filed because it opens the way for corruption where members of inquiry committee, colleagues, friends pressurise the victim to

conciliate because they are assured that if they are successful they will certainly get their share from both parties.

- Provision of imposing penalty on complainant if complaint is found malicious or false is completely unjust should be amended. Already the issue of sexual harassment too sensitive issue, less than 20 per cent of women are coming forward to report such incidences. Law itself is the main obstacle in delivering justice. First of all somebody hurts the dignity of victim by his heinous act after that if she complaints without caring of social insult she is going to face, she is threatened for life, rapidly faces the questions she do not wants to remember and last but not the least if she fails to prove what has happened with her she will be economically penalised. Is this law is enacted for?
- State machinery which has to deal with the issues of crime against women should be directed to deal it sympathetically and sensitively.

Conclusion

From above discussion we can conclude that rights available to women against the crime of Sexual harassment at work place are very limited. It is true that law enacted in this regard is in very initial stage but narrow thinking of law makers is easily reflected through the provisions of act which are not only unjust but makes the women think twice about to complaint or not. Our law makers and the courts have to rethink. Law meant for those should not torture them in any way.

Only reforming the law will not be the solution for the problem, we have to hit the root cause of the problem which lies in the downfall of our moral values. Media especially advertisement film makers have posed the image of women as a consumable item meant for enjoyment. This attitude of society is to be changed and the people with this attitude should be boycotted along with legal proceedings. All the women working in particular organisation whether on lower or superior post should unite together and try to develop a sexual harassment free environment in company. They should believe that anybody can break a stick but it is not easy to break the bunch of sticks.

References

- Chibbar M.(2013) Sexual harassment act: 8 months on, govt yet to act on law, Indian Express, 26 November 2013, www.archeive.indianexpress.com

- Farnandis D. (2013) 17 per cent women are sexually harassed at work place, Times of India, 28 November 2013, www.timesofindia.indiatimes.com
- Heathfield S. M. Preventing sexual harassment at work place, www.humanresource.about.com (retrieved on 21 April 2014)
- Krishna B.G. (2013) Impact of sexual harassment at work place, www.live,law.in
- Perappadan B.S. (2012) Sexual harassment at work place high, The Hindu, 29 November 2012, www.thehindu.com
- PTI (2013) Sexual harassment at work place : how equipped is India? India Today, 01 December 2013, www.indiatoday. indiatimes.in
- Sexual Harassment of women at work place (prevention, prohibition and Redressal) act 2013, The gazette of India, no.18, Published on 23 April, 2013
- Sexual Harassment of women at work place (prevention, prohibition and Redressal) act 2013, www.wikipedia.org
- Sinha A.(2014) Sexual harassment at Work place - An overview, www.legalserviceindia.com The protection of women against Sexual Harassment at work place Bill 2010, Bill no. 144 of 2010, www.prsindia.org
- Sexual Harassment of women at work place (prevention, prohibition and Redressal), Bill 2006, National Council for Women www.ncw.nic.in
- The protection of women against Sexual Harassment at work place Bill 2010, Bill no. 144 of 2010, www.prsindia.org
- Medha Kotwal Lele and others Vs Union of India (2013) 1 S.C.C. 311
- Sema Lepcha Vs State of Sikkim, (2013)11 S.C.C. 641
- Vishaka vs. State of Rajasthan (1997) 6 SCC 241

13

Critical Evaluation of Criminal Law Amendment Act-2013 with Special Reference to Eve-Teasing in the NCT of Delhi

Sandesh Yadav and Aayushi Chaudhary

Abstract

There was huge hue and cry over the social security of women after the Delhi gang rape case, 2012 (popularly known as Nirbhaya case) throughout the country. In such a chaotic environment, the Parliament of India passed the Criminal Law Amendment Act, 2013 with a hope that it will improve the social security level of women in India. The act amended certain provisions and also introduced the new things and thus, the domain of law expanded and encompassed the all possible aspects related to crime against women. The act included the provision of FIR on even slightest of stalking, voyeurism and molestation. The present chapter deals with the critical evaluation of the Criminal Law Amendment Act, 2013 in the light of crime against women with special reference to eve-teasing and examines the extent to which the Criminal Law Amendment Act, 2013 have achieved the success in curbing the social menace of eve-teasing. The present article involves the Pre–Criminal Law Amendment Act, 2013 study and Post–Criminal Law Amendment Act, 2013 study in order to trace out the legal history of eve-teasing and attempt has been made to bring out the actual picture of social environment and effectiveness of Criminal Law Amendment Act, 2013.

Keywords: Social Security, Eve-Teasing, Stalking, Voyeurism, Molestation, Indian Penal Code, Criminal Law Amendment Act-2013

Introduction

Social security of women has always been a highly sensitive and questionable issue across the country. The major role in the degradation of social environment is played by the most ubiquitous and insidious act of eve-teasing. The concept of eve-teasing emerged during the 60's and 70's and can be defined as a euphemism used in India for public sexual harassment or molestation of women by men. Sometimes feminist writers have referred eve-teasing as "little rapes" due to its highly ubiquitous and insidious nature.

Before stepping out of their homes, women are supposed to make-up their mind against the several anti-social elements and hooligans which are involved in the act of eve-teasing. In this way, the eve-teasers make the social environment highly insecure for women and consequently hinder the general mobility of women and accessibility to public places. Most recently, Delhi Gang Rape case (popularly known as Nirbhaya rape case, 2012) was the escalated version of eve-teasing.

The Indian Journal of Criminology and Criminalistics (January-June 1995) have categorised eve-teasing in following five major head:

- Physical eve-teasing.
- Verbal eve-teasing.
- Psychological harassment.
- Sexual harassment.
- Harassment through some objects.

Women, in Delhi, experience all the above mentioned multiple types of eve-teasing at the hands of men. Physical eve-teasing encompasses physical intimacy on buses (DTC, Metro rail etc.) and on busy roads/ markets and on the other hand, verbal eve-teasing includes the heinous acts like singing obscene songs, unwelcome sexual jokes, remarks about female body, showing obscene gestures, winking, whistling, staring and stalking are the types of abuse which are faced by all women with varying degrees at different stages of their life. The more escalated version is psychological harassment through the use of obscene and suggestive words uttered on the telephone or through internet. This is limited to the section of women which have accessibility to such services. The escalation continues and takes the form of sexual harassment which involves the forced and outright groping, mostly prevalent at workplace. The last and most heinous is the harassment through some objects like mms clipping, showing pornography by various means etc.

The major causes that lead to such a crime in Delhi can be listed as under :

- Migration of illiterate rural people to highly advanced and urbanised region of Delhi. These migrants are mainly from the states of Uttar Pradesh, Haryana, Rajasthan, Bihar, Madhya Pradesh etc.
- Lack of respect for women's privacy.
- Unemployed youth with a lot of free time do indulge in such activities.
- Media is having a great impact on young minds by umpteen advertisements and various scenes of Bollywood movies. Further, they portray women as "a substance to be enjoyed".

The places in Delhi which are more prone to eve-teasing can be classified under the following major heads:

- Public places like shopping malls, cinema halls, streets, markets like the one in Sarojni Nagar etc.
- Public transport like buses like DTC and Delhi Metro.
- Private places like Restaurants/Pubs, Women Colleges, Girls School, Universities and Workplaces.

Offenders, in Delhi, may be of all age groups ranging from teenagers, young adults, and middle aged males. All the three age groups are basically involved in verbal and gestural eve-teasing. Moreover, offenders are from both low socio-economic and high socio-economic conditions.

Legal Provisions to Curb Eve Teasing

Eve-teasing is a crime against women and need to be discussed in the light of the constitution of India, Indian Penal Code (IPC) and other legal provisions. Constitutionally, eve-teasing violates the **Article-14** which talks about equality before law, **Article 15** which talks about prohibition of discrimination on grounds of religion, race, caste, sex or place of birth and **Article 21** which talks about the right to live with dignity and honour. Legal provisions to curb the social menace of eve-teasing are–

- The culprit can land into prison for a maximum tenure of three months for obscene gesture, recitation or remarks.
- Showing pornographic materials, pictures etc. can lead to two years of imprisonment along with the fine of Rs. 2000.
- There are provisions under the Indian Penal Code (IPC) - sections 294, 354 and 509 to punish the accused.
- The most recent is the Criminal Law Amendment Act, 2013 which contain certain provisions regarding stalking, voyeurism and molestation.

There was huge hue and cry over the social security of women after the Delhi Gang Rape Case, 2012 (popularly known as Nirbhaya case) throughout the country. In such a chaotic environment, the parliament of India passed the Criminal Law Amendment Act, 2013 with a hope that it will improve the social security level of women in India. The Act amended certain provisions and also introduced the new things and thus, the domain of law expanded and encompassed the all possible aspects related to crime against women. The act included provisions of FIR on even slightest of stalking, voyeurism and molestation.

Criminal Law Amendment Act, 2013

The Criminal Law Amendment Bill, 2013 was passed by the Lok Sabha i.e., Lower House of Parliament of India on 19th March, 2013 and by the Rajya Sabha i.e., Upper House of Parliament of India on 21st March, 2013. It received the assent of the President of India on 2nd April, 2013 and came into force from 3rd day of February, 2013. The Justice Verma Committee Report (2013) served as the base of all amendments done in the Criminal Law Amendment Act, 2013.

The Criminal Law Amendment Act, 2013 provides for the amendments of the following:

- **Indian Penal Code (IPC), 1860**. It amends sections 100, 228A, 354, 370, 370A, 375, 376, 376A, 376B, 376C, 376D and 509 of IPC, 1860. Further, inserts new sections 166A, 166B, 326A, 326B, 354A, 354B, 354C and 354D in IPC, 1860.
- **The Code of Criminal Procedure,** 1973. It amends sections 26, 54A, 154, 160, 161, 164, 173, 197, 273, 309, 327 and first schedule of The Code of Criminal Procedure, 1973. It inserts new sections 357B and 357C of Code of Criminal Procedure, 1973.

- It amends the section 114, 119 and 146 of the **Indian Evidence** Act, 1872.
- Lastly, it amends the section 42 of the **Protection of Children from Sexual** Offences Act, 2012.

Pre- Criminal Law Amendment Act-2013 Study

The Pre- Criminal Law Amendment Act-2013 study aims to analyse the legal status of eve-teasing and the effectiveness of legal provisions (Prior-2013) in curbing the social menace of eve-teasing. The analysis performed in the Pre-CLAA, 2013 study is based on the statistics of National Crime Record Bureau, Delhi and the legal provision of Indian Penal Code, 1860.

Firstly, we will like to discuss various sections of Indian Penal Code, 1860 dealing either with molestation or eve-teasing. In Indian Penal Code, 1860, we have section 294, section 354 and section 509 and out of these three sections, complaints regarding eve-teasing are registered under either section 294 or section 509 while section 354 deals with the acts of sexual harassment and punishment for sexual harassment.

Section 354 IPC says that *"Whoever assaults or uses criminal force on any woman, intending to outrage her modesty or knowing it likely that he will thereby outrage her modesty, shall be punished with imprisonment for a term which may extend to two years, or with fine, or with both."*

Prior 2013, section 354 IPC specifically dealt with the sexual harassment or molestation and aspects like stalking or voyeurism were not mentioned. Further, section holds that sexual harassment can only be committed against women as in Girdhar Gopal (1953) Cr L J 964, it was held that under section 354 IPC only women possess modesty that may be outraged. Thus men are inviolate and not the repository of socially recognised attributes that shames them or society. It is interesting, however, that the judgment holds that both men and women are capable of outraging women's modesty.

Section 294 IPC says that *"whoever to the annoyance of others: (a) does any obscene act in any public place or (b) sings, recites or utters any obscene song; ballad or words, in or near any public place, shall be punished with imprisonment of either description for a term which may extend to three month, or with both."*

Section 509 IPC says that, *"whoever intending to insult the modesty of any woman, utters any word, makes any sound or gesture, or exhibits any object, intending, that such word or sound shall be heard, or that such gesture or object shall be seen, by such woman, shall be punished with simple imprisonment for a term which may extend to one year, or with fine or with both."*

In both the sections of IPC, the burden of proof lies on the prosecution to prove that the accused committed any obscene act or the accused sang, recited or uttered any obscene song, words or made the sound or gesture and that such word, sound or gesture was intended by the accused to be heard or seen by some woman. Henceforth, it is very difficult to establish that the accused had committed the obscene acts (verbal, non-verbal, or both) and consequently, the wrong doers are left unpunished.

Now the question rises **"why do wrong doers (eve-teasers) are left unpunished?"** The answer to this question lies in the fact that there was absence of effective mechanism for monitoring and to follow up such acts. Further, indifferent attitude of people towards the eve-teasing makes the situation worst.

The legal history of eve-teasing can be traced in the following manner:

- Up to 1991, there was no specification regarding the crimes against women except rape and kidnapping. Moreover, laws related to sexual harassment, sections 354 and 509 are subsumed under the category of "*other* IPC *crimes*". Thus, there was absence of classificatory grid which shows that harassment of women was not yet viewed as a serious crime.
- In 1992, the semantic category of "*crime against women*" was coined and a new chapter entitled "Crime against Women" was added to Crime in India Report-1992. The report listed the following crimes against women as enunciated in the IPC. Rape (376 IPC); kidnapping or abduction for different purposes (363-373 IPC); homicide for dowry, dowry deaths or their attempts (302/304-B IPC); torture, both mental and physical (498A IPC); molestation (354 IPC); and eve teasing (509 IPC).

In 1992, eve-teasing (509 IPC) attained the present legal status.

Post- Criminal Law Amendment Act-2013 Study

The Post-CLAA-2013 study deals with the amendment of various sections and insertion of new sections in IPC, 1860. Further, study aims at the analysis of the effectiveness of CLAA, 2013.

Section 354 IPC deals with molestation. The Criminal Law Amendment Act, 2013 amends the section 354 IPC in the following manner:

"In section 354 of the Penal Code, for the words "shall be punished with imprisonment of either description for a term which may extend to two years, or with fine, or with both", the words "shall be punished with imprisonment of either description for a term which shall not be less than one year but which may extend to five years, and shall also be liable to fine" shall be substituted".

The amendment in section 354 IPC clearly describes the lower limit of imprisonment as one year and increases the upper limit of imprisonment up to maximum of five years. Thus, it will create a fear psychosis in the minds of criminals and consequently, demoralising them from getting involved in such crimes.

Further, sections 354A, 354B, 354C, 354D are inserted which expands the domain of section 354 IPC. The most important is the section 354C IPC which deals with *"voyeurism"* and can be read as:

"Any man who watches, or captures the image of a woman engaging in a private act in circumstances where she would usually have the expectation of not being observed either by the perpetrator or by any other person at the behest of the perpetrator or disseminates such image shall be punished on first conviction with imprisonment of either description for a term which shall not be less than one year, but which may extend to three years, and shall also be liable to fine, and be punished on a second or subsequent conviction, with imprisonment of either description for a term which shall not be less than three years, but which may extend to seven years, and shall also be liable to fine."

The introduction of section 354C broadens the definition of molestation, encompassed the most prevalent act of breaching women's privacy and thus, ensures respect for women's privacy.

Another new section i.e., 354D IPC is inserted and the section talks about "stalking" and can read as:

1. Any man Who

- follows a woman and contacts, or attempts to contact such woman to foster personal interaction repeatedly despite a clear indication of disinterest by such woman; or
- monitors the use by a woman of the internet, email or any other form of electronic communication; or
- watches or spies on a woman in any manner,

That results in a fear of violence or serious alarm or distress in the mind of such woman, or interferes with the mental peace of the woman, commits the offence of stalking.

2. Whoever commits the offence of stalking shall be punished with imprisonment of either description for a term which shall not be less than one year but which may extend to five years, and shall also be liable to fine.

The section 354 D broadens the domain by encompassing "stalking" as crime against women and thus, ensures the maximum possible social security for women.

Similarly, section 509 IPC got amended and can be read as:

"In section 509 of the Penal Code, for the words "shall be punished with simple imprisonment for a term which may extend to one year, or with fine, or with both", the words "shall be punished with simple imprisonment for a term which may extend to three years, and also with fine" shall be substituted."

The amendment of section 509 IPC sets the upper limit of imprisonment as three years and thus, showing zero tolerance towards the criminal activities against women.

The section 166A IPC is newly inserted section, which can be read as:

"Whoever, Being a Public Servant,

(a) Knowingly disobeys any direction of the law which prohibits him from requiring the attendance at any place of any person for the purpose of investigation into an offence or any other matter, or
(b) Knowingly disobeys, to the prejudice of any person, any other direction of the law regulating the manner in which he shall conduct such investigation, or
(c) Fails to record any information given to him under sub-section (1) of section 154 of the Code of Criminal Procedure, 1973, in relation to cognizable offence punishable under section 326A, section 326B, section 354, sub-sections (2) and (3) of section 354A, section 354B, section 354C, sub-section (2) of section 354D, section 370, section 370A, section 376, section 376A, section 376B, section 376C, section 376D, section 376E or section 509,

Shall be punished with rigorous imprisonment for a term which shall not be less than six months but which may extend to two years, and shall also be liable to fine."

The insertion of section 166A IPC imposes a boundation on government officials to take necessary and sufficient action whenever needed. Thus, section 166A IPC guarantees that grievances will be heard and wrong doers shall be punished.

In section 161 of the Code of Criminal Procedure (Cr.PC), in sub-section (3), after the provision, the following provision shall be inserted, namely:

"Provided further that the statement of a woman against whom an offence under section 354, section 354A, section 354B, section 354C, section 354D, section 376, section 376A, section 376B, section 376C, section 376D, section 376E or section 509 of the Indian Penal Code is alleged to have been committed or attempted shall be recorded, by a woman police officer or any woman officer."

The section 161 of Code of Criminal Procedure makes the proceedings favourable to women because they will feel free to give detail information of the crime committed against them and thus, ending the fear psychosis, feeling of shame in describing the criminal activity against women.

Conclusion

The critical evaluation shows that CLAA-2013 contains much more strict provisions and severe punishment for crime against women especially eve-teasing (Section-509IPC). But still we find people saying "Government have no strict provisions to curb the social menace of eve-teasing". This raises question that, **"why people are saying so?"** Answer to this question is the lack of awareness among people (especially among women) regarding the legal provisions to curb the crime against women.

Now the question raised here are, **"why awareness is important?"** Awareness regarding the legal provisions will serve the two fold purpose. Firstly, it will make the women to realise that they are socially secure and secondly, the most important one, it will demoralise the roadside Romeos, hooligans and anti-social elements from getting involved in such heinous crimes.

Now, **"What Should be done to Spread awareness among men and Women?"**

- Pasting the newer provisions in printed form outside every government building.
- Distribution of pamphlets containing the newer and amended provisions in public areas, colleges, universities campus.

- Use of loud speakers to convey verbally the newer provisions of CLAA-2013.

In this way, we will be able to spread awareness to each and every hook and corner of our society.

Most of the times we find people criticising the police personnel and saying that *"police don't do anything to stop crime against women"*. But they fail to realise the fact that police personnel is dealing with huge number of crimes taking place simultaneously everywhere so it becomes really very hard to entertain every possible crime. Moreover, it becomes really very tough when eve-teasing (highest degree of uncertainty) comes into scene. To deals with this, community participation is of utter importance and is the need of hour. This social menace of eve-teasing with highest degree of uncertainty and its ubiquitous nature needs a highly uncertain and ubiquitous mechanism in the form of community participation.

In spite of CCTV's surveillance and help line numbers, we need community which matches the degree of uncertainty and ubiquitous nature of the crime. The community participation is the only and sure shot way not only to curb but end the social menace of eve-teasing.

Lastly, strict implementation along with immediate action by the police personnel lies at the core to curb the social menace of eve-teasing.

References

- Shah G (2000). Crime against Women and Police, New Delhi
- Singh K A, and Choudhary J (2012). Violence Against Women and Children- Issues and Concerns. New Delhi, Serials Publications, p.13.
- Akhtar, Chesfeeda (2013). Eve Teasing as a Form of Violence Against Women: A case Study of District Srinagar, Kashmir. International Journal of Sociology and Anthropology, 5(5), 2013
- Crime in India Report, Crimes Record Bureau, Government of India, 1994, 1995, 1996
- Bashir, Aadil and Khurshid, Shobana (2013). Eve Teasing and Molestation-A Case Study of District Srinagar. International Journal of Science and Research, 2013
- Baxi, Pratikhsha. Sexual harassment

14

Eve Teasing - Crime against Women: Human Rights Perspective

Baij Nath

Abstract

All human being are equal. Everyone has the right to live with dignity (including women) without discrimination of any kind. Many international convention, treaties, etc. declared that everyone is equal both men and women. There is special convention on women termed as Convention on Elimination of All forms of Exploitation Against women, 1979 which prohibits any kind of discrimination against women. The constitution of India also provides for right to equality to its all citizens and also made various provisions for the empowerment of women in order to bring them at par with men. In spite of all these protection in national and international law the crime against women is increasing day by day, including the crime of eve teasing. Women face eve teasing while going to schools on the streets, bus, school, working places, etc. by cheap men of the society. Now a day women are also facing eve teasing through mobile phones, social networking websites like Facebook and other applications. Eve teasing affects the life of a woman. Some women even suicide due to this. Almost every girl is the victim of eve teasing. It results in drop-out of girl students from the educational institutions, quitting of job of working woman. However, there are various constitutional and legal provisions for safety and protection of women and punishment for the wrong doer but the offence of eve teasing does not seem to end. The Indian Penal Code Specifically made provisions to deal with these kinds of offences. Many culprits are punished by the Judiciary but many are freed due to lack of evidence. Members of the society need to understand that women are also human beings like men, they have also right to live with dignity and without fear of any kind. Many NGOs are working to deal with the eve teasing. Media is also playing important role in generating awareness among the society for the human rights of women. Women must come forward if any kind of violence they are facing and approach the appropriate authority. This paper focuses on the violation of human rights of women due to eve teasing, it also suggest measures for solving the same.

Key words: Eve teasing, crime against women, human rights.

Introduction

Sexual exploitation of women is not a new phenomenon in the society. There are various types of violation against women. Eve teasing is one of them. Almost every women is the victim of eve teasing in this age. Due to the advancement of technology the crime against women particularly crime of eve teasing is increasing. Women are facing sexual exploitation in the educational institutions as well as at work places. Many times women remain silent because while exposing the culprit the society questions the character of the women. If she is unmarried she may feel that after exposing the incidence no one will marry her.

Almost half of the population are women. If the half of the people of the society are victims of violence than how can we ensure that we are civilised. Most of the sexual harassment cases remain unreported due the fear of further physical and sexual harassment, being socially rebuked. Now a days eve teasing is a burning issue because of its long term effects on women. Due to this women are discontinuing their studies, working women are quitting their jobs. The aim of the researcher is to highlight the violation of human rights of the women due to crime of eve teasing against them and to aware the public of its effects and providing solution in the form of suggestive measures. The researcher has collected the material from various books, websites, Journals (including online journals), books, reports and articles published in various newspapers.

History

The problem first received public and media attention in the 1970s. In the following decades, more and more women started going to college and working independently, meaning that they were often no longer accompanied by a male escort as had been the norm in traditional society. In response, the problem grew to alarming proportions, despite this not being the case in other cultures where women go and come as they please.

Meaning of Eve Teasing

Generally speaking Eve Teasing is teasing a girl or woman. It refers to public sexual harassment or street harassment to a girl by a boy, when it turns in to a serious issue. It is common in India and its neighbouring countries. It is not a recent problem. It is a social problem. Eve-teasing is a crime against women. It is the violation of human rights of women enshrined in the Constitution of India and many international covenants, treaties, declarations etc. It is a serious problem, which creates law and order problem in the society. Mostly young and school going girls are the victims of eve-teasing. Crime of eve-teasing should be dealt with strict laws and penalties.

Eve-teasing is a kind of sexual assault. Acts of eve-teasing includes whistle, catcalls, sexually evocative remarks, brushing in public places to outright groping, teasing by mobile phones, etc. Effects of eve-teasing are disrupted girls education, fear, social stigma which sometimes compel them to commit suicide. Eve teasing of school girls often resulted in increased drop-out rate and some times suicide.

Who are Eve Teasers?

Eve teasers can be any person on the street, in front of school, colleges, in the bus, train, lift, shopping mall teases girls by gesture, physical assault, etc. According to a report the probable eve-teasers are teenage boys, traffic police, rickshaw pullers, bus drivers, supervisors or colleagues of the working women. These teasers wait outside schools, colleges, streets and as soon as they saw the girls they start passing vulgar comments, filthy jokes, indecent exposure, etc.

Definition of Eve Teasing

Prohibition of eve teasing Act 1984 defines eve teasing as "when a man by words either spoken or by sign or by visible representation or by gesture does any act in public place, or signs or utters any indecent word or song or balled in any public place to the annoyance of any women.

Eve teasing means any indecent conduct or act by a man which cause intimidation, fear, shame or embarrassment to a women, including abusing or causing hurt or nuisance to, or assault, use of force on a woman.

Causes of Eve Teasing

There are no specific causes of eve teasing. It is a form of violence against women among others. Eve teasing is not a new phenomenon, it was there and it is and it will be but the pattern, definition and intervention are changing.

Some of the common causes of eve teasing are as follows:-

(i) Women's subordination
(ii) Bad impact of electronic media
(iii) Negative attitude towards women and girls
(iv) Lack of security for women
(v) Misuse of technology
(vi) Lack of morality and social ethics
(vii) Influence of electronic media and films
(viii) Time passing because eve teasers have no job to do
(ix) Having a curious attraction to opposite sex
(x) Lack of family education and culture
(xi) Lack of social values
(xii) Drug addiction
(xiii) Attitude towards girls and
(xiv) No respect for women

Types of Eve Teasing

There are various forms of eve teasing. Some of them are :

(i) **Eve Teasing with Girl Student:** Eve teasing generally occurs nearby girl's school. Young boys wait nearby girls home and started following when she goes to school. Sometimes they pass bad comments, sometimes they throw letter with bad proposal, sometimes they force and threat thee girl to make relationship with them, sometimes they propose the girl to marry. If the girl refuses, they threat be raped or kidnapped. As a result the girl has to leave the school and forced to do early marriage just to rescue her from the unsecured situation.

(ii) **Teasing by Mobile Phones:** It is caused by misuse of mobile technology. Due to the misuse of this technology the girl's lives are becoming hell. The teasers send SMS in an ornamental, rhetorical language as a result the adolescent girl are easily trapped with the false appreciation of the teasers. The girls sometimes take it as a love with a boy and become the victim. The boy capitalised the innocence of the girl by recording some intimate moments or dialogue by using mobile camera or video recorder.

(iii) **Sexual Abuse through Internet:** Through social media or in chatting young boys and girls are coming closer to each other. It often leads to exploitation of girls with some photographs by inserting with the use of modern technology, blackmailing them, often boys encourage the girls to watch some restricted website, as a result they fall victim of sexual extreme world. It is a most dangerous form of violence through technology.

Effects of Eve Teasing

(i) Dropout from the schools. This result in deprivation of girl's right to education.

(ii) Reduce mobility of girls or women. Due to this women are losing their mental mobility which destroys their independent thinking.

(iii) Early marriage. Due to this their physical and mental health becomes weak.

(iv) Hindered development of women.

(v) Psychological problems. Often due to this many girls commit suicides.

International Laws and Crime of Eve Teasing

There are various international conventions and human rights instruments which provide equal rights of women. India ratifies many of the international conventions. The most important among them is the Convention on Elimination of All form of Discrimination against Women (CEDAW), 1979. India ratifies Convention in 1993.Convention sets a framework for national action for ensuring women enjoy, on equal footing with men, their rights in all fields including employment, education and administration of property, and for ensuring the protection of women, especially against the threats to their physical safety and against rape and sexual exploitation. Convention was adopted in 1979 by the United General Assembly is often described as *international bill of rights of women.* It consists of Preamble and 30 articles. It defines what constitute discrimination against women and set up an agenda for national action to end such discrimination.

National Laws and Crime of eve Teasing

Constitution of India :

All human being (both men and women) are equal. Constitution of India provides right to equality under various articles. It also empowers the state to adopt measures of positive discrimination in favour of women for their empowerment. The government of India adopt various policies and plans in various spheres for the welfare and empowerment of women.

Various constitutional provisions for women are as under :

- Both men and women have equal rights and opportunities in political, economic and social spheres.
- Prohibition of discrimination against any citizen on grounds of religion, race, caste, sex, etc.
- Equal opportunities in matters relating to employment or appointment to any office under the state.
- Both men and women have equal rights to a means of livelihood.
- Equal pay for equal work for both men and women.
- State to make provisions for ensuring just and humane conditions of work and maternity relief.

Indian Penal Code 1860

The word eve teasing is nowhere defined in the Indian Penal Code. However victims of eve teasing could take recourse to certain following sections of Indian Penal Code :

Section 292 - prohibits Sale, etc., or obscene books, etc.

This section says that :

1. For the purposes of sub-section (2), a book, pamphlet, paper, writing, drawing, painting, representation, figure or any other object, shall be deemed to be obscene if it is lascivious or appeals to the prurient interest or if its effect, or where it comprises two or more distinct items the effect of any one of its items, is, if taken as a whole, such as to tend to deprave and corrupt person, who are likely, having regard to all relevant circumstances, to read, see or hear the matter contained or embodied in it.

2. Whoever

(a) Sells, lets to hire, distributes, publicly exhibits or in any manner puts into circulation, or for purposes of sale, hire, distribution, public exhibition or circulation, makes, produces or has in his possession any obscene book, pamphlet, paper, drawing, painting, representation or figure or any other obscene object whatsoever, or

(b) Imports, exports or conveys any obscene object for any of the purposes aforesaid, or knowing or having reason to believe that such object will be sold, let to hire, distributed or publicly exhibited or in any manner put into circulation, or

(c) Takes part in or receives profits from any business in the course of which he knows or has reason to believe that any such obscene objects are for any of the purposes aforesaid, made, produced, purchased, kept, imported, exported, conveyed, publicly exhibited or in any manner put into circulation, or

(d) Advertises or makes known by any means whatsoever that any person is engaged or is ready to engage in any act which is an offence under this section, or that any such obscene object can be procured from or through any person, or

(e) Offers or attempts to do any act which is an offence under this section, shall be punished on first conviction with imprisonment of either description for a term which may extend to two years, and with fine which may extend to two thousand rupees, and, in the event of a second or subsequent conviction, with imprisonment of either description for a term which may extend to five years, and also with fine which may extend to five thousand rupees.

Exception

These section does not extend to :

(a) Any book, pamphlet, paper, writing, drawing, painting, representation or figure :

  (i) The publication of which is proved to be justified as being for the public good on the ground that such book, pamphlet, paper, writing, drawing, painting, representation or figure is in the interest of science, literature, art or learning or other objects of general concern, or

  (ii) Which is kept or used bonafide for religious purposes;

(b) Any representation sculptured, engraved, painted or otherwise represented on or in :

 (i) any ancient monument within the meaning of the Ancient Monuments and Archaeological Sites and Remains Act, 1958 (24 of 1958), or

 (ii) any temple, or on any car used for the conveyance of idols, or kept or used for any religious purpose.

Section 293 - of Indian penal Code prohibits Sale, etc., of obscene objects to young person. This section says that whoever sells, lets to hire, distributes, exhibits or circulates to any person under the age of twenty years any such obscene object as is referred to in the last preceding section, or offers or attempts so to do, shall be punished on first conviction with imprisonment of either description for a term which may extend to three years, and with fine which may extend to two thousand rupees, and, in the event of a second or subsequent conviction, with imprisonment of either description for a term which may extend to seven years, and also with fine which may extend to five thousand rupees.

Section 294 - provides for punishment of obscene acts and songs

This Section says that whoever, to the annoyance of others :

a) Does any obscene act in any public place, or
b) Sings, recites or utters any obscene song, ballad or words, in or near any public place, shall be punished with imprisonment of either description for a term which may extend to three months, or with fine, or with both.

Section 354 - makes provision for punishment for Assault or criminal force to woman with intent to outrage her modesty.

This section says that whoever assaults or uses criminal force to any woman, intending to outrage or knowing it to be likely that he will thereby outrage her modesty, shall be punished with imprisonment of either description for a term which shall not be less than one year but which may extend to five years, and shall also be liable to fine.

Section 509 - prohibits Word, gesture or act intended to insult the modesty of a woman.

This section says that whoever, intending to insult the modesty of any woman, utters any word, makes any sound or gesture, or exhibits any object, intending that such word or sound shall be heard, of that such gesture or object shall be seen, by such woman, or intrudes upon the privacy of such woman, (shall be punished with simple imprisonment for a term which may extend to three years, and also with fine.)

Tamilnadu Prohibition of Eve Teasing Act, 1988

Act provides that whoever commits or participate in or abets eve teasing in or within the precincts of any educational institution, temple or other places of worship, Bus Stop, road, railway station, cinema theatre, park, beach, place of worship, public services vehicle or any other place shall be punished with imprisonment for a term which may extend to ten thousand rupees or both.

Role of Judiciary

Judiciary has also tried to curb the menace of eve teasing in various judgements.

In a case the accused was a graduate of a university. He wrote a letter to an English teacher containing indecent proposals and sent it to her in an envelope. It was held that the accused had outraged her modesty.

Modesty of women is an attribute associated with female human beings as a class. It is a virtue which attaches to a female owing to her sex. The act of pulling sari, coupled with the request for sexual intercourse, is such as would be an outrage to the modesty of women, and knowledge, that modesty is likely to be outraged is sufficient to constitute the offence without any deliberate intention having such outrage alone for its object.

In a case a female child of seven year old was held to be a women and as the accused had caused injury to private parts he was held guilty of outraged the modesty of women.

Role of NGOs

There are many NGOs working to curb crime of eve teasing. Some of them are

"BLANK NOISE" is a community project that seeks to confront street harassment, commonly known as eve teasing in India. The project, initiated by Jasmeen Patheja in August 2003, started out as a student project at Srishti School of Art and Design and Technology in Bangalore. Blank Noise is run by volunteers both male and female from across geographical locations and age groups work collective. Blank Noise works on the issue of street sexual harassment. They made public debates on eve teasing. Blank Noise spread to Mumbai, Delhi, Chennai, Calcutta,

Chandigarh, Hyderabad, and Lucknow. Through street actions and dialogue, Blank Noise hopes to achieve its aims of achieving a safe and free environment for women on the streets, and enable society to become more egalitarian towards women in general. In Dec 2012, following the brutal gang rape of a young women in a moving Bus in Delhi, Blank Noise started the Safe City Pledge an initiative urging citizens to pledge ways in which they can make cities safer for women.

"TAKE BACK THE NIGHT" is an international event and NGO with the mission of ending sexual violence in all forms. Hundreds of events are held in over 30 countries annually. Events often include marches, rallies and vigils intended as a protest and direct action against rape and other forms of sexual violence. The common purpose is to advocate for the right of everyone to feel safe from sexual violence. Women are often told to be extra careful and take precautions when going out at night. In some parts of the world, even today, women are not allowed out at night.

Role of Media

Media has also played an important role in highlighting the cases of eve teasing. Some of the instances are as follows:

A 38 year old man was nabbed by one of the recently formed SHE teams a Malakpet bus stop for teasing a girl was on Wednesday sentenced to two-day simple imprisonment by the seventh additional chief metropolitan magistrate in Nampally.

The GRP Mughal Sarai arrested a deputy director in education department from Punjab for allegedly teasing women passengers on Rajdhani Express.

Conclusion

Eve teasing is curse in the society; it is a crime against the dignity, self-respect and honour of woman. It must be curbed by social action and strong and tough law by providing tough punishment. It is necessary that society must be aware of the gravity of the crime of eve teasing and its effects on the women folk. It is observed that women were able to overcome the social barriers by their own willpower and with the support of their near ones. Law is also providing safety to women from any kind of discrimination including sexual exploitation and the right to live with dignity. But the problem is that many women are unaware about their rights, especially those who are living in rural areas.

Suggestions

- Need for a comprehensive legal framework
- Strict punishment should be followed
- Generating awareness through media about eve teasing of women. Special programmes should be followed by the TV Channels
- Parents should give equal attention to their children both girl and boy. The parents should stretch their helping hand towards their children
- Engage young generation in social work
- Avoid going in isolated places
- Avoid travelling in crowded bus or train
- Always stay in groups
- Be decent in public places
- Avoid late nights outside
- Aware of people around you
- Self defence training
- Dial emergency phone numbers of cop or family members

References

- Indian Penal Code 1860
- Delhi Prohibition of Eve Teasing Bill of 1984
- Tamil Nadu Prohibition of Eve Teasing Act, 1988
- Jammu and Kashmir The Ranbir Penal Code published by Law Department Codification Cell and Printed at the Ranbir Government Press, Jammu.
- Agarwal, H. O., "Human Rights", 11th edition 2008, Central Law Publications, Allahabad.
- Shukla, V. N. *"Constitution of India"*, 10th edition, Eastern Book Company, New Delhi-110001.
- Sethi, R.P. *"Commentary on the constitution of Jammu and Kashmir"*, 2005 edition. Published at Ashoka Law house New Delhi-110017
- Mishra, Prof. S.N, *"The Indian Penal Code 1860"*, Central Law Publications, Allahabad, ISBN: 978-93-80289-08-3, Seventeenth Edition, 2009.
- Natarajan, Mangai, *"Women Police in a Changing Society: Back Door to Equality"*, Ashgate Publishing, Ltd., 2008, ISBN 0-7546-4932-6.
- Jain, M.P., Constitutional Law of India

- Akhtar, Dr Zobaida, International Women Online Journal of Distance Education October, 2013 Volume:2 Issue: 4 Article: 01 Issue: 2147-0367
- Bashir, Aadil, "Eve teasing and Molestation- A Case study of District Srinagar", *International Journal of science and Research* (IJSR) (Online): 2319-7064 Volume 2 Issue 12, December 2013 (www.ijsr.net)
- Faruq, Farzana "Eve Teasing: A social Disaster for women in Bangladesh", *Estern University Journal,* Volume 3 Issue 3, December 2011, ISSN NO. 9898-7889
- "Women take to streets to stake claim to their rights" The Hindu, New Delhi. September 17, 2006.
- "Eve teasing lands man in Jail", *Times of India,* 20 Nov. 2014
- "Education Department Official held for eve teasing", *Times of India,* 20 Nov. 2014
- www.indiasocial.in/case-study-blank-noise/
- http//Blog.blanknoise.org/2012/12/pledge-makin-coties-safe.html
- http//www.wikipedia.org
- www.ijsr.net

15

Women Must Protest against Eve Teasing!

Shravan kumar and Ankita Singh

Abstract

The immoral act of Eve teasing is social malady in 21st century. It humiliates the prestige of women at public places by eve teasers in form of vulgar remarks, obscene gestures, molestation, physical assaults, and public sexual harassment from which a little girl to young women suffers regularly in present scenario. To overcome this harsh reality the women of today should plan strategies for complete elimination of this social evil rather than to suffer from brutality of eve teasers, because now it is enough for women to live in fear of losing her modesty. The women of 21st century should raise her voice against eve teasing, to fulfil the goal. The present chapter highlights solution regarding "what women can do against eve teasing? It provides guidelines to every woman to defend her dignity by use of self-defence techniques and judicial provisions of Indian penal code, which she can apply in drastic situations when it becomes necessary to punish eve teasers. Further the article deals with some preventive measures for women, which she should adopt as precautions while moving out in society to avoid conditions, which sparks the fire to eve teasing situations. The tactics mentioned in article regarding self-defence mechanism includes judo karate, martial arts, use of mobile phone technology, which helps women to destroy the web of eve teasing. Under the judicial provisions, the sections 292, 354 A, 509 of Indian penal code act as legal aid for women to fight against offenders of her modesty. Therefore, every woman should adopt these techniques of self-defence, legal provisions, and preventive measures for her safety in social context.

Keywords: Eve teasing, modesty of women, self-defence mechanism, Legal provisions.

Introduction

"Women are the real architects of society" these words of Harriet Beecher Stowe are neglected by offensive act of eve teasing which tends to challenge the feministic values and hunts modesty of women in present society by bows of vulgar comments, public sexual harassment or molestation of women by men. It is a social malady, that sparks the fire to create next Nirbhaya in society by some barbaric males who avoided the fact that women are blossoms in autumn of life, they spread smiles over miles in dark strives of unhappiness. To tease them is to tease divine motherhood, as they are creator, nourisher, and survivor of universe of which the men are part.

They need social up gradation rather than molestation by men as Diane Marie Child says, "A women is the full circle within her is the power to create nurture and transform". Only she needs courage to transform her bangles into swords, cut the cords of eve teasing embryo from womb of society because the courage of women can flow rivers from deserts, and sprout the seeds of prosperity from barren land. Therefore, instead of being a speechless portrait she should raise her voice to rebel against eve teasing and its causative agents.

Eve teasing is product of male brutal psychology towards female. Oxford dictionary defines eve teasing as the making of unwanted sexual remarks or advances by a man to women in a public place. Etymologically the word eve had biblical origin means the first women, and to tease means to provoke. The word eve in present perspective signifies the entire females of society and in totality eve teasing stands for their physical, mental, social, and psychological harassment. It is generally the euphemism used for public sexual harassment, verbal sexual taunting, non verbal assaults such as winking, whistling, obscene gestures and bodily touching to physical assaults such as pinching, fondling from which a little girl to young women suffers regularly in public places, transports, malls, parks, office, and schools.

It is a harsh reality for victim. The women of today must make strategies to overcome this offence by her self–defence mechanism but prior to that, she must make quick assessment of its old roots and present complexities. As dynamic properties of eve teasing changes due to situation and time, as not for same reason the eve is teased every time, there are wide varieties of reasons, situation and places for her public insult.

The crime of sexual assaults at public places against women is not new it persist in society from ancient era. The epic of Mahabharata feature Draupadi as victim disrobed by Dushashan.Social epidemic of eve teasing found its root cause in influences of misogynist tradition of patriarchal society were the practice of misogyny prevails from ancient culture until today to mistreat women by hatred, sexual discrimination. Oppression of women and further considering them of weaker gender by misogynist of society may be probable cause of out bust of eve teasing problems, which challenges the modesty of women in 21st century.

The curse of misogyny is foundation in construction of eve teasing psychology of man which needs the proper solution because the doom of eve teasing snatches away the dignity and mental peace of females and even tempt them to attempt suicide is seen in recent years.

The revolutions of media technology had focused public attention to solve this complex issue by seminar, lectures, and anti- eve teasing campaigns but they seems to fade out as crime of eve teasing against women is on increase.

National crime record bureau of Ministry of home affairs had drawn out the figures of assault on women with intent to outrage her modesty(sec 354 IPC) and insult of the modesty of women (sec.509 IPC) of last 5 years (2009-2013) published in its latest compendium released in June 2014, shows the rapid increase in eve teasing crime against women. Although not mentioned separately but sections 354 and 509 of IPC deals with eve teasing.

Records of Assault on Women with Intent to Outrage her Modesty and Insult of Modesty of Women by NCRB

Sl. No.	Crime	Year 2009	2010	2011	2012	2013
1.	Assault on women with intent to outrage her modesty. (sec 354 IPC)	38,711	40,613	42,968	45,351	70,739
2.	Insult to the modesty of women (sec.509 IPC)	11,009	99,61	85,70	91,73	12,589

Further, the above-mentioned facts needs graphical representation for detailed analysis and further study of eve teasing crime because it is the burning issue in today's perspective regarded as offence against women and unlawful act in social context.

Graphical Representation of Crime of Assault on Women with Intent To out Rage her Modesty

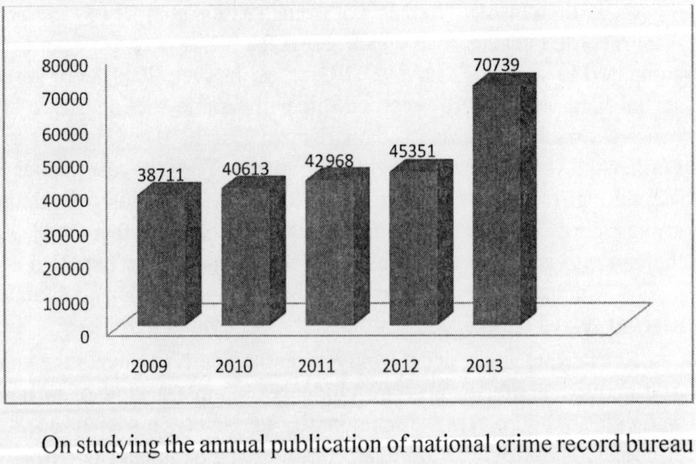

On studying the annual publication of national crime record bureau a total no of 70739 cases of assaults on women with intent to outrage her modesty under section 354 of IPC was reported in year 2013 which shows a increase of 56.0 per cent in comparison to year 2012 having 45351 cases In year, 2011 under the same section (354 of IPC) National crime record bureau recorded 42968 cases of molestation, which shows the increase over the year 2010 and 2009 having 40613 and 38711 cases. The year 2013 recorded highest crime under this section.

On analysis of cases headed under insult of modesty of women too needs graphical representation for further explanation.

Graphical Representation of Crime of Insult to the Modesty of Women

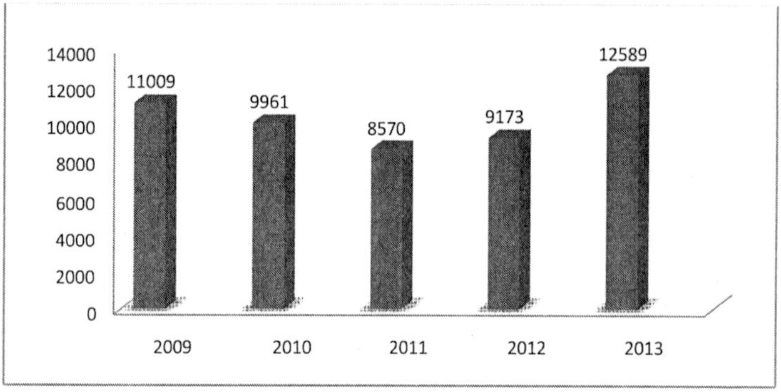

Regarding Insult of modesty of women a total number of 12589 cases were recorded in year 2013 which shows the increase of 37.2 per cent as compared to year 2012 having 9173 cases. In year, 2011 8570 cases of sexual harassment were recorded under the same section 509 of IPC, which shows the decrease in comparison to year 2010 having 9961 cases. Further the year 2009 recorded total number of 11009 cases which was second highest in number than year 2013. These records from national crime record bureau are available till year 2013 only. Further to talk about the current year 2014 too focuses eve teasing and other horrified crime against women as the columns of daily news publications contains the news of sexual harassment of women frequently and rapidly.

Eve teasing as social deformity psychologically paralyzes the victim. The above-mentioned facts are evidences against a kind of torture to women at public places, which horrifies her safety in society inspite of article 21. The Article 21 of Indian constitution guarantees right to privacy as part of fundamental right but the privacy of Indian women is big doubt in Indian society as dozens of roadside Romeo target her by their vulgarity. So now, it is time to begin a countdown, to reform delicate women to the sharp rebellion who can forcefully revolt against the eve teasing crime, but here a question arise what a women can do against eve teasing to untie herself from its evil knots ? The answer for this is she needs three E's for its eradication, which are *Encouragement, Empowerment, and Efficiency.* The encouragement from society, family and friends to empower herself with efficient self-defence mechanism which leads her to fight bravely against eve teasing because if women of today wait for someone to save her from being prey of eve teasing is an unwise act. She needs to be aware of her potential and power to defend her modesty because modesty of women is not a game to play with it; it is a symbol of honour, dignity, and respect, which requires protection from eve teasers.

To begin the functioning of self-defence mechanism it is pre expected from women to raise her voice against eve teasing. It is prior condition for efficient working of this mechanism because the mute women paves way for eve teasers to further conspire against her modesty. As per Indian context, the silence of women is considered as her mutual acceptance to mistreat her in terms of sexual assaults. Therefore, it is required from women to express against eve teasing rather to sit like a dumb doll due to fear of social shame and abuse. Women must recall the article 19(1) (A) of Indian constitution, that guarantees her freedom of speech and expression, which she can use as a weapon to express about the threat of eve teasers towards her social dignity. Women need to be outspoken, courageous and self-sufficient to defend her modesty for that she must learn the efficient working of self-defence mechanism represented below.

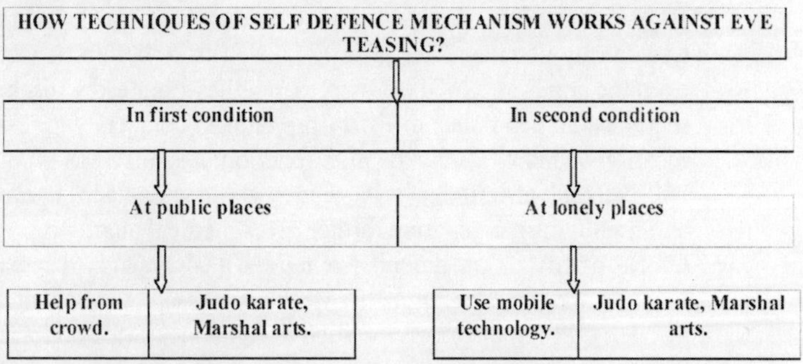

These techniques used under self-defence mechanism works to defend women from eve teasing; it is a kind of initial aid available to her before receiving proper help from law and order. Thus, every women and girl should adopt these strategies. It works efficiently under both conditions to safeguard the women's security at most crowded places and lone areas from eve teasers. Only women requires to use her brain to show little cleverness if trapped in situations of eve teasing. she can use the tactics of judo karate and Martial arts for her self-defence but not every woman knows this art. They are recommended to keep with them the pepper spray, which help them to suede eve teasers and run away to safe place. Further to talk about the most crowded public places like shopping centres, malls, parks roads etc. She can shout to seek help from crowd because some of the gentle men from crowd tend to come forward to safeguard her modesty. As diamond cuts diamond, the handful of good people will protest against eve teasers to protect women, but who comes to protect her in those drastic situations when she alone returns to home from work at dark nights? The answer is no one. In those situations, women should be alert because most of the crimes against her happen in darkness of night. She needs to use of her smart phone and send exact location of her to cops and family by just one touch of GPS setting and location maps. Now with advancement of mobile technology, there are various app on Android, Blackberry and Nokia smart phones, which guarantees women's safety and protect her from eve teasers. Thus, women of today should download some of these apps, which can track her location by GPS and send SMS to list of people chosen as per app setting in emergency. Some of these apps are Raksha–women security alert, life 360, family locator, fight back, circle of 6, SOS whistle that act as a bodyguard to women's security. Let's have a look on their functioning:

- **The Raksha** : Women security alert few months back launched by BJP take cares of women's safety by sending her exact location to trustworthy people of her priority chosen from before. It works even the app is switched off by pressing the volume key for three seconds and send alert to list of pre chosen contacts with exact location on map. Having the SOS function, it sends SMS if not in internet zone also, it also tells women about safe places to move and highlights danger zone further gives medical alert.
- **Circle of Six** : Can defend women as it also sends her exact location and pre programmed SMS alert message to six contacts through GPS. Some other app such as fight back, life 360 locator performs the same function to send exact location of women to her desired contacts.
- **SOS** : Whistle triggers a whistle to secure women instead of sending her location to family and friends. As its name suggest it triggers the whistle to secure women by gaining the attention of people in public places who can come forward to save her. The best quality of this app is that it works effectively although the phone is in silent mode.

These apps hamper the evil interest of eve teasers and act as a shield to safeguard women's modesty at public places, so in present perspective every female is suggested to make use of smart phone technology in her protection, beyond the other self-defence tactics.

The innovations in technology of telecommunication are boon to feministic world. It guides girls and working women to use mobile phones for their safety but it is a bitter truth that eve teasers due to their vulgar mentality, convert this boon to curse for females by their obscene calls and make use of their phones for harassment of women. They talk abusive, make vulgar calls, and make her scared to outrage her modesty in future at public places. To get rid of these situations the states of Uttar Pradesh provide help to females by women help line number named as women power line to handle obscene calls. The females only requires to dial 1090 to get relief as the service works for 24x 7 against obscene caller and roadside Romeos, further the 1091 women help line number also serves to women in distress in state of Delhi and other parts of country to deal with roadside Romeos . Same as these two states, the other states of India too have their own women help line number, which helps women in situation to distress. After threatening, the dignity of women at public places the act of eve teasing is not limited to worlds of mobile only, it make women prey of eve teasers in context of social media also. Therefore, it is necessary for females to be aware of social media sites on internet. They must not post their most personal information like phone number, address, with photographs frequently on social media sites, and share it with some strangers or even sharing with members added to contact list should be in limit not information of each second should be told to them as in many situations friends tend to become foe. Women should remember that eve teasers are more active and smart then her .They collect all information of hers and make plans for future conspiracies regarding blackmailing, eve teasing and pornography. The crimes related to cyber worlds are on increase so females should save themselves to becoming victim of it and should report to cyber cells if found any threat against them.

Further, in worse and uncontrolled situations of eve teasing were females found them to be helpless can take help of law and order. Even they can file case against eve teasers who tends to harm their modesty. For this, first they require to know about laws in India about eve teasing. The word eve teasing is not separately defined as per Indian laws but the section 292, section 354, a section 509 of IPC deals with it.

The section 292 of Indian penal code deals with obscene act and song at public places, .which can create annoyance to others. It strictly prohibits to sing, recites, utter any obscene songs, balled or word, at or near by public place and if offender founds to be guilty under it shall be punished with imprisonment of either description of a term which may extend to three months with fine or with both.

The section 509 of Indian penal code deals with word, gesture, or act intended to insult the modesty of women. It punishes the offender with simple imprisonment for a term which may extend to one year, or with fine or with both if found to be guilty of intending to insult modesty of women by uttering any word, making any sound or gesture, or exhibit any object, intending that women should hear such word or sound, or see such gesture or object, or intrudes upon the privacy of such women.

The section 354 A of Indian penal code deals with assault or criminal force to woman with intent to outrage her modesty. Under this section offender should be punished with imprisonment of either description for a term, which may extend to two years, with fine, or with both if found guilty of assaults, or uses criminal forces to any woman, intending to outrage her modesty. The criminal law (Amendment) act was passed in year 2013 makes amendment in section 354 A of Indian penal code by includes sexual harassment as new offence. It protect women against physical contact and advances involving unwelcome sexual overtures (ii) a demand or request for sexual favour, (iii) making sexually coloured remarks, (iv) forcibly showing pornography (v) any other unwelcome physical, verbal or non-verbal conduct of sexual nature. For all these crimes imprisonment up to five years is given or with fine or with both in cases of offence described in clauses (i) and (ii) Of sub- section one and imprisonment of either description that may extended to one year, or with fine, or with both. In case of person who commits offence under clause (iii), (iv), (v) of sub-section one.

Regarding the disrobing of women which is considered an unlawful act , the criminal law (Amendment) act 2013 under the section 354 B severely punish offenders if found guilty of disrobing a women with imprisonment not less than three years but which may extend to seven years and with fine. The above-mentioned Legal provision of Indian penal code helps women to fight against the culprits of eve teasing for whom to tease eve is the matter of lust and leisure.

Further, the sexual harassment of women at work place is on increase for that the parliament of India passed The sexual Harassment of women at workplace (prevention, prohibition and Redressal) Act, 2013 to protect women from being sexually harassed at all work place weather it is public or private and create mechanism for redressal of complaints. As per context of woman's safety, these laws act as a weapon to punish offenders of her modesty and safeguard her social dignity. In case of the drastic situations where the self-defence mechanism stops working it is recommended to females to take shelter of law and order to live safe and happy.

The legislative provisions, techniques of self-defence mechanism and aid from women help line are answers to question asked before "what women can do against the eve teasing". The modern women of 21st century can rebel against eve teasers by use of it, but these techniques are not enough. A woman requires additional protection, for this they may use some preventive measures to secure themselves. As it is the old saying, "prevention is better than cure "so beyond learning the tactics of self defences and legislative measures provided to them, the women should learn those measures to prevent the conditions which tends to out bust eve teasing in certain circumstances. There are some do and don'ts for women that alert her prior, to become prey of eve teasers. The dos are guidelines for her safety and don'ts are the code of ethics that prohibit her to become victim of eve teasing.

Dos for Women

- Do inform the family members while going out, just keep in touch with them.
- Try to come home at time.
- Do activate the GPS and location maps of mobile phone while going out as it tracks the exact position of victim in case of emergencies.
- For quick defence from attacks of eve teasers keep peper spray in purse.
- Keep in speed dial the police control room number 100.
- Keep in speed dial the number of family members.
- Try to give priority to recharge Boucher rather than facility of e-recharge to avoid obscene callers.
- Before, hiring the taxi note down its number for future safety.
- While, returning from office to home at late night, make it sure that office cab drop at home instead of coming from public transport.
- Be alert while standing in lines at railway stations, airports and to pay bills etc, because some man tends to push woman from back in intention of touching her body.
- Be alert while walking on streets and keep an eye on activities of people moving around.

- Use ladies compartment while travelling in trains instead of general compartment.
- Just avoid going in fairs and cultural celebration alone when there is too much rush, as eve teasers tends to active in these situations.
- Try to gather some important information about the place prior to visit it, like nearby railway stations, bus stand, and police station.
- Moving to any unfamiliar places whether in city or out of station, females should not tell the taxi driver or any stranger that she is unfamiliar with it and must pretend to know the place years back.

Don'ts for Women

- Do not were indecent outfits which tends to give green signals to eve teasers. Although it is true that eve teasers harass even the girls wearing shalwar kameej, but girls on their own should avoid wearing such outfit, which gains the attention of eve teasers.
- Do not go alone out of home after nine at night, and if necessary go with some family members.
- Do not sit alone in public transports like bus and taxi while travelling at night.
- Do not go out of home in night for fun sake like for movies, hanging out with friends.
- Do not date with friends of social media sites.
- Do not share personal information on social media sites.
- Do not mix up with strangers while travelling in bus and train.
- Do not share taxi and rickshaws with strangers.
- Do not consume any drink or meal offered by strangers in public transport.
- Do not react to vulgar comments; just avoid them until it is possible.
- Do not be scared of vulgar messages and calls from obscene callers; just take the help of women help line number to sort out this problem.
- Do not be too intimate and share personal information with colleagues at workplace, maintain dignity in professional contacts.
- Do not hesitate to tell family members if mentally and physically harassed by someone.

Women should take action against eve teasing if trapped in any such situation , but prior to that she must adopt do and don'ts as preventive precautions to protect her to get trapped in such conditions which gain the attention of eve teasers towards her. she must be alert in public places and use the third eye of intuition to discriminate between good and bad intentions of strangers as well as known persons towards her, because in some situation dear ones tends to threaten with their wrong intention the dignity and social image of women. To cure social epidemic of eve teasing, it is essentiality of today to cut the weeds of man's brutal psychology regarding women and make him respect the dignity of women by stop considering her the material of lust for complete eradication of this complex issue, but task seems quite difficult to counsel some brutish men whose game is to play with dignity of women. In such condition, women instead of living in darkness of fear should step forward with courage and revolt against the eve teasing by techniques of self-defence, help from legal provisions and women power line because living safe and happy is her birthright and nobody can deprive her from it.

A modern woman of 21st century should not bear the pain of eve teasing and raise her voice against roadside Romeos who tends to destroy her glory by molestation, sexual harassment at public places because now it is enough. Situation needs to be changed, eve teasers should compel to realise that whole street is not only for them, they cannot move freely on it and tease a women in whatever way they want. For their misdeeds, they will be punished either by law or by entire female society. So now it's time to stop crime against women and give her due respect as being human because women are the pearls in ocean of life.

References

- Criminal law (Amendment) act 2013 http://indiacode.nic.in/acts-in-pdf/acts-in-pdf.htm
- National crime record bureau compendium (2013) Section 292 of Indian penal code http://indiankanoon.org/doc/1704109/
- Section 354 of Indian penal code http://indiankanoon.org/doc/203036/
- Section 509 of Indian penal code http://indiankanoon.org/doc/68146/
- The sexual Harassment of woman at workplace(prevention, prohibition and Redressal)Act, 2013 http://indiacode.nic.in/acts-in-pdf/acts-in-pdf.htm

16

Time to Introspect

Vidya Vati

Abstract

The evil of eve teasing is rampant and ubiquitous in India violating fundamental human rights of women to live with dignity. The term 'eve teasing' itself is degrading for females. All women whatever the social and educational profile may be are vulnerable to sexual harassment. Eve teasing includes acts like lewd remarks, ogling, touching, outright groping etc. These acts have deep impact on life of females. To know the perspective of victim, parents, police and public about the phenomenon of eve teasing, a mini research was conducted with the help of interview guide. Samples were selected randomly from Delhi and a few from other states. The opinions are varied and diverse in respect of reasons and solutions. Our Courts have also shown great concern for this menace and issued elaborate guidelines to curb eve teasing. Many of the respondents agree that law should be effective and swift in implementation. Generally the girls' strategy to deal with the problem is found to evade the offender. The real solution lies in socialisation of child. Education system should also promote values of respect, justice and fairness.

Key Words: eve teasing, harassment, menace, curb

Introduction

The evil of eve teasing is rampant all over the world cutting across religious communities, cultures and regions. In India general attitude towards this evil is baffling and complex which in itself reflects great paradox so far as the issue regarding females is concerned. India is a country which worships female power for nine day as 'Navratris' twice a year, a country in which more than two thousand years ago Kautilaya, a renowned intellectual and author of Arthsastra says, "If a person ogles a woman, his eyes should be extracted."

Here I would also like to quote words of an eminent writer Kerry Brown that she said in famous book Essential teachings Of Hinduism-'In Hinduism a woman is looked after not because she is inferior or incapable but, on the contrary, she is treasured. She is the pride and power of society.' In that country one will find rarely a woman who has not ever experienced sexual harassment which is called eve teasing in general terms.

It is said that status of women in a given society is a mirror of the level of its refinement. If treatment met out to women is the yardstick, it can be said that our society has become very cruel and barbaric. In general women are not respected now. The Nirbhaya incident in Delhi on December, 2012 tells the sordid tale of savagery and sexual violence. This 49 per cent of country's population lives in constant fear of being abducted, molested, raped, and beaten and perhaps being murdered. A female is not safe anywhere. There is need for her to be on guard all the time. It is disgusting that we live in a society where neither 80 years old woman nor 2 years old girl is safe. Even foreign woman travellers are not spared. Recently a Swiss woman was gang raped. A British woman had to jump off the balcony of her hotel to escape from sexual harassment by a hotel employee in Agra.

Sexual assaults are still on rise among India's women. According to the WHO a woman in India is raped every 20 minutes. The professionals, commoners, and high profile women- no one is spared. During my study even some woman constables revealed that they feel unsafe after 8 pm. on the roads of Delhi. Headline Today reporter Ms. Anjana Kashyap was hackled near AIMS flyover in Delhi by three men when she carried out a reality check on the streets of the capital to gauge how much Delhi is safe for women.

Definition of Eve Teasing

Eve teasing is a euphemism used in India, also in Pakistan and Bangladesh for sexual harassment of female by male. Eve teasing describes the acts of name calling, following, stalking, touching, brushing, sexually suggestive remarks, lewd gestures, pulling dupatta and even groping of woman. The disturbing factor is casual attitude the people have for these acts, as it strips away the seriousness of the act of sexual harassment. The word 'eve' has been taken from the Bible who was temptress, who led Adam from the path of righteousness. The term itself implies that it is the woman who is guilty, who provokes man to indulge in such acts and 'tease' gives the act innocent tone and perpetrator deserves to be pardoned.

The views of Danjani Iyer Mohanty are worth quoting here: The term 'eve teasing' must die. We have to use more effective dysphemism 'Sita bullying'. This strike home to many Indians as Sita is pious wife of the Hindu god Rama and above moral reproach; she is still seen as the exemplary daughter, wife and mother. The term 'Sita bullying' could be useful and necessary in changing our thoughts, conversations and actions.

In reality eve teasing at public places is a menace, rather disaster, which humiliates a female, hurts her self-respect and leaves permanent scar on the psyche of the victim and even results in suicide also. It strips away a woman from her right to live with dignity.

Eve teasing is a dehumanising act. It is subtle and blatant but its impact is profound and far-reaching on the status of women in society. Though parents in India love girl as a child , even then they prefer son to daughter. Inter-alia eve teasing and other forms of violence are responsible for female foeticide resulting in adverse male-female ratio. The parents of girls remain in constant fear of safety of their daughters and loss of family honour, as she is vulnerable and physically weaker than man. About 70 per cent parents say that now dowry is not a big issue. Daughter's safety is bigger issue.

Eve teasing indirectly affects development issues also. 'Violence against women is manifestation of the historically unequal power relations between men and women which have led to the domination over and discrimination against women by men and to the prevention of full advancement of women [UN1993]. Fear of violence is a permanent constraint on the mobility of women and limits their access to resources.

Eve teasing and other forms of violence harms not only woman as individual but also deprives society of their valuable contribution economically, politically and culturally. Existential circumstances compel women to restrict their activities to household and family. As Ganghiji had said 'women have vast potentiality. When their energy and strength is tapped in nation building, only then India will become a great nation.' Robert Ingersoll says–there will never be a generation of great men until there has been a generation of free women, of free mothers.

It is right of every human being to enjoy fundamental freedom. Eve teasing is violation on fundamental right. A girl's childhood is lost when we teach her how to avoid victimisation. Known, unknown, uncles, bhaiyas, rickshawallas, shopkeepers, neighbours, teachers, students, class fellows, colleagues, peon–anyone may violate the sanctity of her body. Women suffer in career, for they have to struggle both as a person and as a female. It is a crime easy to commit but difficult to prove.

The Scope of Study

The present study aimed at examining the attitude of victims of eve teasing, parents, police and public towards eve teasing. Four sets of interview guide were prepared.

The sample consisted of 150 students and women. 135 females were in the age group between15-26. They are the most vulnerable group. 15 women were in the age group between35-45. Total 17 persons from Police Department [two of them recently retired] were interviewed holding post of ACP, SHO, SI, Head Constable and constable including female officers. 30 parents of young girls were interviewed at random. The opinion of 20 persons of both sexes in various professions was taken, as–male students, principal, social worker, mali, newspaper seller, water woman, security guard, teacher, driver, shopkeeper and politician. The interview guide comprised of open ended questions.

Perspective of the Police

The police differ, to some extent, on issue whether the incidences of eve teasing or violence against women have risen over few years. 75 per cent respondents believe that incidences of eve teasing and violence have risen, but all respondents agree that reporting has increased after the changes in IPC after Nirbhaya incident in Delhi. 80 per cent of them feel it is due to enhanced awareness among public and increased confidence of girls/parents in reporting such cases. Only 20 per cent think that people's trust in police has increased. Some respondents [both male and female] also confided that 70 per cent of reported cases are false. The real issues are other than eve teasing like mutual animosity, brawl over rent, property, encroachment, tiff in extra-marital relationship etc. Hardly 30 per cent cases are real. A large chunk of society still does not want to expose their females by reporting to the police for the fear of humiliation. All the respondents think if general public fulfils social responsibility by being active in defence of girls/women, the problem of eve teasing, at least what is happening in visible way, will be solved to great extent. Parents are also responsible for this state of affairs, for they have lost control over their children, esp. sons. Only 25 per cent respondents feel that western ways of life, revealing dresses of girls and erosion of traditional family values are leading to moral chaos in Indian society.

On the condition of anonymity one of the officers revealed that police department lacks manpower. A constable has to patrol a large area."We receive requests from girls' school for PCR patrolling to curb eve teasing in the vicinity of schools. Sometimes we are unable to spare staff and vehicle for the said purpose. There is dire need of recruitment in police department." Another police officer says easy access to knowledge through mobile and internet is leading more and more teenagers and young boys to the web of crime against women. Sometimes people with vested interests push them to crime to fulfil their own agenda. Migratory population is another dimension in the capital city. Since time immemorial, social pressure has played crucial in preventing him from violating the social norms in Indian society. Here people have no cultural pressure to behave properly and existing laws do not fear them. Laws are not commensurate with the nature of these crimes. In some cases police works hard to nab the culprit, but they get scot free in court. Sons of powerful and rich persons threaten the victim. These factors demoralise the police, encourages males to indulge in acts of eve teasing and girls do not come forward.

Surprisingly, one of the officers asserted that there should be no change in Juvenile Act regarding the sentencing of perpetrator of crime. Three of the total respondents supported 'adult sentencing' age should be reduced to 14 years, others favour 15 year, while all woman officers advocate that there should not be any condition of age. Sentencing should be in proportion to the seriousness of crime, not the age.

So far solution is concerned, all respondents feel that real solution of violence against women and of eve teasing lies in homes and upbringing of the boys, in the attitude of public at large, in the attitude of girls/women.

If girls become bold and get self-defence training, problem will be solved to large extent.

Some Case Studies of Victims

Out of 150 girls/women, barring three girls all respondents have experienced eve teasing or sexual harassment in one form or the other. Some shocking stories have come up. Ms. Arvinder 36 years old revealed that before marriage her maternal uncle [mama] used to ogle her. One day he tried to touch her bottom in undesirable way. She brought it into the notice of her mother but the latter ignored. Another girl of 18 years is still facing sexual advances of her cousin.

I was chilled to the bone to hear painful story of Samaira [name changed] of 23 years who is in government job and come from a respectable family. She lives in constant fear of sexually perverted brother, who is educated and doing job. Her brother has no qualm in expressing desire to have sex with her. Her mother has information about it. She simply advises her daughter to be cautious. That poor girl is desperately waiting for her marriage so that she may live without fear. 80 per cent girls say that drivers of van or rickshawallas tried to touch in bad way when they were younger at one time or the other.

Jasleen, one of the respondent students had another story. One day she saw a girl of eight or nine crying bitterly while returning from tuition centre at 7 pm. The girl told the name of her neighbor who took her in the far corner of the street and injured her private parts. The impact of this incident was so profound on Jasleen's mind that she did not talk to her brother and father for many days.

Victims' Views

Total 150 girls were interviewed. 90 per cent respondents are in the age group between15-26; Ten per cent are of 35-45.

The data of my study is mirror of the malaise our Indian society is afflicted with. 98 per cent respondents have faced sexual harassment what is termed as 'eve teasing' and swallow humiliation in their daily life. Boys pass lewd remarks, pull their 'dupatta', touch their body parts while on bikes, and ask for their phone numbers. 72 per cent girls ignore them because it is common occurrence. Secondly, if they tell their parents, they put more restrictions on them. Thirdly, they feared the consequences. They may be abducted or be harmed dangerously.

Public is apathetic. 90 per cent girls say no one comes to their help to save them from ugly situation. People just ignore them as if it nothing new or bad. Many stand and watch the 'show', rather they begin to comment on their dress or just pass vile smile. Only 12 per cent girls shared incidence of teasing with their parents. nine per cent have slapped the teaser. Only six per cent reported to the police station.

In the opinion of 13 per cent respondents, those who are not educated and belong to lower middle class are inclined to indulge in acts of eve teasing, but 76 per cent females believe that age, social and educational profile have no link with eve teasing. Young or adults 40-60 years old - all gratify their senses by ogling/ smirking eyes. Notably, 10 per cent females think that the rich and the educated are bigger culprits; only their ways are subtle.

Regarding dress 62 per cent girls feel that dress matters to some extent in case of eve teasing in our society. Males begin to interpret revealing dress as message for sexual provocation and they do not hesitate in violating the line of decency but 38 per cent vehemently opposed this notion. In their opinion, it is mind-set not dress that matters. Even girls of three or four years old or females in traditional dress are also molested.

The solution of the problem, 83 per cent girls/women believe, lies in homes and upbringing. The mindset of males is shaped by values inculcated by parents or other members of family. The girls crib that there is no sanction for boys, only because they are 'males'. The boys' sense of superiority leads them to consider eve teasing as part of their rights. A few respondents argue parents need to control both sons and daughters to curb this menace. On the other hand, 17 per cent respondents do not support this point of view. They say parents are no controlling authority for children in this age of western model of individualism and technology. Mobiles and internet have made youngsters more susceptible to external negative influences. The parents have become helpless.

Attitude of Parents

About 30 parents of young girls were interviewed belonging to different strata of society. 80 per cent parents believe that incidences of eve teasing are rising due to media, internet, film industry and mobile phones. Entertainment industry with glamour and corporate culture is one of the major culprits. Reality shows, dance programmes, award functions, item songs- everywhere females are projected as commodity. News reporting in sensational tone and crime related programmes affects viewers of young age. They learn new methods and ways and try to experiment.

90 per cent parents say our law does not deter perpetrators of crime. Not only law is insufficient, implementation mechanism is also poor. Only six per cent respondents disclosed that their daughters complained against eve teasing. Two of them brought it into the notice of boys' family; one beat the boy. Only one parent reported to the police. After those actions boys did not harass their daughters. Generally parents are found to advise their daughters to evade such elements.

General Opinion of People

Total 20 persons from wide spectrum of vocations were approached to seek their opinion on eve teasing. 25 per cent respondents claim that they have not noticed any act of eve teasing; while about 50 per cent accepted that they noticed misbehaviour with women but they did not intervene for fear of reprisal; only 20 per cent once in life tried to help the woman.

One of them, who is consultant in an NGO, thinks that 'market forces, urbanisation and cultural aggression have led to erosion of both social control and traditional values resulting in male chauvinism and objectification of women.' Another respondent, who is a teacher in a Girls' school, says 'Human being is a potential angel but can be a brute also, if he is not civilised by family, society or education. Now agencies of socialisation–education, family, religion–do not play positive and effective role in the growth of a child. Education is devoid of moral values in this pseudo-secular system. Joint family system, which used to watch deviant behaviour of children, is falling apart at baffling speed. Social pressure used to be a powerful antidote to perversion in Indian society. It is no longer there'.

An NGO [IPAC] Director feels that' to address this menace of eve teasing the law should be simple and swift in implementation. A nationwide campaign should be undertaken with full force. From a long term perspective, the efforts should start in beginning as both young girls and boys are victim of patriarchy. Parents should emphasise on socialisation of boys and girls that promote the values of justice and equality. The mindset which sees woman as weaker being in power dynamics needs to be changed.'

One college student thinks differently. He thinks 'that problem lies in prohibition of free interaction between boys and girls. The boys resort to eve teasing and bullying to get girl's attention. The boys usually do it in front of their friends to become some kind of hero. We need to inculcate the notion among boys that women are different but equal to men.'

The Legal Concern

The provisions of the Constitution clears that dignity of womanhood has been the salutary cynosure of constitutional concern. Sex equality in public employment and public office is assured. Exploitation, moral and material abandonment of youth are frowned upon by constitution. If law's promises were facts of life, India would be paradise for woman. Yet masculine realities and gender perversities haunt our culture that Indian womanhood has to make a long march to reach a level of justice, equality and good conscience.

On 30.11.2012 the Supreme Court as reported in the Deputy Inspector General of Police and another versus S. Samuthiram 2012[11] SCALE 420, directed the Central Government to legislate effective legislation to contain eve teasing.

The Indian Journal of Criminology and [Jan.-June [1999 Edition] has categorised in 5 heads, viz. [1] verbal eve teasing [2] physical eve teasing [3] psychological harassment [4] sexual harassment [5] harassment through object.

In Vishaka and others V. State of Rajasthan [1977]6 SCC 241, the Supreme Court has laid down certain guidelines on the sexual harassment. In Rupal Deol Bajaj and another Vs KPS. Gill[1995]6 SCC 194, the Supreme Court has explained the meaning of 'MODESTY' in relation to woman and said that more and more girl-students and women go to educational institutions, work places etc. and their protection is of extreme importance to a civilised and cultured society. In public interest we are therefore inclined to give the following directions :

1. All the State Governments and Union Territories are directed to depute plain clothed female police officers in the precincts of bus stands and stops, railway stations, metro stations, cinema theatres, shopping malls, parks, beaches, public service vehicles, places of worship etc. so as to monitor and supervise incidents of eve teasing.
2. There are be a further directions to the State Governments and Union Territories to install CCTVs in strategic positions which

itself would be deterrent and if detected, the offender could be caught.

3. The persons in charge of educational institutions, places of worship, railway stations, metro stations, cinema theatres, shopping malls have take steps as they deem fit to prevent eve teasing within their precincts and on a complaint being made, they must pass on the information to the nearest police station.
4. Where any incident of eve teasing takes place in public service vehicle either by the passengers or the persons in charge of the vehicle, the crew of such vehicle shall, take the vehicle to the police station.
5. The State Governments and Union Territories are directed to establish WOMEN HELPLINE in cities and towns so as to curb eve teasing within three months.
6. Suitable boards cautioning such acts of eve teasing should be exhibited in all public places including precincts of bus stands and stops, railway stations, metro stations, cinema theatres, shopping malls, parks, beaches, public service vehicles, places of worship etc.
7. Responsibility is also on the passers-by and on noticing such incidents, they report to the nearest police station or WOMEN HELPLINE to save the victim from such crimes.
8. The State Governments and Union Territories of India shall take adequate measures by issuing suitable instructions to concerned authorises including Deputy Collectors and Superintendents of Police so as to take effective and proper measures to curb such incidents of eve teasing.

The Delhi High Court directed Delhi Police to do a "crime mapping" in the capital in order to know the reasons for the menace.

Acting Chief Justice B.D. Ahmad and Justice Sidharth Mridul ruled, "They want to know whether the phenomenon of sexual aggression against females was a social or policing problem." The Court said the government could consider introducing lessons against eve teasing in school books.

The Court was hearing a PIL filed by advocate Gaurav Bansal. A survey claimed a spurt in crime against women and sought directions for taking adequate steps to prevent it. The PIL submitted a press release issued by Delhi police in April, 2013 which said incidents of molestation and eve teasing had recorded 600 per cent and 783.67 per cent rise respectively in recent years.

As above discussed, people have diverse and varied opinion on eve teasing. The reasons which can be attributed to increasing incidences of eve teasing are many: deteriorating law and order problem in many cities and towns massive influx of immigrants giving rise to faceless offenders, governance system, and apathetic attitude of citizens to incidents of common concern. Barring a few respondents all agree that male centric socialisation is one of the major factors which reinforces male chauvinism and female inferiority. The statement such as given by Abhijeet Mukherjit echoes the same jeering attitude of males must be condemned –'Women who are participating in candle light vigils and those who are protesting have no connection with ground realities. These pretty ladies coming to protest are highly dented and painted, who go from discos to demonstrations.'

Eve teasing is not a new phenomenon. This evil has existed all over the world. It has been a matter of social concern for a long time. However in India, its scale and severity is a matter of great concern for all because its impacts are deep and disastrous. A substantial amount of news space in daily newspapers and TV channels is occupied by this phenomenon. This social abnormal behaviour had both latent and manifest social sanction. As many parents also grumble, film industry is also responsible for fanning this evil. Bollywood perpetuates the myth that girls like to be teased. In our films heroes venture on such acts through courting and persuasion. The villains act in outrageous way. This type of attitude attracts teenagers and the young.

As more and more women are coming out of homes and joining workforce in different vocations, the incidences of eve teasing are not only increasing in terms of its frequency, forms and severity, eve teasing is also multiplying. It needs to be addressed effectively keeping in view the fundamentals of justice, equality and fairness. Whatever the lifestyle of a woman may adopt, no one has right to dehumanise her by touching without her permission. It is time that Indian society introspected and gave its women their due place in society.

17

End Eve Teasing; A Voice Through Words

Manvi Yadav, Neetu Yadav, Preetu Srivastava

Abstract

The issue of violence against women i.e., sexual harassment, molestation, domestic violence and eve teasing is deeply rooted in our societal norms and economic dependence. The recent gang rape of a woman in Delhi on 16th December 2012 has led to a outpouring of anger and frustration of people in such a way that they came out on streets in large number calling for justice and change. As female participation in outside world is increasing and laws have been amended to protect them and give security but still Indian women have a long way to go for protection and justice. The challenge an Indian woman has to face includes misogynistic society, defective governance structure, an inefficient legal system and socio political structure which is heavily dominated by the men. Actually the reason behind is the mindset of society for treating women as object. Can this mindset be ever changed the answer is yes but we need to change the society first, it cannot be done overnight. This paper analyses the psychology of the eve teasing and how education and society can work hand in hand in solving the problem of violence against women.

Introduction

How a society confronts the issue of violence against women depends upon how women experience the security and freedom to move in the society. Freedom from violence and the threat of violence is the first measurement of women's capacity for survival and empowerment. The United Nations Declaration on the Elimination of Violence against Women states in its preamble that violence against women is a product of the "unequal power relations" that characterise gender relations in all parts of the world. The declaration recognises that in addition to individual acts of violence, it is this history of unequal relationships that is at the core of widespread and pervasive nature of violence against women. The experience or threat of violence affects the lives of millions of women worldwide. Every form of violence that is domestic or public threatens all women and limits their access and ability to make choices about their lives. The fear of violence, including sexual harassment, molestation or even eve-teasing can be a permanent constraint on the mobility of women and limits their access to resources and basic activities. Of all the forms that violence against women can assume, eve teasing is the most ubiquitous as she has to face it on daily basis.

Eve Teasing is a term which usually involves young men annoying or disquieting girls or women by making sexual advancement against them in public or in work place, it is considered as a 'normal' behaviour and not an assault to females. It is so common that we have become desensitised to offensive behaviours. Eve teasing begins as an attempt to irritate a girl or catch her attention a lewd stare, a whistle, a well-timed clap, an unwarranted bump, a seemingly casual touch, a lingering look at a vulnerable time, the humming of suggestive song, cheap gestures, display of indecent snaps or videos, giving "unwelcome call" or "missed call", sending indecent texts, all these are typical example of eve teasing. Now the question arises, who are eve teasers and who are real victims?

Who are Eve Teasers and Who are Victim?

The eve teasers include all types of student like school, college and university going it also includes jobless young man, rickshaw pullers, street traders, bus drivers, bus conductors, labourers, security guards etc. Young and adult, rich and poor, educated or uneducated all classes are involved in this heinous act. The victims are also from various classes like factory workers, domestic workers, students and high class professional women. Eve-teasing may be cores for poor income group, but richness does not guarantee free from eve teasing. We just mean to say that an eve teaser can be anyone, he doesn't belong to any particular community, caste or class. Basically an eve teaser is a person who basically govern by a mind set of considering women inferior to males and thus deserving of less than equal treatment and where he think he can treat her in any way whichever is convenient to him. But here question arise is it women coming from various section and classes of society, forever remain targets and victims of eve teasing? Do we really don't have the solution to this problem? Before all these question are addressed, one needs to explore and analyse why, irrespective of the dress women wear, or despite of their ages, their looks, their educational, professional and marital status, irrespective of time or place, women are being subjected to all kinds of harassment. An obscene telephone call, following women in streets, passing intolerable comments and last but not the least so many incidence of eve-teasing which is taking place daily that are not reported. Now a days there are so many laws to combat the violence against women but eve teasing is such a issue where laws fail to control the situation. If a person passes a obscene comment on a women will she be going to police station to file the complain and if she dare to go and file a complaint will she be able to prove it. There are so many if and buts in dealing with the legal issues of the eve teasing incidence. But one important thing which we often overlook is the psychology behind this eve teasing. Therefore it is essential to analyse the psychology of eve-teasing.

The Psychology of Eve Teasing

Women are often criticised for 'inviting' molesters by way of their 'seductive' way of dress and make-up and sometimes they are also criticised about their body language. But these theories fails in the face of rustic, illiterate and poor village women who cannot afford to dress seductively and do make up. What does 'seductive' dressing mean? Who is going to decide what 'seductive' dressing is and what is not? Another myth says that girls ought not to step out after dark and if they have gone out, they ought to come home before it is too dark. It is implied that the victims are perhaps to blame for men teasing, and molesting them. This thinking is itself rooted in patriarchy like from childhood, parents bring up their sons and daughters by two completely different rules of censorship on their movements outside the house geographically and in terms of time one set of rules for boys and one set of rules for girls. Yet, when the girl grows up and gets married, she is expected to adjust to the 'outside world' of husband, in-laws and a different family altogether, something they have not prepared her for. The Maitrayani Samhita (Yajurveda) repeatedly says that a woman's body is not her own, so she cannot prevent herself from being molested. Violence thrives in the victim's acceptance of the victimiser's moral right, social superiority and physical power. When women protest against violence other women, social groups or the machineries of the government, they are again victimised. Covert or overt, direct or indirect, visible or invisible, structural or social, women are always both targets and victims of violence across the world. Eve teasing, like rape, molestation and sexual harassment, is generally understood in feminist theory to be an expression not of unbridled lust and desire, but of power. Eve teasing is a form of sexual harassment indulged in by men, without considering their intelligence or their education. Many psychologists believe that sex, love or fun is not the only motive that men indulge in this behaviour. Eve teasing is closely related to the patriarchal mindset of the Indian male. Men are raised to believe that they are more powerful physically and emotionally than women. They feel that they are doing nothing wrong just having some fun. Women on the other hand are made to feel vulnerable and the weaker sex.

A recent incidence, in Delhi when a young medical student was brutally gang raped on a moving bus on 16 December 2012. A historic movement occurred where people demanded justice and action from the government. But some policy makers and government leaders have given the statement revealing their traditional bias against women and their acceptance of all that eve-teasing implies. Statements like, "Skirts should be prohibited keeping in view the rise of social crimes against women." or "I think that girls should be married at the age of 16, so that they have their husbands for their sexual needs, and they don't need to go elsewhere. This way rapes will not occur." and "One of the reasons behind the increase in incidents of eve-teasing is short dresses and short skirts worn by women. This in turn instigates young men."

These attitudes are deeply embedded in the fundamental social expectations of men towards women throughout India, As a result of these pervasive attitudes, survivors of rape are often blamed for the sexual assault. They are said to have brought it on themselves by being out alone, or dressing provocatively or becoming too "westernised".

A biggest problem in our society is that these incidence of eve teasing are seldom reported because it is well known fact that these reports will never be addressed and if it is been addressed then the victim is harassed in such a way that she starts feeling as a culprit rather a victim. Therefore it becomes important that the attitude and mindset of our society should be changed.

Attitude towards Women Need to be Change

Various laws have been made already, but all those laws will only be effective in curbing eve-teasing if we, as a nation, change our attitude towards women. Normally the attitude towards eve-teasing is that the woman herself is attracting attention and so it's her fault. Women have to be looked upon more respectfully in the society. For this social values have to change". In changing these social values our education system will play an important role. Most the people do not respect females. This is the important desired moral values which is depleting in our society. But what are the moral values? A general perception is that if you respect your elders and females, if you are a good citizen and a human being in every sense then you are a moral person. To be a moral person every belief and thought should be strong and determined. We must have the courage to do right and fight for the right. Therefore one must be trained in the same from the beginning of life. Therefore moral values must be taught and should be an indispensable part of our education system. Apart from teachers and schools, parents must play an active role in teaching moral values to their children. As it is often seen that in most of the cases where sexual assault or molestation has taken place parents often discourage their children not to complain because of many reasons. But we should not forget that many parents are role models of their children therefore they should set an examples in front of their children. Education must focus on the all round development of a child. As education prepares an individual for their future role and these moral values help in making complete human beings and not just an individual. The lack of moral values is the root cause of various kind of corruption. Until and unless our own vested interests surpass the societal good this corruption will be manifested in all forms in our society. We have to stop this immediately because if the moral values keep on deteriorating then it may lead to the complete downfall of the society.

School management should understand that education is not a business. Teachers should realise their responsibilities and they should work hard to bring the desire change in the society as they can only mould the future. Hence school education system must include moral and social values.

Conclusion

In India, it is hard truth is that even today, women are struggling for their own identity, shouting for their own voices and fighting for their self-esteem. Every day, they come across the fears and fraught for individuality self-respect and dignity. Despite our constitution guarantee of equality of sexes, no discrimination still the exploitation of women in India continues. The incidence of dowry deaths, woman sexual harassment, cases of domestic violence, molestation and ill-treatment of women are on increase. It is high time now that women should get a respectable and dignified position in the Indian society which they have the right to deserve. Awareness among the masses particularly in women as well as in society should be created and their equal rights should be effectively implemented. In this era of globalisation privatisation and liberalisation with revolution in means of communication and information technology, role of media becomes more crucial for women empowerment in Indian modern society. In modern society changes have been taking place in everywhere in almost every field to protect rights and dignity of women. A number of women organisations have been working for women freedom, security and empowerment. But all of those are external in nature. As we all know the mentality, attitude and mind set are the product of society and culture. In the same family, boys and girls are treated differently, boys are given all sorts of freedom where as girls are imposed with restrictions. We have to give equal freedom to both of them in any society and in any circumstance, if we want to become a developed nation. The only tool which can empower women is education. Education will only give them strength and societal status. This will increase the women smooth living in modern society. Education will make them aware about their rights. Every woman has a fundamental right to be safe. If a woman is educated and aware she will be able to protest in the right manner. Socio economic empowerment of women must be ensured by the nation to minimise the exploitation which can help to improve their status. The recent gang rape has created a fear among women, which is a very unfortunate and serious thing. But recent verdict of Supreme Court to give death sentence to accused is appreciated by most of the people as this kind of harsh punishment will create fear in the mind of the person. An individual will think twice before committing such a crime. The fear should be in the mind of the offenders not the innocent people. We hope our judiciary will understand the gravity of the situation and will ensure that the correct judgments is given in all such cases without taking much time.

Suggestions

1. *Community and Society*

- Present status of women is because of lack of well-planned educational, economic and social programmes. Despite of so many laws we are unable to protect them because of negligence on the part of our own system as well as on the individual who cannot get justice.
- We need communities and individuals to go hand in hand and become a part of this change of mindsets, attitudes and beliefs. We together can compel the government to do everything in their hand to, ensure justice and to deal with robust public services to make women's lives more safe and secure.
- Society need to create healthy environment for women and girls everywhere by supporting efforts to end violence against them, promoting their political participation and leadership in order to increase their economic empowerment.
- Create awareness everywhere to end exploitation against women and girl through the education and strong social, moral, and cultural values and make strong laws to punish victim immediately in present Indian society.
- Healthy family atmosphere, progressive family education and the trust between the members of the family are necessary.

2. *Education System*

- Education policy should ensure equality between girls and boys. Curriculum has a strong role to take initiatives to portray girls and boys equal.
- In the textbook, moral education should be included immediately and should have a chapter on the violence against women by giving emphasis to establish eve teasing as a social curse.
- Teachers in the class should be aware of treating both boys and girls equally. They should talk about morality about violence to make them understand the gravity of violence on total humankind.

3. *Laws*

- Law should be implemented with the same zeal with which it has been formulated. Local police and school security can play a strong role in controlling the issues related to violence against women.

4. *Media*

- Electronic media and printing media should be sensitive enough to handle the issues related to women. They should be aware about the consequence and negative impact of eve teasing. Journalist should have training how to handle gender issues. They should be careful as some news in the newspaper due to the week presentation of the newspaper makes the girl vulnerable and the boys as a hero. They should take extra care to avoid presenting the stereotypical image of boys and girls

References

- Verma, R.B.S., Verma, H.S., Hasnain, Nadeem. (2007). *Towards Empowering Indian Women: Mapping Specifics of Tasks in Crucial Sectors.* New Delhi: Serial Publications.
- Verma, R.B.S., Verma, H.S., Hasnain, Nadeem. (2009). *Study of Women's Problematic in India: Assessing Contemporary state of the art.* New Delhi: Serial Publications.
- The United Nations (1993). Declaration on the Elimination of Violence against Women, General Assembly Resolution.
- Akhtar, Chesfeeda. (2013). Eve teasing as a form of violence against women: A case study of District Srinagar, Kashmir. *International Journal of Sociology and Anthropology, Vol 5(5),* 168-178.
- Akhter, Zobaida. (2013). Eve Teasing, Tears of the Girls: Bangladesh Open University towards Women Empowerment. International *Women Online Journal of Distance Education, Vol 2(4),* 1-23.

18

Eve Teasing of the Marginalised Women: Experiences from Cachar (Assam)

Ruman Sutradhar

Abstract

Eve teasing, the exact manifestation of a gender biased patriarchal society, treats women as nothing more than a sex object who are used for sexual pleasure and enjoyment of the dominant sections of society, the men. While women in general have been victims of eve teasing, women from the marginalised groups like dalits, slum dwellers, and the mentally imbalanced insane are mostly exposed to the divulgence of varied forms of eve teasing due to the nature of work they do which basically rests on wage earning, house maids, waste picking or begging. Such a ludicrous form of enjoyment is not concentrated to the women of a particular age group rather women across all age groups are victimised by such acts with varying magnitude and dimensions. In this regard, experiences of women from the age group of 13 to 35 have been shared. This paper is the outcome of personal (unstructured) and focused group interviews accompanied by keen observation of the researcher, conducted from 8/11/2014 to 29/11/2014 (twenty one days). For the work, areas of Silchar, (the main town of Cachar) where the marginalised women live, work and are generally found have been selected for the purpose of collecting primary data. Attempt has been made to bring forth the nature of eve teasing, by analysing some of the experiences of women belonging to the marginalised groups in the district of Cachar. Certain measures as a response to minimise extent of eve teasing have also been suggested, because a total eradication of such an act is not possible in a day that require to go under a series of reform measures.

Key words: Sexual pleasure, Gendered socialisation, Patriarchy, Marginalised, Dalits, Insane

I

How eve teasing affects the marginalised women in Cachar? The present study begins with this question in mind, which considers those women as 'marginalised' who either have been the members of, or are the direct victims of the complex process of marginalisation, whereby individuals or groups of people are relegated to the lower or the outer edge of the society, 'that operates and promotes through the practice of discrimination, oppression, subjugation, and domination, which gets legitimised and reproduced through the normative and institutional arrangements of society' (Singharoy, 2010). Under this framework, the dalit women, women from the slums, the mentally retarded and insane women of Cachar have been considered as 'marginalised women', stigmatised by the intersecting circles of multiple forms of marginality. The rationale behind is the fact that although women in general share certain commonsensical problems like eve teasing, the problems of the marginalised women remains specific, given their diverge patterns of marginality.

Eve teasing, the public sexual harassment or molestation of women by a man or gangs of men including 'verbal assaults like making passes or unwelcome sexual jokes; nonverbal assaults like showing obscene gestures, winking, whistling, and staring; and physical assaults such as pinching, fondling, and rubbing against women in public places such as the streets, public transportation, parks, beaches, and cinema halls' (Akhtar, 2013), is the exact manifestation of a gender biased patriarchal society that treats women as nothing more than a sex object, used for the sexual pleasure and enjoyment of the dominant sections of society, the men. And such acts, in the words of Catherine Good, are used in order to 'exert power over women', where women are subjected not only to remarks or gestures laden with sexual innuendo but also to actual physical molestation, signified by the grabbing of breasts and buttocks, tugging women's braids, jostling against them (although this is made out to be accidental), or spitting on their faces or clothes (Good, 2007).

The act of eve teasing found its first impression in India during the colonial period, when women tried to come out of the traditionalism and began to share the public space with men. It was not acceptable to the men according to whom the actual place of women was private, the home, and their actual role was that of a traditional Sati like submissive wife, and not merely a professional lady who has the ability to compete with them in the same plane of public arena. With the increasing social mobility of women due to urbanisation and globalisation, vulnerability of women to forms of violence such as eve teasing has also raised in a society where patriarchy remains implicit in the social system as is the case of India. Such ideological constraints have also affected the society and culture of Cachar, where women are treated as the secondary- the 'others' in the private as well as public spheres that holds to preserve women within the four walls of home, daring which they encounter commonsensical ubiquitous problems like eve teasing.

II

Eve teasing is not a new phenomenon for the women throughout the country, and such power manifestations of patriarchal society did not leave the women of the North eastern state of Assam. The district of Cachar situated at the Southern most part of Assam between 92° 24' E and 93° 15' E longitude and 24° 22' N and 25° 8' N latitude, includes a number of groups whose marginal state has been rooted historically. Of those groups, 20 women from each of the three Dalit groups, Kaibarttha, Patni and Sutradhar have been choosen for detailed examination on eve teasing. As to the mentally retarded, the analysis is based on the observation of the researcher. It should be noted that the women living in the slum area who constitute a marginalised group also belong to the Dalit community. Regarding the experiences of the women, a few cases have been depicted with anonymous names in order to retain confidentiality of the victims.

Eve Teasing of Dalit Women

Dalit women in Cachar, alike the Dalit women throughout the subcontinent have been the victims of marginalisation. Excepting a negligible proportion who could be benefitted from the government policies of affirmative action, majority of the women live in a state of immense backwardness, ignorant of the caste based discrimination prevalent in the district reflected from the nature of work assigned to them which are mostly the lowl paid works. For instance, majority of the house maids of urban Cachar belong to the Dalit community, not excepting the daily wage earners. It is worth to mention here that for the purpose of writing this paper the 16 marginalised groups identified as Scheduled Castes (Chart I) have been considered as Dalits.

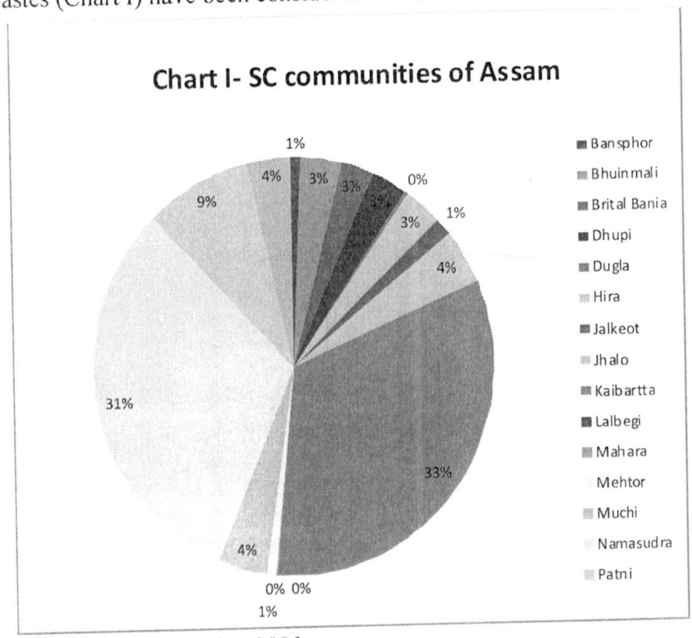

Source: *Census of India, 2001*

The Dalit families are strongly patriarchal and the women here are the victims of Dalit patriarchy. Of the 60 Dalit women interrogated, everyone reported of having faced eve teasing in some way or other irrespective of the age, although the intensity is decreased with increase in age. It remains at its peak from the age of 18 to 28. Regarding the perpetrators, majority of the women admitted that the teasers were mostly middle aged men. As to the young boys, they found that boys from backward areas like those who came from inner village (as understood by their dressing pattern and languages) were the teasers in busy roads and buses. But in case of young girls of the age group 12 to 17 (the initial years of facing such acts), the teasers they observed were mostly from nearby places who passed unwelcome comments or jokes or winking, excepting a few who move for sexual assaults. In a later stage, pinching is found to be the most common form of physical assault in a crowded place, and buses are usually the most common and advantageous places for the teasers. Eve teasing, in some cases may go to an extreme point, leaving the girl with deep psychological trauma as happened with Rita (Case I), a 12 year old Patni girl and Sarbani (Case II).

Case I

Rita Das, aged 12 lives in Silchar, is a victim of eve teasing. Hailing from an extremely poor background, Rita has often encountered verbal comments from a group of young boys living beside her home. Initially the simple girl could not identify the obscene gestures of the guys but gradually she learnt about the things when some obscene posters were shown to her from some distance. One day while she was coming from school one of the boys of the same group pulled her skirt from behind and the others enjoyed the harassment of the girl. She cried and ran away to her home. Next day she took her mother along with her, which continued for few days. Her mother thought it was now ok, because the boys didn't turn up there for those few days. This made her mother to leave Rita alone. As usual she went and returned from school alone and her fear was little less when she could safely return home for two days. The third day, the boys again appeared in her way to return home from tution. That evening Rita was grapped by those guys in the street (it should be noted that the street remain quiet at that time) who physically molested her, to the extent of opening her skirt in the road and trying to see what's inside. The girl began to cry and cry and when they saw one of the passer by near, they fled away. That man took her home. The entire things had such an impact on the girl that she remained silent for days and refused to go to school any more.

Case II

Sarbani Sutradhar aged 28 lives in Silchar with her parents and siblings. The 10th pass Sarbani, who work in a local firm as receptionist, recalls her experiences of eve teasing. Till this moment she experienced several acts of eve teasing, the most common of which includes passing unwelcome comments from the teasers which to her has become a regular phenomenon. From around class VIII, she began to experience forms of teasing, of which she narrates one, and the impact of the incident can be understood from the fact that narration of those incidents brought tears to her eyes which reflected the trauma she faced at that time that will perhaps rest for entire her life. The incident happened when she was a 19 year old teenager. At the very evening, Sarbani went to see some celebrity singer arrived at the heart of the town with her best friend Mita Nath. That evening entire the town was lighted as if diwali, to welcome the star to his hometown, people were ready to welcome him with full excitement, everyone rushed like anything just to have a look of the star. The rush was a form of benefit to the men groups, the benefit that could send a girl to deep trauma, for it was their turn to tease the girls and no one would be able to do anything. In the roads where it was not possible to keep their feet, Sarbani and Mita were walking alike the other girls where the men were teasing and molesting the girls as they could, someone grabbing the breasts, someone the hips and wherever their hands go, someone's dupatta is torn out, some girls were forcibly made to fall in the ground, where, above her were the hands of 10-11 men together. That was what happened to Sarbani, when Mita somehow managed to pull her back with the help of a man who was standing behind. I should mention here that while she was narrating the same, and even now when I am putting these words to ink, I can feel the trauma she might have faced and the reason why she cried at the time.

The experiences of these two women are such that these in no way would be acceptable to a girl, but still are accepted by the victims as well as their near ones. Such extreme cases are found in lower numbers in the course of interrogation. Regarding the Kaibarttha women, they are found in a slum colony near the railway tracks. While the traditional occupation of the community is related to agriculture and some where fishing, the Kaibartthas in Silchar work as wage earners. Educationally backward, the women work as house maids; or wage earners in constructions or small industries like beedi making, candle making; or as small vegetable vendors. In this regard, Sneha (Case III), a girl living in the slum area shares her experiences of eve teasing.

Case III

Sneha Das, aged 19 belongs to a family of a poor rickshaw puller and maid of Kaibarttha community. At the age of 10 she left her studies and began to work as a maid in a Bengali Kayastha family, where from she worked at three houses at a time. The house she lived was a single roomed with a partrition in between, having no security of lives and property. When asked if she was ever teased by a boy, either verbally or physically, she replied with a ironical smile at her face, "These are very common to us for we work from home to home, unknowing of the nature of our maliks, and if we see all these we have to sit at home that we can't do because we need money to feed the stomach. Even my mother had lots of experiences of such acts, but we have to stay mum". She further hold that the boys nearby who often do the work of picking metals and irons from road or sometimes glass bottles also do not leave the girls without teasing, which is mostly verbal in nature. During the mela (large gathering of people at a nearby field) also, she encountered groups of boys passing her, one of whom rubbed his crotch with her, and such incidents occurred not only with her, but with many of her friends.

Case IV

Priya Das, a 23 year old Patni girl is university graduate and belong to a middle class family. Amidst immense problems, Priya managed to study by the support of her parents, but faced eve teasing alike the other girls. She say "Eve teasing is something every girl experience irrespective of the caste, but the ones who looks somewhat timid and shy type face more than the ones who walk boldly. Initially I used to be very timid as I was always taught to be in my home. It was during that time when I was victimised more. But as time passed on, I understood who can be the possible targets of the teasers and I walked boldly with somewhat arrogant expressions whenever I move from any crowded place, or go somewhere in a congested vehicle". When asked about whether the teasers should be punished, she agreed to that point but to her, it was not possible to punish them. Priya say that it's better to escape from the situation or such physical assaults rather than a tight slap the teaser deserve.

The condition of women living in the slums is not very different to that of Sneha. Rather it can be worse off in many cases, where they are not only the victims of eve teasing in public places, but also reside in unsafe homes, or work in places that may or may not increase their levels of vulnerability to eve teasing in public or sexual tortures in private. As understood by Priya, eve teasing can be avoided to some extent by being bold, but not in all cases boldness serves the purpose. For instance, if Sarbani's case is taken into consideration it will yield reality for she too was a bold woman despite which she was severely stigmatised by a group of men. However, to some extent being timid makes the woman more vulnerable to acts of eve teasing which is also revealed in the work of Akhtar. Having its roots in the old testament of Bible, the archaic term 'eve teasing' is often taken very simply to have happened or will happen to a girl in its verbal or non verbal forms as it is sometimes taken as mild romantic gestures, and not necessarily as derogatory to their dignity. But such mild gestures when takes its severe form like physical assaults leaves the girl or women in a lifelong depressed state of mind as happened to Rita and Sarbani. While the young girl, unable to bear such acts of severe sexual assaults was left with the feeling of intense fear and insecurity that deprived her of the fundamental right to education, Sarbani was left with lifelong mental agony. Sneha, on the other side, was left with no other option than to live an unsafe unsecured life. Such are the situations of the victims of eve teasing, whose anxious mind cannot avail to development opportunities thereby limiting their scope; restricting their freedom of movement; depriving them of resources (intellectual like education, or virtually the socio-economic-political ones); thereby pushing the marginalised women to a state of perpetual marginalisation.

Eve Teasing of Mentally Imbalanced and Insane Women

Among the marginalised groups, the mentally imbalanced or the mad women who loiter around the streets, unconscious of even their state of being are the ones who remain outside the purview of policy makers, social scientists or even the common citizens elsewhere. These women who need greater care and special attention due to their imbalanced state of mind are not only devoid of any special care or sympathy, but are also the most vulnerable groups due to their inability to identify or speak out their problem or the social injustices met out to them. The town of Silchar very frequently witnessed varied acts of tortures of these women and girls. Around a month back, while walking in the road, a lady sitting in the corner of a shop near the busy day time road was observed. With her half tangled hair, the muddy body of the woman was half covered by a dirty piece of cloth that left the lower part of the body uncovered. Trying to search something in the polythenes near her, the woman was sitting in front of a shop, where every passerby had their eyes on her. Some passed on and some were turning back again and again. The unfortunate part is that even these women are also not relieved by such dirty acts. A keen observation of those men made it sure that they were looking at the uncovered part of her body, thereby passing lewd comments and smiling at each other.

In another instance, a woman of the age limit of 30s was found to loiter through the streets. Fully naked with a piece of sari in her hand and a bowl on another, the woman went on walking. Two women who were passing her felt ashamed to see such a state but none could manage to make her wear the sari, probably due to some sort of fear. Most of the people ignored the woman, but among them were a few young men who made jokes of the lady, gazing and laughing at her pitiable condition. Such acts show lack of humanity, when few men find enjoyment in teasing a woman as such, where in cases, the women were seemed to be much elder than them. This happens not only to these kinds of women, but also to those half conscious girls who do know their homes but are not aware that they were girls and certain acts may lower their dignity. Apart from eve teasing, the mentally imbalanced women, whether they loiter around roads or stay at home, are more vulnerable to sexual molestation in private. The truth of this can be estimated from this case, which was observed months back, and obviously not for writing this paper.

An insane woman loitering around or sometimes sitting near a temple in the bazaar was often seen by people residing nearby. The women used to give her old clothes which she wrapped somehow in her body. When she was seen for the first time, it was a normal look. Around two months later she was seen in a pregnant state, and her last visit was not alone but with a baby girl. She was not fully conscious but seemed to be little aware of the fact that the baby was hers, and that she should not give her to anybody. After that she was never seen in the place. The overall things made it clear that some man or men made use of her insane state but in private. This is because if such act was done in public, People won't tolerate such shameful acts. The point is that if this woman can be used at such extent for the sexual enjoyment of a man or some men, it is obvious that they are often harassed in private or may be in some lonely street. Alike the other conscious women, they are also exposed to teasing by some men who do not even hesitate to take advantage of their insane mentally imbalanced state.

III

Eve teasing in any of its form is the manipulation of power relationships between men and women in a patriarchal society like India, which do not anyway exclude the district of Cachar. The level of damage it can cause to a woman was explained best by Ms Rashida Manjoo, The UN Special Rapporteur on Violence against Women, according to whom, eve teasing is a personal attack on women's minds and bodies that instills fear and violates a woman's right to 'bodily integrity, education and freedom of movement'. Regulated as a powerful mechanism of control and intimidation to preserve and maintain women's subordinate status in society, eve teasing causes immeasurable damage to her self-esteem. From a girl of 12 to a senior woman, the social epidemic of eve teasing is rampant in the district, although in varied forms and intensity. Such an act manifest the gender subordination of society where even a younger boy can tease a much elder woman due to the fact that he knows that he can exert some sort of power over that woman. The reason behind is the way of gendered nature socialisation, whereby the males are usually socialised in a way to dominate the females, be it wife, daughter or mother or a stranger women, provided she should be a 'woman'-the secondary citizens and the subordinate others. This not only violates the moral notions that guide a society but also the legal and constitutional provisions that guarantee freedom of movement of every citizen by declaring the same as a fundamental right. Hence it is a threat to the success of the democratic features of a society that not only hampers the development of the women, especially the marginalised, rather pushes them to the outer edges of the state and society of the district and virtually the country by the denial of opportunities, resources, and a life of liberty and dignity. It thus becomes pertinent to deal with such acts of violence seriously, for which certain measures have been mentioned.

1. Since the very roots of eve teasing lies in the patriarchal notions of the society, passed on by the process of gender biased socialisation, whereby males are taught to be dominant and hard; and women are taught to be submissive, soft and tolerative; it is essential to socialise them in a way that teach both boys and girls equally from the early childhood, which in later years will help the boys to treat women with respect and not as a submissive dominative individual to whom power should be exerted.

2. Apart from the gradual process of socialisation, it is essential that the individuals, both men and women, should be aware of the fact that eve teasing is not a simple phenomenon to be left unnoticed and tolerated silently rather it is an act that prohibit certain group of individuals a life of dignity and liberty. Even if some educated women remain little confident to face eve teasing, women belonging to the marginalised groups, most of whom remain already stigmatised by poverty, illiteracy and poor sanitation facilities (as

is the case with slum women), often take it as a fate to be teased. It thus would be fruitful if awareness camps can be arranged. In this regard, women's organisations and NGOs can play a vital role around the city and villages. Since students remain one of the most significant part of a society who can bring out change, various students organisations like minority students organisations, SC/ST organisations or even the general ones can spread awareness by distributing leaflets, or workshops to deal with eve teasers.

3. Media is an agent that encourages eve teasing of women in public places. The depiction of eve teasing as mild romantic gestures by the hero in various shows and movies greatly lead to the subconscious acceptance of the act by women in general that enhance the chances of such acts to accept silently. It's very important that media should play a positive role in combating the act of teasing the 'Eves', because media continues to be one of the most influential agent for human psychology as boys (to tease) and girls (to silently accept teasing) often tend to imitate the things as shown in the movies or serials.

4. Last and the most important is that government should pass legislations because such acts of teasing prohibit women's freedom of movement which is not only their basic right but also a fundamental right guaranteed in Article 19 (d) of Indian constitution, violating which may question the constitutional security of the citizens of the nation. For the purpose, state governments of India should also take steps, as there is no such legislation in the state of Assam. Excepting the Prohibition of Eve-teasing Act of 1984 of New Delhi and the Tamil Nadu Prohibition of Eve-Teasing Act, 1998, no other state has so far passed any legislation in this regard. These acts also have limitations as they do not contain any measures for the mentally retarded and insane women, who need special care in special homely atmospheres and not in streets. However, since legal remedy without enforcement bears no significance, such laws need to be implemented properly for which administrators (both central and local) should be strict and such legal provisions should be made legally binding, so that women, especially the marginalised who are already victimised by the social and historical processes, can exercise their basic right to live a life of dignity.

References

- Akhtar, C. (2013). Eve teasing as a form of violence against women: A case study of District Srinagar, Kashmir. *International Journal of Sociology and Anthropology,* 5(5), 168-178.
- Akhtar, Z. (October 2013). Eve Teasing, Tears Of The Girls: Bangladesh Open University Towards Women Empowerment. *International Women Online Journal of Distance Education,* 2(4), 1-23.
- Chatterjee, S. (2000). *A Socio-Economic History of South Assam.* Jaipur: Printwell Publishers Distribution.
- Good, K. A. M. (2007). *Eve-Teasing and Gender Equality in the Post-Colonial Framework of India.* M.A Thesis, Cornell University.
- Singha Roy, D. K. (2010). *Surviving against odds: The Marginalised in a Globalised World.* New Delhi: Manohar.
- The United Nations (1993). Declaration on the Elimination of Violence against Women, General Assembly Resolution.
- Yadav, M. (2013). SC on Eve-Teasing: Human Rights of Woman in India. J Indian Acad Forensic Med., 35(2), 98-100.

19

Eve Teasing: Outraging the Modesty of Women

Deepa Awasthi

Abstract

Despite of various efforts from various NGOs, women groups and members of civil society, the criminal act of eve teasing still exists in society. Not only continuous but also expanding its wings. Not a single place, not a single woman is left which has not witnessed or faced the incidence of eve teasing. Society may consider it as a crime of light nature but remember that in some of the cases victim or her companion who is usually friend or her family member may lose their life or get badly injured as a consequence of opposing the acts of eve teasers. In this chapter with the help of number of real life stories author has tried to explain the expansion of eve teasing in all the fields of society. As soon as women steps out of the fourwalls of home she is in danger. She has to pay the price for her liberty to get education or involved in some economic activity. Stories and experiences also suggest that women to face it boldly with courage rather than facing it with their eyes down. It is responsibility of all of us – family, society, schools, police and government to stand together and do the needful to eradicate the evil of eve teasing from society. Author also mentions the better ways to deal with the crime rather than suggesting the women to keep knives or pepper spray in their purse, learning martial arts, avoid wearing modern dresses, avoid going out singly.

Key Words: Expanding, Witnessed, Consequences, Eradicate, Stories.

Introduction

In recent years eve teasing has emerged as one of the most heinous crime against women. The shocking truth about the crime is that it is committed in day light. Public witnessing it but prefers to remain silent. Usually victims of the incidences of eve teasing also do not report it to police. This tendency encourages the eve teasers to repeat the incidence with the same or other women. All the aspects psychological, social, legal are responsible for making this crime so vibrant. What women can do to save themselves from eve teasing? Answer is nothing; they cannot make themselves save from eve teasers as they are present everywhere at every moment. Actually eve teasing is the result of unequal gender relation in society.

Stories and Experiences from Victims

Here are some stories as retrieved from internet, for the sake of hiding the identity of victims the name of the victim and date has not been mentioned.

- At Rajeev Chowk station I entered in the Metro unfortunately with mob of 50 to 60 persons inside. Ladies compartment was overcrowded, no chance to step in and I was already late to office. After few minutes I found that I am the only lady inside the compartment. As my destination was just one stop away so I neglected it. Suddenly I found that a group of male age about 25 to 30 years surrounded me and start squeesing and pressing me all over the direction. I yelled at them. Everybody in the compartment was looking at me and enjoying their act with smile on their face. Till mean time train stopped, I moved to the gate. Suddenly I found myself half naked, one of them pulled my t shirt down and other one pressed my hips. I just jumped out of train adjusted my dress and thought it is every girl who travels in the general compartment faces it or it happened with me only.
- On a sunny day, I was coming back from my college driving my scooty through a posh area of Lucknow city known for its

civilisation and tradition. Certainly I found a luxury SUV is following from more than one kilometre. They were very near to me suddenly the guy sitting neighbour to driver's seat thrown a cigarette at me. I was shocked by their act almost slipped but fortunately adjusted my balance and speeded up. They followed me started throwing paper balls at me. I was just driving my scooty helplessly with full throttle. One of the other car driver who was watching the whole incidence from long time, by over taking them and stopped his car in front of their vehicle. He called the police and complained against them. Later on it was found that boys driving the SUV were closely associated with the ruling political party in state. Police was also helpless like me they lodged any FIR under motor vehicle act for reckless driving not for eve teasing. I reached to home standing in front of God thanked the person unknown to me but saved me. Question still lies in my mind why not every victim of eve teasers fines a right person on right time to help her.

- When I was pursuing my graduation, I use to give tuitions to some students to manage my own expenditures. It was about six o'clock evening, I was returning to home. I took a bus, took a seat. Within ten minutes bus was overcrowded, passengers were standing in the gallery. I found a strange movement by a person standing neighbour to me, with every jerking of bus he was trying to come more close to me and trying to touch my breast with his hands. Situation was very embarrassing for me. In the mean time conductor came to me I byued a ticket, he followed me and demanded ticket for same destination. My tension grown as I thought this person will be with me at bus stop also. In mean time I made a detailed SMS to my friends called them at bus stop, crying for help. Without knowing my intentions that person followed me and left the bus with me. As bus moved away I grabbed the collar of that man and shouted at him "now touch me." My five friends already present at the bus stop slapped him without count. He started begging for forgiveness promising that he will not repeat it with any girl. He ran away in an instance.
- I am a 19 year old girl from Noida, works at my general store. Just like other days it was a hot summer days. As there was no customer in shop I was reading a story book. Suddenly a boy of age 20 or 25 came in the shop and asked for toothpaste and toothbrush. I moved back toward rack to get the toothpaste and

toothbrush. I moved back, I was stunned as that boy was standing with his pant open showing me his.......... he remained there for about one minute and said that "I have no money to bye tooth paste, but if you want you can take it" with my tearful eyes down, I could not speak a word. He suddenly ran away from shop and started his bike and ran away with his three friends. He repeated the story after ten days. I told the incident to my mother, we both are afraid as we are the two people in our family and shop is the only means of earning for us.

- Last year I attended a marriage of my friend's sister. As she was very close to me so I was just equally well dressed like other family members. At the time of barat every one of us was stunned as twenty males fully drunk were leading the barat. As soon as they entered the pandal they started passing ugly comments towards girls of bride side. All of us decided to remain quiet as we don't want to spoil the occasion. Time passed and dinner started. We friends decided to have early dinner so that we can enjoy after that. After taking dinner we moved to Ice cream counter, it was over crowded, hands on each other. Suddenly one of the barati standing behind me pushed his hand in my blouse and pressed my breast. Before I could understand he pressed in with full strength. I cried and pushed myself back with full strength. That individual turned back and smiled at me. My eyes were filled with tears. My friends came to me and asked me "what happened?" I said "nothing." Later on when I discussed it with my friends they told that some unsocial elements entered in barat and a number of girls have complained about such incidences.
- I am a post graduate student from Delhi University. Three month before my father expired in a road accident. I decided to help my family so I joined a part time job at a retail showroom after my classes from five pm. to nine pm. Showroom was on fourth floor so usually I chooses lift for going and coming down. One night when I was going back home from my job I entered the lift along with three other guys. As lift started one of guys put his hand at my waist, I turned at him and hold his hand but others too joined the party and started touching my body all over every where they wanted. Hardly can I stop them with my two hands as compared to their six hands. Certainly lift stopped as on second floor some people were waiting to enter the lift.

Above stories are good enough to find the intensity of crime of eve teasing. No place is safe for women on this earth.

Nature of Eve Teasing Prevailing in Society

Discussing the nature of eve teasing prevailing in society one must consider that all the steps or acts that harasses the women or fears her is taken as a matter of enjoyment by the eve teasers. They feel proud in inventing a new or innovative ways of teasing girls. Usually popular one are :

- Wolf whistles
- Mild casual touch
- Verbal comments
- Staring continuously
- Trying to come close more than permissible limits.
- Groping or attempt to grope
- Unwanted talking
- Well timed clap by group
- Cheap gestures
- Singing a suggestive song
- Double meaning talks
- Bike chasing
- Physical attacks

The most unfortunate thing about eve teasing is that usually incident takes place at crowded public place where hundreds of men as well as women prefer to remain mute spectators. Some time policemen are also present in crowd but they also behave similarly allowing the eve teasers enjoying by outraging the dignity and modesty of women. What is the reason behind this negligence? Answer is our centuries old male dominated social structure where males consider it as their right to establish her inferior through words or acts or by both. Challenges post by eve teasers to victim are much deep and wider.

General Patterns Followed by Eve Teasers

Usually a common pattern is followed by eve teasers :

- Eve teasing is more prominent when males are in their peer group. Hardly any man has courage to harass a girl when he is alone.
- Eve teaser enjoys helplessness of victim.
- Silence of girl encourages the eve teasers confirming them that they cannot harm them.

- They are always afraid of police and reaction from public.
- They try to involve in eve teasing at stranger place as they wants to hide their identity from family. They don't want their family to know what their son is doing in society.

Myths and Reality about Eve Teasing

S.No.	Myths	Reality
(1)	Eve teasers are macho man.	They are very coward and psychologically weak person. A simple slap or even a loud call can make them run away.
(2)	Eve teasers are uncivilised man.	A simple looking guy, well dressed and educated with good educational, cultural or economical background.
(3)	Eve teasers are very bold.	They represent the frustrated personality. They try to hide their identity at any cost.
(4)	Eve teasing usually happens at lonely place.	It's not true. Eve teasing can take place any where whether lone or crowded such as market, bus, train, outside school, college.
(5)	It is better to avoid incidence of eve teasing.	Rather than avoiding the crime of eve teasing must be faced boldly and aggressively.
(6)	There is no law to protect the women from eve teasers.	There is strict legislation to stop eve teasing, usually victims do not report the crime to police for further consequences. Sometimes they report initially but withdraw their complaint after some time.
(7)	Nobody comes forward to protect a victim from eve teaser.	Whom do you expect to come forward when victim herself fears to step forward?
(8)	Modern dresses or gestures of girls invite the boys.	Even most well dressed women e.g. wearing saris or Burka as in case of Muslim women also faces eve teasing.
(9)	Generally young girls of age group 15 years to 30 years are the victims of eve teasing.	Its not true, experiences suggest that even women in age group 40 years to 50 years also faces the eve teasing.
(10)	Eve teasing is an act usually enjoyed by young boys of age group 15 years to 30 years.	Males of all the ages even above sixty never let the chance loose to harass a female even she is as young as their daughter.

Psychological Aspects of Eve Teasing

Eve teasing is social and psychological problem rather than a legal problem. Proper counselling of eve teaser by parents, relatives, police and professional psychologists can really make the difference. As suggested by a psychologist— "Eve teasing is a distorted expression of a normal impulse to be noticed by opposite sex." As in younger age every boy or girl naturally wants to establish their identity and wants to be noticed by everyone especially by opposite sex, in the same way eve teaser want them to be noticed by opposite sex unfortunately they want to get it through wrong path. They also suggest that boys who have healthy interaction with girls have less chances of harassing a girl on street as compared to the boys grown up in a close environment where they have little or no chance to interact with the opposite sex.

Psychologists also view that generally boys are confused and believe that their unusual words or behaviour makes them noticeable and they can easily attract the girls towards them. Psychologists also suggest that rather than sending these teasers to jail they should be brought to them so that the real problem could be diagnosed. Just punishing them without understanding the psychology behind their criminal act is not going to solve the issue completely.

Eradication Measures to Stop Eve Teasing

Eve teasing is a curse, not only to women but for all civilised society. It must be stopped, but it is possible when everybody in society including victim, parents, schools, teachers, police, government must stand together and opposes the act of eve teasing-

Role of Parents and Family

Family is the foremost solution to eradicate the problem of eve teasing. Psychology of an individual largely depends upon how parents brought up their children. Every parent must make their son understand that they will become real men on the day when they will save a innocent girl from eve teasing not by harassing a girl on street. Beside this they must teach their daughters to face the evil of eve teasing boldly with eyes and head held high. They should teach the girls that courage, and determinations are the only arms they have to fight against eve teasers.

Role of Society

Society can play a vital role in discouraging the acts of eve teasing. Usually eve teaser wants to live a double life. On one side they wants to enjoy the act of eve teasing while on other side they want their white collared image to remain intact with them. If the civilised members of society follow a strict norms against eve teasing, no doubt not a single female will have to face the danger of their dignity and modest being outraged by a stranger.

Role of School and Colleges

Serious efforts by Schools and colleges can really put a full stop on the crime of eve teasing because eve teasing is the one of the first sexual act that is performed by young boys as soon as they enters the age of adolescence. Inculcating the essential moral values among new generation can have control over the problem.

Role of Police

Police can play a decisive role in complete eradication of crime of eve teasing. Inspite of giving psychological and legal support to victim police itself start harassing her. Generally unnecessary questions asked by policemen are against the dignity of women. First of all victims hardly come forward to report the incidence of eve teasing to police but if someone dare to come forward police generally choose a middle way bring settlement and negotiation between both parties. Police must act as per the law rather than hiding the incidence considering it as a crime of light nature. This settlement based behaviour of police encourages the criminals to repeat the crime as they are confirm that they will get away with the ill consequences either by paying bribe or through high political connections.

Role of Government

It is the government who is fully responsible for law and order situation in society. Government must protect the dignity and self respect of every citizen including weaker sex of society. Government should compel its agencies to take immediate action against the individuals violating the rights of women. This will help to create an environment of safety and security to almost half the population of country.

Conclusion

From above discussion we come to conclusion that not a single woman in society is free from the fear of her modesty being outraged by the eve teasers who are present all over. Who is responsible for the problem, certainly all of us who have given the enormous chance to the crime of eve teasing to grow in all the directions with full pace. First and the biggest liability is of the victims, they should not hide the incidence, report it to police, media and administration.

References

- Dutta, N. (2014). Eve teasing: A curse on society. www.udaipurblog.com
- Eve Teasing Evils. www.ken-foundations.blogspot.com (Retrieved on 7 Nov 2014)
- Federick, P. (2002). Hassled but helpless, The Hindu, 10 September 2002, www.thehindu.com (Retrieved on 4 Nov 2014)
- Ray, S. (2011). Letter from India: Outrage over an eve teasing tragedy, 19 February 2011. www.newamericanmedia.org (Retrieved on 22 Nov 2014)
- Subham, F. (2012). Eve teasing: How women are tackling it. www.amedarkotha.com (Retrieved on 7 Nov 2014)

20

Eve Teasing: Eradication Measures

Goldy Gupta

Abstract

Today women of all ages, races, religions, classes, nationalities experienced violence all over the world. Eve teasing is also a sort of violence against women. It ranges from sexually coloured remarks to outright groping. It includes all type of assaults i.e., physical, verbal and non-verbal. This shameful act against women impoverishes our society culturally, economically and socially, as it limits the women's participation in the development of societies. Here are the some suggestions for eradication of eve teasing from society. Providing a healthy and friendly environment at home, helps the kids to build strong values and reduces the tendency to react violently. Parents have to inquire their children's behaviour inside and outside the home. Excessive use of liquors, drugs should be prohibited, preventing the misuse of mobile phones and internet. Media glorified verbal and gestural eve teasing and the message sent is that it is acceptable. There should be appointment of censor board for small screen. Some women feel shy to report such incidents for the reason that it would attach stigma to them. The victim is not responsible for this incidence. It is a need of hour, to tackle this problem with courage by victim itself. There are so many Safety Alert Apps are available in play store. These are specially designed to enhance the safety for women. Women can make her safe by simply downloading it. Providing religious, moral values and sex education along with regular education system can work in good way. Practicing yoga helps to rectify this negative approach from society. Whosoever is found guilty must be punished. The offender must be kept under the ambit of law. The family and society of the victims should have courage and resolve to support them.

Keywords: Women, Eve teasing, Society, Safety, Education, Family.

Today women of all ages, races, religions, classes, nationalities experienced violence all over the world. Eve teasing is also a sort of violence against women. It ranges from sexually coloured remarks to outright groping. This term is generally used for sexual harassment of women in public places like park, lane, cinema hall, busy markets and public vehicles. Eve teasing is defined as 'the making of unwanted sexual remarks or advances by a man to a woman in a public place' (Oxford Dictionaries, 2014). It includes all type of assaults i.e., physical, verbal and non-verbal. Physical assault such as rubbing, touching, fondling etc., verbal includes passes sexual jokes, vulgar comments etc. while non-verbal includes staring, whistling, expressing obscene gestures.

A lewd stare, a sly whistle, a well-timed clap, an unwarranted bump, seemingly casual touch, a lingering look at a vulnerable time, the humming of a suggestive song, passing downright uncouth comments, cheap gestures, the display of an indecent snap or video, bikes flying close with hands stretched to grope you, passing by in slow moving cars blasting loud music with many eyes inside measuring you up…all these are typical examples of eve teasing (Banwasi, Prakruthi .N.)

This shameful act against women impoverishes our society culturally, economically and socially, as it limits the women's participation in the development of society. So it is the time to eradicate it completely from our society.

The following are the suggestions for eradication of eve teasing from society:

Provide Quality Family Education

Family is the first school of learning and the mother is the first teacher for a human being. The mothers must teach their sons to treat women with respect. The traditional Indian thinking considers boys are superior to girls. Boys who see their father treating their mother with respect will automatically grow into men who think likewise. Providing a healthy and friendly environment at home, helps the kids to build strong values and reduces the tendency to react violently. Quarrel between parents, neighbours or relatives make a negative environment and shows negative impact on children. A positive environment is the only antidote to a negative environment. As the child receives the first impression of life at home and ideas formed at this young stage continue to linger in the later stages too. Home environment should be conducive. If a person achieves right values, ethics, knowledge etc. from his family from very young age, he never indulges in immoral activities like eve teasing. So, right family education is must for children if we want to make our society free from crimes like eve teasing.

All Guardians have to be Cautious

Today is the trend of nuclear family. Parents have no time for their wards. To overcome from this problem of eve teasing, they have to inquire their children's behaviour inside and outside the home. If any fault is found then necessary steps should be taken against it. A lot of freedom and power should not be given to boys. A sense of accountability should be inculcated in them. The moral sanctions imposed on girls to protect them from the ill consequences of this unlimited freedom given to boys, if only half of them are imposed on boys, the girls would regain their identity by enjoying enough freedom to live like a human being.

Limit Open Sky Culture

People see free sex, obscene material, open mixing of men and women through various television shows, magazines, movies and consequently try to do the same thing, which causes eve teasing (Aminul Hoque, 2013). Man, who lives in fantasy world of movies, lose all sense of reality. He fails to see that his favourite hero on celluloid behaves differently in actual life. In fact, he is gentleman. Pub culture, club culture, casino, bars, late night parties; all these has made fashion today. The drunkenness leads to many incidents of eve teasing. Media should ban on highlighting 'macho' image of men, who make a public display of affection towards unwilling girls. So, this so called open sky culture has to be limited.

Prohibition on Use of Alcohol and Drugs

Uninterrupted alcoholism and drug addiction is a major cause of eve teasing. When a man takes any intoxicating material, he loses his conscience and at that time, he can do anything unfair like eve teasing. Bashir and Khurshid (2013) found in their study that 50 per cent of respondents are of the view that peer group is responsible for inculcating bad habits, as it is due to bad company youth get addicted to antisocial crimes like drinking of alcohol, drug addiction which are the root causes for such issues in society. Consumption of alcohol at an early age should be avoided. Excessive use of liquors, drugs should be prohibited. Rehabilitation homes and support programmes are available for those who need professional help.

Avoidance of Indecent Outfits

Women should avoid wearing indecent and revealing outfits. Dresses which expose the parts of the body often give men a wrong signal. But wearing this type of outfit is not a justification for a man to assault her; after all he is not an animal to give the justification that he assaulted a woman as she was an easy prey to him. Any female wearing scanty dress doesn't give license to men to harass her. Even burqah doesn't guarantee safety. Many cheap men tease decent looking females also. But exposure of body leads to more teasing. So everyone should wear decent clothing. It will minimise this evil to some extent.

Prevention of Misuse of Mobile Phone and Internet

Present age is the age of ICT. Every person has inclination towards it. The mobile phone and internet are frequently used tools in various crimes. Mobile phones have become mobile cinema having free call, SMS and talk time. Without showing his actual identity, a man can do friendship with opposite sex which may lead a lot of eve teasing. There are so many pornography sites on internet. Now a days, mobile has become in the hand of people as a store house of pornography. 25 per cent of total search engine requests in a day is pornographic (Pornographic Statistics, 2012). Proper steps should be taken by our government otherwise eve teasing would not be stopped.

Appointment of Censor Board for T.V. Programmes

In India, there is a censor board for big screen but not any authority for T.V. channels broadcasting. Various programmes of different channels are full of vulgar materials. There should be check on foreign channels. China and many other countries have banned some channels in their country. Our government should also take serious steps in this direction, as these channels are seemed to be harmful for our culture. Media is glorified verbal and gestural eve teasing and the message sent is that it is acceptable, desirable, suitable and humorous for people. Media should not portray men as powerful and women as powerless to be exploited, sex object or item and eve teasing as harmless act. There should be appointment of censor board for small screen.

Tackle Eve Teasing Fearlessly

Some women feel shy to report such incidents for the reason that it would attach stigma to them and would be embarrassing for them. If a woman feels shy and reserved to defend herself and keep the suffering to herself, eve teasers may get back next day with reinforcement."Being too shy and reserved to speak up is just going to work against you. You've got to look your offender in the face and speak up as loud as you can."(Indian Women Welfare Foundation, 2009). Silence on this type of act, not only encourages the offender but also gives wrong message to other prospective teasers. If a woman just look straight into the eyes of eve teaser and speak up, he would run away. So, it is a need of hour, to tackle this problem with courage by victim itself. Women should tell the teasers that they are better equipped with reactions instead of being stunned when they are eve teased.

Empower Women to Fight Back

The women should carry pins, pepper powder, chilli powder, pen-knives etc., to protect themselves. Carrying small safety weapons not only make a woman safe but also help in avoiding any type of evil act. Self defence classes like karate, martial arts etc. should be joined. These techniques will not only make the teasers to learn a lesson but will also give some strength to the other females for future of how they can defend themselves from those non-humans. Akhtar, Chesfeeda (2013) found that 100 per cent respondents held the opinion that the women, who looked timid are easy targets of physical teasing as this offence is committed underhandedly and the offenders fear disclosure by the victim. As a result they prefer timid victims. So looking bold, poker faced is an effective strategy, to some extent, to protect women.

Download Women Safety Apps

Present era is technology era. Smart phones are quite handy. There are so many Safety Alert Apps are available in play store. These are specially designed to enhance the safety for women at anytime and anywhere. By it, the relatives or authorities are able to pinpoint the exact location in seconds. Safety and security is just a couple of swipes away with these iphone and smart phone apps. Whether a woman in immediate trouble or get separated during a night out and don't know how to get home, having these apps on your phone can reduce the risk and bring assistance when needed. Several safety apps are originally developed for reducing the risk of sexual assault (Lowen, N. D.). The offender never would think about this type of act again in future. To reduce the chance of becoming a victim, get quick help with these safety apps. Women can use technology in this way to safe themselves.

Open More and More Co-Education Schools

Aminul Hoque, (2013) found that 62 per cent school girls are victims of eve teasing. So, there should have more co-education schools, so that males are exposed to female from a very young age and grow to mutually respect each other. School is a place, where boys and girls interact with students and teachers of opposite sex. The physical proximity of the girls and boys has made free interaction. They should be allowed to mingle freely so that they learn to respect each other's individuality from a very early age. They should be involved in group activities involving both the sex so that the curiosity and inhibitions regarding the opposite sex can end. It would also make them to look on each other rather than feeling shy of each other. Sharing and shouldering the responsibilities together thereby respecting and caring equally. Right attitudes should be developed in boys so that they abstain from any kind of objectionable behaviour.

Include Sex Education in Curriculum

According to Wikipedia, a sex education curriculum is a sex education programme encompassing the methods, materials and assessments exercised to inform individuals of the issues relating to human sexuality, including human sexual anatomy, sexual intercourse, reproductive rights and responsibilities and other aspects of sexual behaviour. Common sex education curricula include an abstinence-only approach, implemented in academia via the internet, peer education, games, health care organisations and school instruction.(Wikipedia, 2014)At the stage of puberty, it is the natural tendency of male and female to attract each other, when openly see each other. Sometimes males cannot control them and indulge in eve teasing. Sex education should include understanding of emotions, behaviour of opposite sex. Traditionally, adolescents are deprived of this type of education and discussion regarding this type of issues being considered taboo. So there should be a provision of sex education.

Inculcate Moral and Values through Education

The educated youth don't necessarily involve in this uncouth behaviour. But, the people who are uncivilised, uneducated indulge in this type of act of eve teasing. But, just getting academic knowledge is not right education. Daily there is news of molesting or sexual harassment in any educational institutions. It means our present education system is lacking of values. Moral values should be imbibed, so that the factors, which cause moral degradation, are counterbalanced by moral and values provided by education. It should be imparted at all stages, especially at very young age, so that the seeds of moral values planted in children at a very young age take deep roots. By inculcating morals and values in our education system, eve teasing can be eradicated from society to a great extent.

Provide Religious Education

Religion teaches a person morality, ethics, values, code of conduct, manners, good behaviour etc. In the absence of religious education, people are not aware about what is permitted and what is prohibited. They have no knowledge about punishment of bad deeds of life. For this reason, they are doing evil acts frequently without any fear. Religious teachings and preachings should be followed by everyone. In every religion, men are not allowed to take a second glance of a woman. And he should not be unethical to another woman. But, unfortunately it is the most forgotten religious teaching. By following it, men would not be able to justify their violence by finding faults with women. In our religions, Eve teasing is considered as a crime which is punishable not only in this world but also in the life hereafter.

Practice Ashtang Yoga

Every person in this world has craving for peace and happiness. Whatever we do, it is with the ultimate goal of achieving happiness. Not only individuals but every nation, the entire world is praying for world peace. The magical solution that promises individual's joy, peace and prosperity in their personal lives and shows them a path to world peace that they can adopt fearlessly is Yoga. The path of Ashtang Yoga which has been propagated by Maharishi Patanjali is a complete way of life.

There are eight principles of Yoga. It is only Ashtang Yoga that can stop the violence in today's world. The first principle is Self-restraint. Observance of celibacy is included in it. Abstaining from the food which arouses sexual desires, avoiding situations of sexual temptations, sexually provocative audio and visuals, sexually provocative sights and dresses is called celibacy. Looking at the opposite sex with lust, touching, meeting alone, talking, discussing the subject, enacting the sexual acts, thoughts of a sexual nature and keeping company of people who distract or tempt, are the eight types of intercourse. A celibate should protect himself from the above and use five sense organs for noble objectives. Lust and anger attach themselves to the body for a short time. In that period the whole body is shaken after which the body becomes charmless, weak and pale. So follow celibacy and become brilliant, clever, intelligent, strong and courageous (Balkrishna, 2008). Practicing yoga helps to rectify this negative approach from society.

Organisation of Workshop, Seminar and Awareness Programmes

Slogans should raise against this shameful act and should make aware people about seriousness of this issue. Its great need to highlight this issue in society again and again. Seminars, workshops should be organised to aware women about dealing that difficult situation and how to fight back. The bad effects of eve teasing should be described to the mass people. The media should take up this responsibility and educate the public on how to tackle this social evil i.e., eve teasing. Programmes need to be carried out by social service organisations, NGO on large scale to sensitise the boys, who are prone to such type of shameful behaviour. These boys can be helped because most of the time they are not bad, not a rapist or a murderer. They are just misguided and lost their way.

Spread Awareness about Gender Sensitisation

Around the world gender is taken as primary classification between people. These labels of male and female carry images and expectations about how we should act. Gender roles are attitudes and activities that a society links to each sex. Gender sensitisation refers to the modification of behaviour by raising awareness about gender equality concerns. By modification of behaviour of parents towards children can lead to causal effect on gender equality. When the kids are young i.e., before the puberty age, both boys and girls play with each other with no thought of gender difference. But, as they start reaching adolescent period, parents, society keeps them reminding about gender differences. At this stage, a boy starts becoming aware a girl as a 'girl'. Throughout our modern world the woman is portrayed as docile, beautiful creation in need of protection and care. Thus the gender sensitisation should be explained in every sphere of lives. This stereotyped image should need overhauling. Men should be taught to respect the women. They should be made aware about the contribution of women in the development of society and co-existence of both sexes. None is less than other. School curriculum should include gender related studies which glorifies the achievements and capabilities of women. So gender sensitivity should instill in society.

Provide Exemplary Punishment to the Offender

There has been undergone so many amendments in anti eve teasing laws in past one year. There is no specific legislation in the country except the state of Tamil Nadu which has enacted Tamil Nadu Prohibition of Eve-teasing Ordnance, 1998 which later became an Act, namely, the Tamil Nadu Prohibition of Eve-Teasing Act,1998.(Singh,2012).Under Indian Penal Code the term eve teasing is not used. There are three sections under which action can be taken. Section 294 punishes any obscene act or recital of any obscene songs or ballad or words in a public place with a punishment of three months or fine or both. Section 509 of the Indian Penal Code, a word, gesture or act intended to insult the modesty of a woman is punishable for one year imprisonment, fine or both. Another section is 354 (IPC) according to which anyone who uses forces or assaults a woman to outrage her modesty will be punished with two years of imprisonment or fine or both (Devi and Jasrotia, 2013).

But, there is no use of this type of law, unless and until offender is punished. It is not a secret that the police don't take eve teasing incidents seriously. It is so common that even the police are terrified with the flood of number of complaints, they might receive if they did register them. It is a matter of shame. Whosoever is found guilty must be punished. The offender must be kept under the ambit of law. If he remains free, the crimes will spread vigorously. Publish photo of eve teasers in local newspapers along with their shameful act. Every person will be feared if exemplary punishment is provided to offender.

Time to Change the Attitude of Family and Society

The family and society of the victims should have courage and resolve to support them, the victim is not responsible for this incidence. In most of the cases, whenever a victim informs the family members about it, they misunderstood her. We must tell females that not to keep silent about this matter. The society and family should support her mentally (Santosh). Everybody has to come forward and hinder the occurrence if he observes any such incident of eve teasing at any place. Its not her fault. She has the right to live her life freely in the world. "The change begins at homes where the parents must teach their sons to respect women. We must educate our sons." (Parshathy, 2013)

Creation of Social Responsibility

Man is a social being. As a social being, many men have their subordinates. If a man properly take care of his subordinate persons and prevents them from doing bad deeds, then no society can do evil deeds. Men themselves should tell their friends, who tend to tease girls ,that this behaviour is unacceptable. If they catch their friend passing a vulgar comment they should tell him that this is insulting to women. If responsibility will be grown in the mind of people of a society there is a less chance of eve teasing. Each and every member of the society must be aware, educated, enlightened and devoted to their roles, responsibilities and duties. Every person shouldn't shut his eyes while witnessing an eve teasing incident. It is the time to teach the eve teasers, they will not be let free if they disrespect women. The concentrated efforts can take away the menace of eve teasing slowly.

Thus eve teasing is a form of sexual harassment indulged in by men, never mind of women's age, social status, intelligence level, marital status or their education. It is spreading like cancer disease in our society. Strong laws and punishments are not only strong enough to eradicate it. All of us have to stand up, speak out and act against it instead of mere mute witnesses to such type of issues. Women need to be aware, courageous and fight for their rights. It is a time to bring changes in the thinking pattern of the males who are indulging in such type of crimes. The males are indoctrined to develop a wrong attitude towards females from an early stage. They are taught things like 'Don't cry like girls', 'Don't be shy' etc. Males think that females are inferior, weak and vulnerable. The problem started from here. So, it is necessary from a very early childhood, boys and girls should be treated as equal and girls should be taught that they are not inferior in any way.

References

- Akhtar, Chesfeeder, (2013). Eve teasing as a form of violence against woman: A case study of district Srinagar, Kashmir. *Academic Journals,* 5,168-178.Retrieved from http://www.academicjournals.org
- Aminul Hoque, Mohammad (2013).Eve teasing in Bangladesh: Causes and impact on society, A study from Islamic perspective. *The International Journal of Social Sciences,*15(1). Retrieved from http://tjoss.com
- Balkrishna, Acharya (2008). Yoga : Its philosophy and practice, Hardwar, Uttaranchal, Divya prakashan.
- Bansal, Rehaan, (2014). Short Essay on Eve Teasing. Retrieved Oct 15, 2014 from http://www.shareyouressays.com/84409/short-essay-on-eve-teasing.
- Bashir, Aadil, and Khurshid, Shabana (2013). Eve teasing and molestation - A case study of district Srinagar. *International Journal of Science and Research.* 2(12).Retrieved from http://www.ijsr.net.
- Banwasi, Prakruthi. N. (n.d.). Eve teasing evils. Retrieved Nov 15, 2014 from http://www.banwasi.com/html/ete1.html.
- Devi, Reena and Jasrotia, Anu (2013).Eve-teasing in the panjab university campus:A study of girls hostel students. *Asian Journal of Multidimensional Research.* 2 (8). Retrieved from http://www.tarj.in.
- Eve Teasing (n.d.) retrieved Nov 01, 2014 from Retrieved from http://www.womenwelfare.org/Eve per cent20 teasing.html
- Lowen, Linda (n.d). Best apps for women concerned with safety and security. About News. Retrieved Nov 15, 2014, from http://womenissues.about.com/od/violenceagainstwomen/tp/Best-App-For-women-Concerned-With-safety-And-Security.html.
- Oxford Dictionaries (2014).Oxford: Oxford University Press. Retrieved Oct 01, 2014 from http://www.oxforddictionaries.com/definition/english/eve-teasing.
- Parshathy, J. Nath (2013,Dec 16).All about eve teasing.The Hindu. Retrieved from http://m.thehindu.com/features/metroplus/society/all-about-eve-teasing/article 5466089.
- Pornography Statistics. Retrieved Oct 10, 2014 from http://www.familysafemedia.com/pornography_statistics.html

- Santosh (n.d.). Eve teasing evils .Retrieved Oct 10, 2014 from http://ken-foundation-awareness2.blogspot.in/p/eve-teasing-evils.html?m=1
- Singh, A. R. (2012,Dec 29):Supreme Court on eve teasing of woman and its guidelines. Retrieved from http://e-pao.net/epSubPageExtractor.asp?src=features.Spotlight_On_Women.
- Wikipedia,The Free Encyclopedia."Sex Education". Retrieved October 20, 2014 from http://en.m.wikipedia.org/wiki/sex_education_curriculum.

21

Eve Teasing: How Much is too Much?

Fatima Rizvi

Abstract

There are lots of women who are tortured by eve teasing every day but keep silent after such incidents. There is an unfortunate silence surrounding this issue. And because it is not in the public arena of debate, not being discussed or analysed, it is a misunderstood issue. This study intended to explore the attitude towards eve teasing in university students. Ten In-depth interviews were conducted in university of the Lucknow. The participants were selected through purposive sampling. The thematic analysis was done. There were mainly Seven themes; meaning, important as a social issue, personal experiences, reasons, reactions, impact and suggestions for eradication of eve teasing.

Introduction

The modern society is crisis ridden on all fronts and at root of all the ills is the crisis of values. Be it the infamous Damini case of Delhi or hundred of similar shameful incidents, the numerous political scams that stare at every other day or the various terrorist activities. The list is endless; hardly a day passes without news indicative of social, moral, cultural values at all levels which has led the spread of selfishness, unlimited greed, corruption, violence and destruction. In these system women related issues are often neglected. Within this patriarchal social fabric women face different types of harassment in every sphere of their lives. "Eve-teasing" refers to public sexual harassment or street harassment to a girl by a boy. Eve teasing is the most common crime against women as it's easy to do and hard to prove. This is the harsh reality in India; No girl has been spared from being a prey of eve teasing. And those who are not suffered to it yet they live in a constant fear of happening something bad to them.

Eve-teasing is a threat to women's empowerment and should be eradicated. This is not simply a matter of an incident which happens one day and is forgotten the next day. It's a traumatic experience which can leave deep psychological scars and has negative consequences it may be that serious that it could lead a woman to commit suicide due to the harassment and torture that she might have undergone. Eve-teasing is a serious offence against the honour, dignity, and self respect of a woman.

Situation is getting worst and worst, day by day. In public places we often observes that guy teasing girls, commenting bad words or holding their hands forcefully and everyone around there are just watching the scene peacefully. Not even a single man moves forward to help the girls in such situation. Leave men, not even other girls comes forward to help the victim girl. There is no specific legislation in the country except for the state of Tamil Nadu which has its own legislation to deal with this offence. Eve-teasing is a topic worthy of analysis because it prevents women from being active participants in public aspects of Indian society and because the assaults that women face in public can affect the way in which women view themselves as members of society.

Sample Selection

The researcher conducted her study in university of Lucknow. Women were selected through purposive sampling method under which used convenient sampling from the university of Lucknow. The data was collected through in-depth structured interviews with each participant between 15 December 2013 and 30 December 2013. Interviews were conducted on a one-to-one basis. All interviews were audio-recorded and transcribed verbatim. The participants were all given a pseudonym to protect their identity and ensure confidentiality. The sample consisted of women between the ages of 18 and 28 years. The educational level of the participants was high, five were students of masters, and two were M.Phil and three were PhD scholars. My gender also facilitated my access to the women, as several participants made it clear that they would not have participated had I been a male researcher. For this article data were drawn from Ten in depth interviews. Researcher selected in depth interview because in-depth interviews are used when seeking information on individual, personal experiences from people about a specific issue or topic, when to capture people's individual voices and stories. It is important of gaining a detailed insight into research issue from perspective of the study participants themselves. This reflects the emic perspective that is essence of qualitative research.

Data Analysis Procedure

The researcher used nvivo for analysis in making nodes and themes. The interviews were reciprocal: both researcher and research subject were engaged in the dialogue. Therefore, duration of interviews and the number of questions varied from one participant to the other. Interviews were audio-recorded, with the permission of interviewees, each interview was assigned a code, and notes were taken during the interviews. For the very purpose of phenomenological analysis researcher transcribed key words, phrases and statements to consolidate the emerging themes. The systematic procedure of transforming the data through interpretations was followed. The researcher concluded the explicitation by writing a composite summary of themes emerged under seven major themes; meaning, important as a social issue, personal experiences, reasons, reactions, impact and suggestions of eve teasing.

Thematic Analysis

Thematic analysis was used as the method for analysing the qualitative data. We identified various themes from analysing the data and counted the frequency of each theme in the participant's answers to the open-ended questions.

Meaning of Eve-Teasing

There are the different meanings and views about eve-teasing :

A coarse stare, a sly whistle, a seemingly casual touch, The smooching sound, remarks about your body the humming of a suggestive song, passing downright uncouth comments, cheap gestures, bikes flying close with hands stretched to grope you, passing by in slow moving cars blasting loud music with many eyes inside measuring you up... all these are eve teasing.

Another Sensitive Girls Says

Imagine walking towards your campus knowing you are being watched, analysed, and talked about. This is the thing which makes me uncomfortable, self-conscious.

One of the Respondents States that

Eve-teasing is a mean to disturb girls. It is practiced in public places and university campus even inside classrooms. It is common; yet talk of the experience is taboo. Girls have been socialised to keep the details of their victimisation private.

Another Girl Says

Eve teasing is an attempt to irritate a girl or catch her attention, probably by a whistle or a clap, or by obscene messages sent on the cell phones or through internet. Anything from catcalls to violence comes under one simple term Eve teasing.

One Respondent Tells that

Eve-teasing is like 'fun' for the boys. It is a difficult crime to prove and the eve-teaser takes advantage of this. You know you're being eve-teased when you hear those wolf whistles behind you when you go out shopping or are jabbed while getting on a bus. There are hundreds of ways to do it.

Another Participant States that

Eve-teasing reflects a gender bias in society, proving that males are dominant while females are helpless. In eve-teasing, a man, knowing that he is stronger than the opposite sex, uses his power to bully women. It is a power game in which the man is the predator and the woman is preyed upon. Perhaps the most alarming thing about eve-teasing is that it is the first rung on the ladder of sex crimes.

Important As a Social Issue

Eve-teasing is not taken as seriously as it should by women. Actually, it has far-reaching consequences. After all, something that has been labeled 'little rape' by certain feminist writers cannot be mere pestering.

As One of the Participant Mentions

It is really serious issue but you know I am always told that this is very common thing and no need to give attention at this.

Another Woman Gives the Similar Response

Nobody think of it as a serious problem. Girls are supposed to get habitual of it. Only a girl can understand what we girls have to face in our routine life.

One Respondent Tells that

At every place, women and girls have to move with a fear. Right from their home to streets, streets to their office, from their school to their college, at each place men are there to spoil their dignity. This is really serious but society takes it very lightly considered a joke or fun activity of boys.

One Respondent Tells that

It is the cruel truth of the day and the conditions are getting worst and worst, day by day. Earlier I just used to ignore these incidents but as I heard raising cases of rapes and acid attacks I don't know what to do. To ignore them is not safe at all; at other side to face them include the risk of serious violence.

One Respondent Shared her Personal Experience

I went to my brothers college for meeting my school friend, there I saw him sitting in the canteen passing cheap comments on girls. When I shared this with my mother in the evening she said it's common for this aged boys. He will be fine later I was just shocked. How could she take this thing that much lightly?

Personal Experiences

Respondents were asked if they experienced such incidents in their life, they could shared their experience. It was also found that an incidence occurred long back still has a strong impact.

One Respondent Shared her First Encounter with Eve-teasing

When I was in school, a boy on a bike used to follow me daily to school and one day offered me a ride, I was too small to even gauge it as unwarranted, eventually ran ahead to join a group of girls from my school. The incident had affected me so much that for months after that I insisted on being accompanied to school.

One of the Respondents States that

Two years back a guy started to follow me at every place from home to campus Loitering around my college, tortured medially by mouthing obscenities, whizsing past on bike, touching me and by coming near my house late at night and screaming lascivious things near my room window. In beginning I did not took it seriously but later when I realise I felt scared. I told at home in result Now I am always accompanied by a male relative, they do not let me hang out alone in public places like movie theatres and shopping malls, because they are always tensed about my safety.

Another Participant States that

This happened when I was 12 years old. My mother and I were walking back home in the evening. I was on the side facing the road. Suddenly a biker comes from behind and hits my butt and flees. I yelled 'hey' which was usually my instinctive reaction but I couldn't figure what happened. I wasn't able to understand that situation. My mom immediately made me switch sides. I did not understand what happened and why.

There is One More Response

I wanted to do my MBA from Delhi University but my mother did not allow as she is frightened to hear about cases of violence against girls in Delhi. She said you will not be able to manage there alone.

Reasons of Eve Teasing

There are various reasons behind this like Illiteracy and carelessness, Students exaggeration in front of friends, Personal grudges and individual relations with the women, Psychological problem, sexually exaggerated nature, to have fun and embarrass women. In this regard there are the different views of respondents.

One of the Respondents States that

I confronted these eve teasers everyday while commuting to my computer classes, horribly sick is what these creeps are, I feel like talking to a hardcore eve-teaser and finding out what cheap thrills he gets out of this.

I think Boys do this behaviour to show their heroism. This is the mistaken concept that every boy has to be a "macho" man and a girl is a conquest to prove his manhood.

One Respondent tells that

I think the perpetrators of eve teasing come of low status family. They are culturally, mentally blocked and to me though the world has changed a lot they have not changed much. Mentally they live in mediaeval ages physically though in 21st century.

But again I wonder when I see those men of letters, men of reputation also being indicted for the offense.

Another Woman Gives the Similar Response

Due to not having socially approved ways to interact with girls freely, boys have misconception about girls and sometimes this realty influences a boy to tease a girl as means of expressing himself in front of a girl. It has also something to do with their upbringing, or some insecurity in him that they take out by targeting girls, a tacky way of feeling macho!

One More Respondent Gives the Similar Explanation and Response of it she tells

Silence of victim and ignorance of the people leads to this behaviour. Society expects that girls should be docile, decent and tolerant, and of course it is because of their vulnerability. Family socialises a girl as per the expectation of the society and naturally she losses her bravery to protest any injustice and abusive behaviour against her. As society labels a girl as vulnerable, parents suggest their daughter to avoid and not to protest against eve-teasing.

What is Your Reaction?

One respondent tells that

I go my college by bus usually. Once A man was standing in front of Ladies seat and on the pretext of balancing himself was touching me. After few moments I started shouting at him loudly and he was like "I didn't do anything". But all the people on bus started confessing him. Felt great and was happy that I dared to take the step.

Another Woman gives the Similar Response

There was a guy who persistently followed me when I used to go to school on a cycle. One day I gathered enough courage to stop and ask him what he wanted as he was really bugging me. He asserted that he was a decent boy and that he wanted to be friends with me. I politely said that my upbringing did not permit me to open up to strangers and requested him to stop following me lest I face its consequences. He stopped following me after that.

Another Woman Gives the Different Response

Eve-teasing is something that is always going to exist in our society, and we have learnt to live with it. Women are often taught that fighting back or making a scene will only give the Eve-teaser the response and attention that he is seeking. This teaches women that Eve-teasing is their fault because they have attracted a man's attention. Since women feel that they are at fault for Eve-teasing.

One of the Respondents States that

I just scream back and abuse the eve teaser, I know that they get scared if you are bold, if we get scared they will continue.

Another Participant States that

Sometimes they sing cheesy songs to hold our attention but we are so used to it that we don't even turn around and look. Retaliation would mean inviting humiliation and embarrassment and even might result in the reversal of blame on us.

Impact of eve teasing

One respondent tells that

An eve teased female feels weak and frustrated and may experience depression and low self-esteem. Being harassed on the streets can prompt her to withdraw or become constantly anxious. Dozens of girls have committed suicide on account of eve-teasing.

Another Woman Gives the Similar Response

It hinders their chances of progress by limiting them to their homes. Eve-teased girls often drop out of school to avoid their tormentors, and because parents fear for their 'honour'. These girls are then forced into early marriages, which have a deep impact on maternal nutrition and health. These girls become mothers at a younger age and give birth to babies with lower birth weights. So, this form of harassment contributes to maintaining the low status of women.

One of the Respondents States that

Even though Eve-teasing is not taken perceived as a serious crime in India, it "...plays a serious role in conditioning a girl's mind into accepting the superiority of the male sex by making her feel that she's just an object to be commented upon, that men folk have a right to make any comments about her body...."

There is one More Similar Response

I try to look like a guy to avoid these creeps stalking me while I am riding on the roads, these cheapsters try to talk to you and irritate you. This messes up your very frame of mind, the irritation affects you after you reach home, your mood is messed and the incident is etched for a while in your minds, even making you crabby with your family. But still I feel hesitant to inform my parents about an incident of eve teasing; as I know from past experience that I would be the only one to be affected adversely. All activities and clothes would fall under scrutiny, late nights would be curbed, wantonly by strict parents and on a sub-conscious level by parents who are supportive.

Suggestions to Stop this:

One Respondent Tells that

Women should take self-defense courses, "It sharpens their reflexes and it gives them practice to be violent... generally we have never taught our girls and women at home to be active as far as defending yourself is concerned. We have never told them to beat up somebody, to use your body or anything to save yourself, we just want them to be silent spectators, silent victims so therefore this training programme... makes them confident ...and it also prepares them to activate their body in such a way that they are able to give an adequate and proper answer to the person who is misbehaving with them".

There is One More Similar Response

People blame the victim's clothes to film songs now. When will we get the courage to actually face the problem rather than finding pointless things to blame? How about we work on making the police force better, improving security, enacting harsh punishments, getting cases to actually finish at court in time rather than being kept pending forever, etc?

One Respondent Tells that

I heard somewhere that *khaap panchayat* passed the diktat of banning girls from wearing jeans I could not believe my ears. Will they stop teasing us if stop wearing jeans? I think they should given moral values first so that they could at least learn to respect women.

There is One More Response

These days people don't help others who are in trouble, I really doubt if they will stick their legs out for unknown women who are victims of eve teasing attacks. I wish that awareness about eve teasing is created in every school to make all girls and guys aware about the harm caused by eve teasing. It will go a long way in transfixing a sense of right behaviour in the generations to come.

One of the Respondents States that

I feel that parents should chat with their daughters and ask them to be bold when faced by such an issue and they should also advise their sons to not ever indulge in such cheap acts. It is the responsibility of parents to educate children about these aspects of life and build them to be better humans.

Conclusion

Today we find that the problem of eve-teasing is growing at an alarming rate and it needs urgent attention. The present study tries to explore the experiences and perceptions of university students. What are the meanings of eve teasing according to them and what is the impact of eve teasing. Findings of the study indicate that students have different viewpoints about it. Majority of the students see it as a serious issue while others see it as a regular part of their everyday lives that was not worthy of analysis and they did not even question why it happens. Eve teasing is an immoral activity against the honours, dignity, and self-respect of a girl. It hurts the adolescent girls as well as the decency of the society immensely. Data also revealed when a girl goes out to a public space, she never feels secure irrespective of her clothes and time. This shows that the existing framework is not sufficient to deal with this problem. Thus, a lot is yet to be done to make the society a safe place for women. We want women of positive existence not as show pieces which enhance society's false pride, family's beauty or newspapers sale. The future is waiting to be made better; all we have to do is to refuse to shut our eyes when we stand witness to an incident of eve teasing. We must stand up and speak and act against this menace. And, above all, women need to be aware of and fight for their rights. As someone has rightly said, rights that are not asserted cease to exist.

References

- Creswell, J. W. 2003. Research design: Qualitative, quantitative, and mixed methods approach. Thousand Oaks, CA: SAGE.
- Dwyer, S. and Buckle, J. 2009. "The space between: On being an insider-outsider in qualitative research." International Journal of Qualitative Method 8(1): 54-63.
- http://articles.timesofindia.indiatimes.com/2012-09-23/chandigarh/34040318_1_eve- woman-constable-pcr.
- Eve teasing to be made non-bailable offence" www.Hinduonnet.com <http://www.hinduonnet.com/2001/09/11/stories/04112232.htm>
- http:/en.wikipedia.org/wiki/eve-teasing (Accessed: 10th October, 2013)
- http://issuesindia.hpage.co.in/eve-teasing_49567401.html
- http://www.mightylaws.in/799/menace-eve-teasing-problem-solution
- http://www.studymode.com/essays/Eve-Teasing-A-Problem-Of-Modern-713756.html
- Journal of the Indian Academy of Applied Psychology February 2011, Vol.37, Special Issue, 100-10, p.1.

22

Eve Teasing in India and Bangladesh a Conceptual Survey

Rukmini U. Jamdar

Abstract

Eve teasing is a burning issue in our Indian society. We witness different types of eve teasing in our day to day life. Eve teasing may be in the form of slight touch to a deadly crime such as rape or sexual harassment of women. Newspaper carries issues related with eve teasing on daily basis. Eve teasing in different forms occurs in all the countries. What are the causes of eve teasing, how the term eve teasing is interpreted, what are the different causes of eve are teasing, and what legal provisions are there with reference to this issue are some of the highlights of this article? The paper deals with the above related issues in the form of a conceptual survey in India and Bangladesh.

Key Words: Touch, Harassment, Causes, India, Bangladesh

Introduction

Eve teasing is a recognised principle of liability or not and if not is it the high time to recognise it as an independent area of liability. Observing the present scenario which is most unsafe for women, this project also puts forward and presses the need of including eve teasing under a new head of liability. Now a day eve -teasing is become critical problem in our country. Social menace like eve-teasing breaking out wave from recently in Bangladesh this project tries to put some light on the grey areas of sexual harassment or what is called eve teasing in Bangladesh. Examining these grey areas also has the intention of attracting the attention of eminent jurists, lawyers and the law makers to this grave civil wrong and to pressurise them to formulate some laws in this direction so as to give some relief to the victim which is otherwise impossible.

What is Eve-teasing?

Eve teasing refers to the temptress nature of Eve, placing responsibility on the woman as a tease. Eve teasing is a euphemism used in India and sometimes Pakistan, Bangladesh and Nepal for public sexual harassment, street harassment or molestation of women by men, with eve being a reference to the biblical Eve. "Eve teasing" is used in India to refer to a wide variety of behaviour including molestation, "flashing" or any verbal/ physical sexual street harassment that falls short of rape. It's an archaic term. The "Eve" part comes from the Old Testament and describing harassment as "teasing" makes it sound almost like a mild romantic overture that should be tolerated - which of course it should not.

As we know our Indian Society has always remained and will always be male dominated. The women in India have suffered a lot through stages. Eve teasing is a menace that has grown to alarming proportions. Not many cities in India are considered safe for women. Though, we are one of the fastest growing countries in world but we have yet to ensure the safety of working women and students. Eve teasing is a huge issue in many metropolitan cities of India. It depicts incidents of public sexual harassment, street harassment or molestation of women by men. Eve teasing also involves sexually suggestive remarks, groping, making lewd gestures and perverted teasing. These disturbing incidents usually take place in public transport, streets, offices and public places. School girls, college going students, working women etc regularly go through humiliating comments by the unruly men. Eve teasing can leave a permanent psychological scar on women. Eve teasing begins as an attempt to irritate a girl or catch her attention, probably by a whistle or a clap, or by drooling behind tinted windows in a car.

Considered a problem related to delinquencies in youth it is a form of sexual aggression that ranges in severity from sexually suggestive remarks, brushing in public places, catcalls, to outright groping. Sometimes it is referred to with a coy suggestion of innocent fun, making it appear innocuous with no resulting liability on the part of the perpetrator. Many feminists and voluntary organisations have suggested that the expression be replaced by a more appropriate term. According to them, considering the semantic roots of the term in Indian English eve-teasing refers to the temptress nature of Eve, placing responsibility on the woman as a tease, as though the aggressive response of the males was normal rather than criminal. Eve-teasing has been a notoriously difficult crime to prove, as perpetrators often devise ingenious ways to attack women, even though many feminist writers term it as "little rapes", and usually occur in public places, streets, and public transport. Some guidebooks to the region warn female tourists that eve teasing may be avoided by wearing conservative clothing, though eve teasing is reported both by Indian women and by conservatively-dressed foreign women.

Eve Teasing in India–Some facts and Figures:

- The expression eve teasing is Indian in origin. You won't find it in most of the dictionaries. Native speakers of English do not use it.
- Studies show that 32 per cent of the eve teasers are students, 35 per cent are anti socials while the remaining 33 per cent are middle aged men.
- The number of registered cases of sexual crimes against women in India increases from 67,072 in 1988 to 84000 in 1993.In 1995 alone, more than 25000 cases of molestation and 12000 cases of rape were reported in the capital city of New Delhi. It is estimated that well over 80 per cent of the sexual crimes go unreported. For example, 7643 of the 50000 estimated instances of violence against women were reported to the police even in Kerala, a south Indian state with the highest women's literacy rate.
- An increasingly large number of college going women taking public transportation in Delhi have resorted to carrying pins, pen knives, and even daggers as a deterrent. Others have taken self defence classes.
- A recent survey revealed that approximately 90 per cent of college women in New Delhi have experienced sexual harassment in some shape or form. Yet , it is estimated that only about 1 in 10000 eve teasing occurrences are reported to the police.
- 98 per cent of the women have stated that sexual harassment on roads has affected their personal or academic development in one way or the other.

These facts may appear untrue and horrifying but they clearly show the plight of women in India. The condition is deteriorating every day. It is high time, therefore, that we include eve teasing as a Tort under a new head of liability and curb this heinous practice.

Eve Teasing – The Psychology Behind

Many psychologists believe that sex, love or fun is not the only motive that men indulge in this behaviour. Eve teasing is closely related to the patriarchal mindset of the Indian male. Men are raised to believe that they are more powerful physically and emotionally than women. They feel that they are doing nothing wrong just having some fun. Women on the other hand are made to feel vulnerable and the weaker sex. Teachers of psychology and social scientists believe eve teasing to be a result of the frustrations suffered by a majority of youth. Disappointed by the unbecoming attitude of teachers and indifferent parents , they yearn for an outlet to vent their aggression and depression. Besides , many who do not inherit good values tend to indulge in acts of sexual harassment. Eve teasing can be seen as a rite of passage for boys on their way to becoming men. Considering that sex is not the only motive, it would be reasonable to conclude that the psychodynamics of eve teasing are closely linked to the issue of masculinity and the masculine agenda.

At the risk of over simplifying a complex phenomenon, it would not be imprudent to say that in our country, the construct of masculinity is usually equated with patriarchy. In other words, masculinity is experienced not so much as a set of emotional or behavioural characteristics unique to the male gender, but more in terms of hierarchical domination over the feminine gender, so that the most man gets a socially dominant position over his female counterpart. Gender segregation from childhood, lopsided parental relationships as well as the representation of man–woman relationship in literature and popular cinema, all serve to reinforce the patriarchal model of masculinity in the mind of the growing male child.

It may appear paradoxical that in a country like India where the mother is generally deified, the growing male child does not learn to respect the members of his mother's gender. But it is because of this deification that the boy finds it easy to slip into the patriarchal mode, for he does not relate to his mother as a woman, but as a helpless and martyred dependent who needs to be pitied and cared for. The vocal emergence of feminism has also pushed the contemporary male a little on the back foot , not only the women are threatening to encroach on his male dominion, but also because he does not have any idea about how he can counter encroach on hers. So he moves squarely into the adversarial position, something he is instinctively comfortable with and, during adolescence, focuses not just on how he can express himself sexually, but also on how he can claim his patriarchal right. As part of his evolution into the patriarchal role, an arena is required in which his valour can be expressed. Organised sport and cultural activities are examples of these, but require some talent and application. Whereas standing with a group of peers at a bus stop or in a Cineplex, passing lewd remarks, gesticulating lasciviously and generally behaving obnoxiously requires mere numbers, and when the helpless girl is in no position to defend her despite visible evidence of distress, domination gets established.

Thus, we tried to understand the psychology of an average eve teaser when he indulges himself in the heinous practice. All this study has been done only to establish the fact further strongly that it is now high time to include eve teasing as a separate Tort so that this injustice and crime against the honour and dignity of the women can be stopped.

Eve Teasing and Tortious Liabilities

Mere thinking would not work in the present era. People should come forward and take strong steps against this practice. Strong laws should be enforced to tackle this problem. Eve teasing should be taken as a grave offence against the dignity and honour of a woman. We can start by making eve teasing as a separate head of liability under the Law of Torts. When included in law as a civil wrong, it would certainly see a decline in the cases of eve teasing also the women will have a weapon in their hands to uphold their dignity. They will feel more empowered and independent.

Eve Teasing as a Tort- A Civil Wrong

Let us examine eve teasing under the light of the three essential elements of Torts. Torts can be conceptualised to include the following essential elements:

This civil wrong is other than a mere breach of contract or breach of trust. This wrong is redressible by an action for unliquidated damages.

Eve teasing is a civil wrong. The eve teaser causes injury to the plaintiff who in turn affects her both physically and mentally. It is an unlawful infringement on the victim's privacy and person. She is tortured in the process. It also hampers her peace and happiness. In other words, curtails her right to enjoy her life and be happy. Eve teasing is neither a breach of contract nor a breach of trust. It is an encroachment on a woman's right and her dignity. Eve teasing is an unexpected incident. There is no question of a contract in it. Thus, its remedy is unliquidated damages which are to be decided by the courts according to the gravity of the injury caused. The courts can also provide a remedy in the form of injunction and detention also. This would force the eve teasers to at least think thrice before they indulge in such Torts

Eve teasing is the worst form of trespass to person possible. It is done intentionally to hurt a woman physically as well as emotionally. It is also done to gain the attention of the woman. It violates the person's elementary civil right to security of person. It is a grave civil wrong against women. It is more torturous for small girls and adolescents. Avoidable physical contact and advances, touching, patting, whistling, pinching, physical assault and molestation by the eve teasers amount to Battery. An unwanted physical touch, an unwanted kiss all amount to battery and are actionable by the Law. The act of putting another person in reasonable fear or apprehension of an immediate battery by means of an act amounting an attempt or threat to commit a battery amounts to an actionable assault. An eve teaser also commits a assault when he commits the shameful act of eve teasing. Thus, we can say that eve teasing amounts to Trespass to person as it constitutes both Battery and Assault.

Compensation and Remedies

The Remedies can be in the following forms:

The eve teasers should be humiliated publically so as to make them aware and feel guilty of the shameful practice that they indulged in. People should socially boycott them as to make them realise their mistake. Their names should be published in the newspapers describing their shameful act in detail so as to make them feel guilty and realise their mistake. Damages should be awarded to the victim in terms of money. It should be big money. It will recover the loss that she must have suffered and also will discourage men from involving in eve teasing. The court can also ask the eve teasers to strictly abstain from indulging in eve teasing in case of repeated acts of similar kind. The court could also arrest a person for eve teasing under article 57, CrPC. This would further discourage people from eve teasing.

Eve Teasing in Bangladesh – Some Facts and Figures

Who is eve-teaser?

Now-a-days Eve-teasing has become intolerable. The harassment can take a variety of forms and the perpetrators come from multiple walk of life. They are rich and poor, educated and uneducated. According to Bangladesh National Women Lawyers Association (BNWLA) the Eve-teasers may be:

a. Teenage boys
b. Rickshaw pullers
c. Bus drivers
d. Street vendors
e. Traffic vendors
f. Often supervisors or colleagues of the working women

It is a matter of great regret that, now-a-days some educated and well-known boys are also enjoying the way of eve-teasing. Eve teasing is not a new problem in Bangladesh. It is a concern since many years. Almost every young girl is a victim of teasing, especially by the local teenagers. The most of the people may avoid it as common phenomena in youth. Yes, it is. But it is not every time. It can be tolerated until no girl is being attacked. But when it crosses the line, it will raise as a problem to us. It is surely a social problem. These days, many girls have committed suicide only to safe themselves from eve-teasing. That means, eve-teasing in Bangladesh has reached its maximum range. No doubt his is against the women rights. Those who are involved with this kind of embarrass stuff can be named as a terrorist. The teasers wait outside schools, colleges or house and as soon as girls walk passed by them they start teasing with ribald comments, smutty jokes, coarse laughter, sly whistles and even indecent exposure. According to a daily newspaper, two girl committed suicide only in October 2010. In the last seven months there four girls were killed and 42 were injured. Well, this is just a rough measurement, which came across the people's attention. There happened many occurrences like this, which were not published in the newspaper. In most of the cases, the victims shy to exposes these incidents.

Various forms of Eve Teasing in Bangladesh

Eve-teasing has attacked our society in various forms. With all its forms it is destroying the society.

1. **Eve-teasing with School Going Female Students:** At the adolescent age, male students while passing by a school make

many indecent remarks hurting the female students. An adolescent young boy follows a girl from her school to her residence just to attract the attention of the girl. Such other ways of eve-teasing are passing bad comments and writing indecent letters etc. In some cases, some eve-teasers venture themselves to make a relation with a young girl forcibly. It puts the concerned girl into such a mental trauma that it is hard to bear. Following such mental trauma some young girls end their lives.

2. **Eve-teasing on Mobile:** Eve-teasing on mobile phone has become the most popular form of communication. A stalker, getting a mobile phone, starts teasing a girl in many ways. At first, he sends SMS in ornamental and rhetorical language to which a young girls easily falls victim as she is also an adolescent. Becoming a victim to this, a young girl develops a relation, on which that particular boy capitalises. Some intimate moments are captured by hidden camera or video recorder and these are later on circulated through the internet. That is a reason why mobile phone sometimes becomes a curse despite its multiple benefits.
3. **Sexual Harassment by Internet:** Young boys and girls in the cities are used to chat through internet by which they come closer to each other. Being adolescent, the boys and girls fall victim to their sensuality extreme world.

Laws in Bangladesh

In post-independent Bangladesh the Dhaka Metropolitan Police Ordinance (DMPO) of 1976 first addressed the women teasing directly. Section 76 of the ordinance defines women teasing as, "wilful and indecent exposure of one person in any street or public place within sight of, and in such manner as may be seen by, any woman, whether from within any house or building or not, or wilful pressing or obstructing any woman in a street or public place or insulting or annoying any woman by using indecent language or making indecent sounds, gestures, or remarks in any street or public place". Women-teasing is punishable with a maximum one year of imprisonment, or with a maximum two thousand Taka fine, or with both. This is for the first time, in Bangladesh, an act other than the Penal Code addressed the teasing offence against women. However, the term 'eve teasing' is still not used. Likewise, the other five metropolitan police acts/ordinances made similar provisions to penalise the offence of teasing women. However, these acts have no jurisdiction outside their respective metropolitan areas that makes the offence exclusively a local and urban phenomenon. Special laws penalising the offence of teasing women having nationwide jurisdiction was yet to be passed.

In 2000 the government enacted tougher law to protect the vulnerable women and children of the country from various typical offences. The Prevention of Women and Children Act-2000 came down heavily on the oppressors of the women. This act, inter alia, defined the now-much-talked-about sexual torture and sexual harassment.

In section 10(1), the law defines sexual torture as, "if a man touches the sexual organ or any other organ of a woman or of a child by any of his organs or by any other objects with a view to fulfilling his illegal sexual desire, such act of the man will be termed as sexual torture". This definition, in fact, includes the attempt of rape or outraging the modesty of a woman by actual physical contract. The law punishes the offender with rigorous imprisonment of minimum three and maximum Ten years and also an indefinite amount of fine.

In section 10(2), the law defines sexual harassment as, "if a man, with a view to fulfilling his illegal sexual desire outrage a woman's modesty or makes erotic gesture, such act of the man will amount to sexual harassment". A rigorous imprisonment ranging from two to seven years and additionally an indefinite amount of fine is rewarded for this offence. According to this definition sexual harassment is an offence that is committed by not coming with actual physical contract to the victim.

However, the section 10(2) was abrogated when the law was last amended in 2003. A new provision has been added under section 9(ka) of the present law that states, if a woman is forced to commit suicide as a direct consequence of somebody's willful dishonor/sexual harassment/assault, then the offender will be liable to a maximum of ten years and a minimum of five years of imprisonment. The amendment actually denied the remedy of sexual harassment of non-contract nature. The new provision though punishes the offender, it will not happen until the victim is dead. A legal ridicule, indeed!

Conclusion

Eve teasing is wrong against the honour, dignity and self respect of a woman. It hurts her immensely. There is a strong need for combating this fast growing problem. Policing should be made more responsive to the needs of women, for instance with dedicated police cells and help lines for victims. State and public institutions should take more seriously the implementation of the directive on sexual harassment issued by the High

Court last year. Civil society organisations and women's groups should be given more resources to support and counsel victims, and launch public awareness campaigns.

By law, the government should make it mandatory that the youth found to be guilty in eve-teasing deaths should be dismissed from the school/college where he is studying and also barred from joining any other school/college even through correspondence. All these punishments should be apart from rigorous imprisonment for a few years. In essence, they should be blacklisted at all levels and made a "zero'! Eve teasing create day by day more problem In our country. so I want to say the upbringing of our country are getting engaged with destructive activities, because they do not have any righteous aim before them. I hope the culprits would be treated with zero tolerance. So the Government must take it seriously.

Hence, there is a immediate need to bring eve teasing as a separate head of liability under the Law of Torts. There should be a provision for a strong punishment for eve teasers. In a country like India and Bangladesh where women are worshipped at par with the Gods, this kind of behaviour against women is unjust, unfair and Hippocratic. We should be respectful to women. Then only our country would be on the lines of happiness, prosperity and success.

References

- Bangladeshis raise voice against sexual harassment - Jun 19, 2010
- Current News, January, 2011
- Dhaka deploys female peacekeepers
- Minister's security guard held on charge of eve-teasing, Date- 13/ 02/2011
- Beauty tips for Bangladesh police
- www.bbc.co.uk
- www.eveteasing.org
- Bangladesh students protest against rampant 'eve teasing, sexual harassment of women '
- www.legalserviceindia.com/articles/etea.htm

23

Condition of Women: A Literary Perspective

Rupali Mirza

Abstract

English literature is full of instances of gender discrimination and sexual assault against women. Aristotle truly said, all art is an imitation of reality in his literary theory of "Mimesis". It was believed that woman was the source of sin. She was called the second sex or the fair and weaker sex. Thus, women were put on the margin, called marginalisation of women. In traditional patriarchy they had only one identity i.e., their physical identity. "Women live like Bats or Owls, labour like Beasts and die like Worms" as marked by Margaret Cavendish in Female Orations (1662). They are prisoners of their house and their own bodies. At times, they are willing slaves. The selected literary works namely; *Tess of D'Urbervilles* (1891) by Thomas Hardy, The Colour Purple (1982) by Alice Walker, *A Room of One's Own (1929) by Virginia Woolf, The Circle of Karma* (2005) by Kunzang Choden and *A Vindication of the Rights of Women* (1792) by Mary Wollstonecraft, all reflect on the condition of women in the social set-up in the eastern as well as western countries. Feminism as a movement has tried to educate the society about the need to bring about an effective change in the mindset of the patriarchy. Women's rights such as the right to get education, freedom of thought, right to vote, right to be independent have all been advocated by feminists. The much needed transformation in the society is only possible if the patriarchal social norms will allow some flexibility and give women the honour and respect that they deserve.

"Dhol Ganwar Shudra Pashu Nari sakal tadan ke adhikari."

These are lines used by Tulsidas in Ramcharitmanas, in which the god of sea, Samudra requests Rama when the latter becomes so angry that he brandishes a weapon to evaporate the sea. The lines literally mean that drums, the uneducated, lower castes of the society, animals and women, all ranking in the same plane, should be beaten so as to put their acts together or better explained, behave in a proper way. Although, the deeper meaning of these lines goes much beyond the surface meaning but the sea deity meant to suggest one to abide by the boundaries set by god. However, the lines sound controversial as women are ranked the same with Dhol, Ganwar, Shudra and Pashu.

This was not just the condition of women in the East. Even in the West, women did not score any better. Middle English Literature talks only about "Caritas" or the love of god. The writers of those times did not refer to women in their writings as they were taught horrors of the flesh. Thus, the middle Ages propagated the woman as a devil. Imtiaz Dharkar, a Pakistan born Scottish female poet has written a collection of poems *I Speak for the Devil.* She talks of defending the female body, according to her there is no shame in being a woman. Such is the treatment of women in literature which is a reflection of their actual state in the society. *I Speak for the Devil* was published in the year 2001, in which Imtiaz Dharkar has used striking titles for her poems and these poems also have an underlying idea of protest in them. According to Susan Bolotin such literature belonged to the postfeminist generation in her article "Voices from the Postfeminism generation".

English Literature is full of instances of sexual violence against women. This kind of violation starts as eve teasing and assumes immesurable consequences. According to Aristotle's theory of mimesis "all art is an imitation of reality". Sexual violation of a woman is significantly discussed in many literary works discussing atrocities on women belonging to different stratas of the society. Tess of the D'urbervilles is a novel written by Thomas Hardy (1840-1928). Tess the girl in question goes to work at a mansion and ends up being seduced and raped by Alec, the son of the owner. It is due to this act of rape that her true love, Angel rejects her and finally she is convicted for the murder of Alec. The book talks a lot about the hypocrisy of the Victorian society. The novel is not far away from reality as women who belong to lower social status are exploited all the time due to their lower economic position in the social set up. The following lines depict Tess' predicament:

After changing her mind about asking Angel's parents for help, Tess despairs after spending the night outdoors. In the morning she spies the dead and dying pheasants and experiences an affinity for the tortured birds. Then, despite her tortured life at Flint comb-Ash, she optimistically rallies and realises that compared with the birds, her life is not bad. Despite her attempts to remain optimistic, however, Hardy's pessimistic views insure that Tess is doomed and that the birds' wrung necks foreshadow her own death by hanging. (Hardy, 312)

The women belonging to the financially weaker sections of the society such as the women in the professions of rag picking, dish washing, domestic helpers and baby sitters are frequently taken advantage of by their male masters. Most of these instances go unreported. The cases which are reported, the accused are usually left scot free as they have enough money to bribe the law-keepers due to their superior economic position. Many women bear the lewd sexual remarks and assault by those who are above them in the social hierarchy as they have to compromise with their personal values on account of being moneyless. They don't want to lose their employment that is their only mode of income.

Another novel, *The Colour Purple* was written in the year 1982 by Alice Walker who won the Pulitzer Prize and National Book Award. The storyline runs on an illiterate black girl, Celie who lives in Georgia. She writes letters to God just after undergoing the most troubled circumstance of a forced incestuous relationship with her step father. Later she gets married to a man called "Mr." and leads a life full of torment till she is able to secure her financial and emotional independence. Celie's true feelings are explained best by the following lines:

Initially, Celie believes that being a woman inescapably means that she has to serve and obey men and she is thus a victim of patriarchy. She is eventually introduced to another way of living by the strong female characters of Sofia and Shug who embrace her in a kind of sisterhood, which is a way for oppressed women to resist patriarchy". (Sundqvist, 2006, p.12).

Similarly, many women in our society are exploited sexually just as Celie within the four walls of their houses which is considered one of the most secure places for a woman. In most cases their relatives or their own fathers and uncles subject them to sexual assault. Women hardly want to complain against their own family and close relatives if they are victimised at home. These women face a traumatic phase of depressions, mental torment and at times they undergo a complete nervous breakdown.

Marital rape too should be considered as an act of sexual assault. Forceful sex or making contact with the spouse without her due consent is equated to marital rape. Women in wedlocks are subjected to such inhumane treatment by their better halves almost every day and this kind of violence against women always goes unvoiced.

In the novel, *Speak* by Laurie Halse Anderson, published in 1999, a high school girl, Melinda becomes a victim of a sexual assault at a party and fails to overcome the trauma that she undergoes. Many girls, especially living in metropolitan towns and cities visit pubs and discos where their modesty is outraged. Many of these girls are subjected to sexual exploitation at parties and club houses where they are unable to raise their voice as such occurrences have become a part of party culture and some women have already come to cordial terms with such outrageous behaviour.

The Lovely Bones is another such literary work by Alice Sebold, published in the year 2002. It is about a teenage girl named Susie who is raped and then murdered while coming back from school. There are numerous examples of girls who become victims while travelling in buses and trains. Commuting is a usual part of their routine thus it is unavoidable if they come out of the confines of their homes.

A rape case happened in Delhi on the evening of nine February, 2012. The dead body of the victim was found in Haryana after four days of her abduction. She was forcibly pulled inside a speeding car, reportedly an Indica by three men who abducted her to mustard fields where they inflicted physical torment on her. She was beaten up, her face and eyes were mutilated by a sharp screwdriver. She was raped time and again over a period of three days and acid was poured over her face and eyes. Finally she was left to die on the roadside. There are umpteen number of rape cases inflicted on the women who travel by public transport. Women are not safe while travelling and sadly neither the law keepers nor the government authorities are doing anything to keep them safe.

The need of the hour is a global movement that can unite all women irrespective of their country or class. Such a movement is Feminism which from the 19th century has demanded equality, right to education and the right to vote for women. Feminist phase was from 1880-1920. This phase believed in the freedom of women, their voting rights as their stepping stone towards free will. They raised their voice against phallocentricism. Elizabeth Gaskell and Gilman etc. are representatives of this age. These were the stepping stones towards women emancipation.1920 onwards the Female phase started which made the women writers independent of any imitation they documented their true feelings and experiences. According to Elaine Showalter woman now indulged freely in gynocriticism as readers and wrote their true experience in feminist writings, gynotexts. Virginia Woolf wrote *A Room of One's Own* (1929) in which she discussed liberation, feminism, and androgyny. She believed that a woman needs an exclusive room so that she could write and thus earn money so that she could get an exclusive status in the society. The woman of today needs to be financially independent if she wants emancipation from the rules, regulations, trials and tribulations of the society. Financial freedom can help the women attain an independent status in the society. Over the years women have borne oppression as mothers, sisters and wives, more so, due to their financial dependence. Most of the urban women are coming out of their shell whereas the rural women are still in a woeful state. The exploitation of women by the traditional patriarchy still manifests itself on women all over the world. The mindset of the society needs to be influenced so that women may gain more leverage to develop themselves in their careers and gain more respect and importance in the society.

Women's problems and their needs have been discussed in textual theories and this debate is called the Feminist Debate, it is also called "The Woman Question". This debate started in the 17th century and it questioned women's place in the society. If we view this question in the traditional light, due to division of labour, man for the field and woman for the hearth was the usual division of responsibility which made women financially weaker and she came to be subjugated due to these reasons as also due to her biology.

It was believed that woman was the source of sin. She was called the second sex or the fair and weaker sex. Thus, women were put on the margin, called marginalisation of women. In traditional patriarchy they had only one identity i.e., their physical identity. Women live like bats and worms in the confines of their house as marked by a staunch feminist. They are prisoners of their house and their own bodies. At times, they are willing slaves. It is said that patriarchy has deliberately created a situation for women in which they are dependent on their men, this is called

Dependence Syndrome. Woman is considered property, earlier of the father and brother later, after marriage, transferred to her husband. There is a double code of conduct, one for the male members of the house and another one for the female members who reside in the same house. Woman is used as a sexual slave, termed Sexual Colonialism springing from the concept of marital rape. All this leads to women always being the Object and never the Subject. Physical pleasure was always the prerogative of the male. In some societies, such as in Africa, FGM, Female Genital Mutilation was done. In traditional patriarchy woman was muted or devoiced. Sexual assault is a method of devoicing the woman.

The reasons for feminist revolt are quite apparent. "Sexism" is the critical term that is used for discrimination done on the basis of gender. Such discrimination against women exists right from the time a girl is born. Imtiaz Dharkar discusses about the bias and prejudice against the birth of a girl child in her popular poem "Honour Killing". This term has a wider connotation than killing a girl when she chooses her own life partner against the wishes of the society. Numerous girls are killed even before they are born or just after they are born to lessen the burden on the shoulders of the patriarchy who consider women as a burden.

When a girl slowly grows up, the society makes her believe that she should depend on her brother and father, later at the grown up age her husband decides her priorities. She has very little power to make her own decisions. In such an atmosphere it is difficult for a female to assert her true feelings and rights. This kind of a situation is aptly described by the critical term "dependence syndrome".

There is a double code of conduct in the society, the norms for a male child are totally different from the norms that are applicable on the female child. For these reasons Virginia Woolf wrote about Judith Shakespeare to express if Shakespeare had a sister what would happen to her. Shakespeare was sent to the grammar school but unfortunately his own sister Judith would stay at home and work in the kitchen. On reaching the age of puberty she would run away and befriend an actor/manager, be impregnated and finally commit suicide. This is a depiction of the treatment of western women.

The situation in the eastern world was full of plight and miseries. Kunzang Choden, a female Bhutani writer, tells the story of Tsomo in The *Circle of Karma.* The novel is set in 1950s, when the attitude towards women remained orthodox even though Bhutan had become a modern society by this time. Tsomo is the third out of her twelve siblings and yearns to be educated. She is denied the right to gain education even though she is an intelligent girl. The backdrop of the novel is a very religious one. Her father, a pious man believed that a girl did not need to read or write. Tsomo had two relationships but both the men seemed to be strangers to her true feelings and needs.

Assertion of female identity can be seen in one of the earliest literary writings by Mary Wollstonecraft in *A Vindication of the Rights of Women* in which she talks about the importance of female education:

we shall not see women affectionate till more equality be established in society, till ranks are confounded and women freed, neither shall we see that dignified domestic happiness, the simple grandeur of which cannot be relished by ignorant or vitiated minds; nor will the important task of education ever be properly begun till the person of a woman is no longer preferred to her mind. (228)

Women will continue to be suppressed if they will not get a chance to get education. The government has launched several schemes for the education and development of the girl child, however, all such efforts by the administrative machinery will be thwarted if the patriarchy will deny her the intrinsic rights that every human should have.

Women are often classified as good women and bad women, though we never see men being graded under any such categorisation. We are told that Duessa is a bad woman in the *Faerie Queene* by Spenser and Una is supposedly a good woman. We also read about the erring women in Jacobean drama. These are prejudiced views about women as their very vices which they are criticised for become virtues when a male exercises them.

As Literature is a replica or picture of real life, all along we see the textual harassment of female writers and the sexual harassment of women in the patriarchal set up. This is a situation most appropriately described by the critical term "textual-sexual" harassment. Taking into consideration all the regulations imposed on women by the community and very little powers given to them, contrary to the norm of rights and duties going together, we can derive a simple conclusion that women are denied the position they deserve in the society. Women are trying to get their rightful position by working harder in their respective fields so that they may become financially independent. It is the responsibility of the society to embolden the women by returning them their lost prestige. This respect can only be regained by her only if the entire world takes the pledge to respect her, honour her and support her in all her endeavours to stand independently, on her own feet. The feminist writings can be instrumental to the extent that they can be a guiding factor in conditioning the minds of the people so that they develop a positive attitude towards women. It is imperative to educate the people about the fact that a woman holds the fate of the world. Only if the mother is educated, will she be able to educate her children, hence women are the shapers of the society and their emancipation will lead to the empowerment of the entire society. William Ross Wallace wrote a poem in 1865, What Rules the World which describes most appropriately what a woman means to humanity:

> ***"Blessings on the hand of women !***
> ***Angels guard its strength and grace,***
> ***In the palace, cottage, hovel,***
> ***Oh, no matter where the place;***
> ***Would that never storms assailed it,***
> ***Rainbows even gently curled;***
> ***For the hand that rocks the cradle***
> ***Is the hand that rules the world" (Wallace)***

Works Cited and Consulted

- Badowska, Ewa. "The Anorexic Body of Liberal Feminism: Mary Wollstonecraft's A Vindication of the Rights of Woman." Tulsa *Studies in Women's Literature* 17:2 (1998): 283-303. Print
- Bodichon, Barbara Leigh-Smith. *A Brief Summary in Plain Language of the Most Important Laws Concerning Women: Together with a Few Observations Thereon.* London, 1854. Print.
- Choden, Kunzang, The Circle of Karma. New Delhi: Penguin Putnam, 2006. Print.
- Dharker, Imtiaz, Purdah, Delhi: Oxford University Press, (1989).
- Dharker, Imtiaz, I speak for the devil, New Delhi: Penguin Books,(2001). de Souza, Eunice, Ed. Nine Indian Women Poets, Delhi: Oxford University Press, (1997). Gate, Henry Louis Jr., and *Appiah K.A., eds. Alice Walker: Critical Perspectives Past and Present. Newyork:* Amistad, 1993. Print.
- Hardy, Thomas. Tess of D' Urbervilles. Penguin Putnam Inc: New York, NY. 2003. Print.
- Mellor, Anne K. *Romanticism and Gender.* London: Routledge, 1993. Print.

- Mellor, Anne. "On the Publication of Mary Wollstonecraft's *A Vindication of the Rights of Woman."* BRANCH: Britain, *Representation and Nineteenth-Century History.* Ed. Dino Franco Felluga. Extension of *Romanticism and Victorianism on the Net.* Web. 12 December 2014.
- Northrop, H.D. Beautiful Gems of Thought and Sentiment. Boston, MA: The Colins-Patten Co., 1890. Print.
- Sebold, Alice. *The Lovely Bones.* New York: Brown and Company, 2002.
- Silver, Anna Krugovoy. *Victorian Literature and the Anorexic* Body. Cambridge: Cambridge UP, 2002. Print.
- Anderson, Laurie *Halse. Speak.* New York: Farrar Straus Giroux, 1999.
- Spenser, Edmund. The Faerie Queene. London, 1609. Early English Books Online. McGill University Libraries. 12 December, 2014<http://eebo.chadwyck.com>
- Taylor, Barbara. *Mary Wollstonecraft and the Feminist Imagination.* Cambridge: Cambridge UP, 2003. Print.
- Sundqvist, S. (2006). *The Emancipation of Celie: The Colour Purple as a womanist Bildungsroman.* (Doctoral Dissertation, Karlstands University, 2006). Print.
- Wollstonecraft, Mary. *A Vindication of The Rights of Woman and The Wrongs of Woman, or Maria. Eds.* Anne K. Mellor and Noelle Chao. New York: Pearson Education - Longman Cultural Editions, 2007. Print.
- Walker, Alice. *The Colour Purple.* London: Women's Press, 1992. Print.

24

Women Power Line-1090: An Initiative against Eve Teasing

Meenakshi Dwivedi

Abstract

With the increased number of cases of eve teasing and sexual harassment against women, the Women Power Line-1090 is a benefaction to modern women and eventually to society . It is a one state-one-number service to handle cases of harassment by vulgar and abusive callers and stalkers in Uttar Pradesh, India. Named as Women Power Line-1090, 1090 is a 24x7 Women helpline. Instead of a victim going to a police station, women cops will now go to the doorstep of the victim to register her complaint, particularly in cases related to physical or sexual harassment and domestic violence. It came into existence on November 15, 2012 and since then it has been of great help to the women in the State. This is a 'one-state-one-number service' being operated by the Uttar Pradesh Police Department against harassment of women by vulgar and abusive callers and stalkers. Women in UP can access this helpline No.1090 from anywhere and can lodge complaints against harassment by obscene callers and road romeos. The identity of the complainant is kept secret for their protection. The victims are not required to come to Police Station for lodging complaint or pursue the matter. This chapter deals with the detailed description of Women Power Line-1090.

Introduction

India is fast emerging as global power but for half of its population, the women across the country, struggle to live with dignity continues. Women, irrespective of their class, caste and educational status, are not safe in the modern society. Women have been the victims of exploitation since long time in different fields of their life physically, socially, mentally and economically. There are several causes of sexual as well as moral abuse which are very often highlighted by the media in Indian modern society and a lot of those also remain unexplored. Violence against women, sexual harassment and exploitation of women are not of recent origin. Its traces are found in the history of ancient India. Women are facing problems in every sphere of life whether employment, access to health care or property rights. India is fast developing but women in India continue to be discriminated. The declining sex ratio in India portrays the discrimination shown towards women at the stage of birth. They are victims of crime directed specifically at them- rape, kidnapping and abduction, dowry-related crimes, molestation, sexual harassment, eve-teasing, etc. It is realised that the long run supremacy of male over female in all respect in the patriarchal society in India is highly responsible for arresting the empowerment of women. Women are being trafficked for sex, harassment at workplaces and tortured in family and society.

Women across the world have tasted all flavours of life, from the glory and respect which she was ascribed in the Vedic period, to the denial and subordination in the post Vedic period and finally to the struggle for equality, recognition and survival in the contemporary world. But one thing that has been common throughout these phases is the disadvantaged status of the women. Women have been made to face all kinds of violence, physical abuse, denial of right to live, subordination and neglect. The acts of abuses like eve-teasing, molestation, sexual abuse and rape cover both physical and verbal abuses. However, they all are different parts of what is commonly known as sexual harassment or sexual misconduct.

Women are the wealth of India and they have contributed in almost every field and made country feel proud at every occasion. They are in front, leading the country, making mile stones and source of inspiration for many. However, another reality of Indian society is that there is systematic discrimination and negligence of women in India, which could be in terms of inadequate nutrition, denial or limited access to education, health and property rights, child labour and domestic violence etc. The fear of sexual violence has been a powerful factor in restricting women's behaviour and sense of freedom. The struggle against violence is actually the struggle against the unequal distribution of power both physical and economic between the sexes.

The concept like eve-teasing gained nationwide attention in the 1960's but today eve-teasing has evolved as a huge issue in many metropolitan cities of India. A large number of Indian women have faced or are facing this menace. Another form of violence against women is that of molestation, or what is commonly known as 'sexual abuse' or 'sexual assault'. It is the forcing of sexual behaviour by a man over the women. Further, rape is one of the most extreme forms of sexual violence committed against women. It is an act of physical violence and assault which is expressed through sexual means.

Eve-teasing is a social evil. Eve-teasing starts from beaches, roads, cinema hall, buses and ends in different educational institutions. The uncivilised people, street hooligans, college boys starts the ragging for girls which can lead to the mouth of deaths for the women or to even anyone whose loved one undergoes this. The educated youth does not necessarily involve in this uncouth behaviour. But the people who are uncivilised, uneducated indulge in this behaviour. The girls don't come outside of their houses due to eve-teasing. Eve-teasing creates mental tension, unconsciousness and even mental disorder too. Eve-teasing deserves to be tackled fearlessly by the women so that they can have an independent and safe access in a society. Carelessness of the police department may lead to public humiliation of women in broad day light. It leads mental tourchers for the parents and to even anyone.

Increasing number of cases of eve teasing in urban places in India compelled the local authorities to take a serious look into the problem. The growing instances of the murders, of women for rejecting the love of the man had rocked the nation and now the serious thought is given on the reasons for these crimes. The expression "eve teasing" is of Indian origin, the word is not found in the dictionaries. And native speakers of English don't use it. As per the popular idea the expression eve teasing is a euphemistic in post-colonial India and refers largely to sexual harassment of women in public places, where a women is an "eve " temptress who provoke men into states of sexual titillation. This popular perception of sexual harassment posits the phenomena as a joke where women are both a tease and deserve to be teased.

Growing incidents like a bike pulling up at college bus stop and the man on the bike shouting lewdly at a college girl, come with me Rs 300 for night; a car loaded with men pulls out of a driveway of a market shouts at a woman- do you need a ride-we will take you where ever you want and pay for it; the woman gets humiliated and outraged. The laughing and passing lewd remarks of an eve teaser can leave a permanent psychological mark on a woman.

Studies shows that 32 per cent of the eve teasers are students, 35 per cent are anti-socials while the 33 per cent are middle-aged men. In India, every 51minutes a woman is sexually harassed; every 21 minutes one woman is molested. Eve teasing is something that a woman has to contend with everyday.

Crimes against women have always been a matter of concern in India's most populous state. Media reports reveal that between August 2011 and November 2011, of the number of complaints of harassment and crimes against women received by the National Commission for Women, the highest were from this state. Moreover, according to the National Crime Record Bureau (NCRB) 2011 data, the state accounted for 12.9 per cent of all violent crimes–the highest in the country. Violent crimes, according to NCRB classification, include murder, attempt to murder, culpable homicide, dowry deaths, kidnapping and abduction, dacoity, robbery, riots, arson, and rape.

For years, thousands of women across the state have been suffering violence and humiliation in silence. Now, the Women Power Line-1090, a one-state-one-number service being operated by the UP police to handle cases of harassment by vulgar and abusive callers and stalkers is an indication that the system is slowly responding to the concern of women's safety. Uttar Pradesh police is all set to gift a helpline number exclusively meant for women facing problem of crank calls, vulgar messages, etc. Most likely, the helpline is called Women 'Power Line'. The number '1090' may appear innocuous to many. But for women folk of Uttar Pradesh, who are have been subjected to molestation, rapes and stalking, it denotes a 'Power Line', quite literally. Therefore anything that contributes even remotely in ensuring safety to women will certainly be welcomed by them.

The idea of Women Power Line-1090 generated from a seminar organised by 'Hindustan Times' on the topic- 'Safety of Women', where Chief Minister of Uttar Pradesh, Mr. Akhilesh Yadav was also invited. The women participants of the seminar met the chief minister and told him that they lack feeling of safety and always have the apprehension that somebody is stalking them wherever they go but they don't have a platform where they could get help from in such a situation. These women remained in touch with DIG, Mr Navniet Sikera and kept exchanging their views with him. And finally, Women helpline is launched on November 15, 2012 throughout the state. Its toll-free telephone number is 1090. On the day of Bhaiya Dooj (a Hindu festival wherein the women pray for the well being of their brothers and they in turn give gifts to sisters), UP Chief Minister Mr. Akhilesh Yadav launched Women Power Line-1090 which aims to provide quick help to women, who have been victims of molestation. The 24-hour Women Power Line -1090 is a potent tool to curb crime against women and is a massive improvement on the current system where the complainant would have to either call police control room–100 in case of emergency or approach the nearest police station for getting police help.

The women folk can access the helpline from anywhere in the state and can register their complaints. A specially trained force comprising women only constables has been formed to attend the calls and ensure timely help to the victims. The UP government decided to launch the Power Line in view of rising complaints of molestation by women as many women lodged the complaints about the harassment through cell phone calls and text messages in the past few years. Here, the identity of the callers is kept secret to protect them. After receiving the calls the women are forced to warn the harassers twice. Afterwards, an FIR is registered against the culprit if he does not mend his ways and continues to harass the woman. The Women Power Line-1090 first aims at counseling and thereafter if necessary takes due legal action against the culprit.

The habitual offenders will be black listed and they will be denied driving licenses and character certificates. They will face problems in getting their passports and government jobs as well. The idea is to counsel the perpetrators initially and punish them only if they continue to harass the women folk. Their family members will also be informed about their deeds.

Raghavendra Singh, in-charge of the Women Power Line-1090, made the statement that a statewide study was conducted by them prior to launch of the service. He revealed that between 2000 and 2012, there was a sharp rise in the use of mobiles to harass women. The victims caught in such situations were usually helpless. They were unable to confide in their family members for fear of being confined to the home. It had repercussions on their freedom and access to education or work. The 1090 number has changed all that. When women call, complete confidentiality is maintained. The software has been developed in such a way that only the women constable who receives the call knows the name and number of the caller. Even senior officials also have no access to their details. This has instilled a high level of confidence and trust among women callers. During the research phase 76 complaints of women who were being harassed were received. Of these, five were cases of severe harassment. Three were involving married women in Lucknow and two were students from other districts. These cases were a learning experience in the development of the Women Power Line-1090. The foundation of the Power Line is based on the experiences of these five women.

Important Features of Women Power Line-1090

- Victim callers are assured of anonymity.
- No Need to visit any police station or office to lodge a complaint or show up for hearing.
- Phone call will be attended by lady police officers.
- Until and unless the problem is solved, police will keep in touch with victim, at least for a month.
- Phone No. 1090 will be applicable for the whole state of Uttar Pradesh.

The services of the Women Power Line-1090 are being rolled out in three phases–the first is already complete and the second phase is currently in operation. Now DIG, Mr. Sekera enthusiastically looks forward to the remaining third phase. A rich database of the harassment cases against women is being prepared and this was used to address the issue of harassment in cyberspace. This comprised the second phase of the project that was launched in March 2013. The third phase will deal with physical violence against women in public places. Using the database of crimes currently being prepared, difficult areas will be tagged using Google Earth.

As till June first week (2013), 1090 centre has registered 72,492 complaints from the women, who were facing harassment through mobile phones and mobile messages. Interestingly, of this, 69,415 complaints have been worked out in the first phase that is at counseling level. Of this, 52134 cases have been completely solved with victims expressing satisfaction. This means that trouble maker has not harassed the victim for the past 38 days. Similarly, the Women Power Line-1090 also received 1795 complaints with regard to social networking sites and domestic violence. Of this, 1163 complaints have been worked out at cyber crime cell and local police level. For the obstinate of the accused, the Women Power Line-1090 registered FIR. Until now, a total of 167 FIRs had been registered, the WPL data showed. Elaborating further on the ways to make more and more women aware about the Women Power Line-1090, the centre got 15 women constables trained by an Ex-faculty, IIM. These women constables were asked to tell about Women Power Line-1090 at all the schools of the city after summer vacation in July.

Sustainable success of Women Power Line-1090, since it came into existence on November 15, 2012 has not only drawn media attention and applauds from politicians and citizens alike but has now become a topic of research. Two students from Indian Institute of Management (IIM) have joined Women Power Line-1090 at Lucknow. Not only this, a private university of Lucknow has also expressed its intention to enroll at least two students from its campus for Ph.D. on the social impact of Women Power Line-1090 after Lucknow University. While the second plan is still at a premature stage, the research programme is on, confirmed DIG (range), Lucknow Navniet Sekera, the brain behind the Women Power Line-1090 concept. It is found that the two students one from IIM-Lucknow and other from IIM-Delhi have joined Women Power Line-1090 to study its effectiveness for the society. On another private university's plan, talks are going on; however, nothing could be said until the plan takes shape. As data shows till June first week, Women Power Line-1090 centre has registered 72,492 complaints from the women, who were facing harassment through mobile phones and mobile messages. Interestingly, of this, 69,415 complaints have been worked out in the first phase that is at counseling level.

The Women Power Line-1090 will however be not a free service though unlike the 100. Hence, normal call charges will apply. It is felt that the power line will prove to be a big help to the women in the state, where crime including eve teasing against them has been rising steadily.

Eve teasing must be stopped. Women deserve respect. Men and women are equal. Our lack of consciousness has lead to a loss of many lives. But we don't want any more lives to say good bye to this world. Women have the right to live freely in the world. Independence is their birth right. They have the right to lead their lives as males. On the other hand, the family and society of the victims or teased girls should have the courage and resolve to support them. Most often, they are misunderstood by their family whenever they inform the family members about teasing. The family and society should support them mentally. So as the government must take things seriously. The country wants both of them to be active in such issues. No doubt, the initiative of Women Power Line-1090 would be very effective in curbing the menace like eve teasing.

References

- Bunch C (1997). The intolerable status quo: Violence against Women and Girls The Progress of Nations. Retrieved from http://www.unicef.org/pon97/women1c.htm
- Chandra, R. (Ed.). (2004). Status of Women in India in Social Development in India. Isha Books, New Delhi.
- Dr. Khokan Kumar Bag, Piyal Basu Roy,(March 2012) Changing Face of Women Exploitation in International, Journal of Social Science Tomorrow Vol. 1 No. 1 ISSN: 2277-6168 March|2012
- Gender Study Group, (1996). A Report on Sexual Harassment in Delhi University, Delhi.
- https://sites.google.com/site/lucknowhelplines/women-helpline-1090
- http://timesofindia.indiatimes.com/city/lucknow/Dial-1090-report-a-crank-caller-to-police/articleshow/16830852.cms
- http://www.firstpost.com
- http://www.thehindu.com/opinion/op-ed/cant-do-without-critical-analysis-of-the-ast/article4326386.ece
- Mukhejee, D. (2005). Women and Urban Crime. Kalpaz Publication, New Delhi.
- Rao, M.K. (2005) Empowerment of Women in India: Discovery Publishing House, New Delhi.
- Tripathi, R.S. and Tiwari, R.P. (1999) Perspective on Indian Women: APH Publishing Corporation, New Delhi.

25

Street Harassment: The all Pervasive Gender Discrimination Problem

Kaneez Mehdi Zaidi

Abstract

Eve teasing is usually portrayed as a compliment, a joke or only a trivial annoyance in our society. The seriousness of the issue is downplayed by the 'playful' connotations associated with the term 'eve-teasing'. To emphasise the seriousness of the issue it would be better to phrase it street harassment. Street Harassment is a form of gender based sexual harassment, an under recognised problem with severe psychological and physical consequences. Street harassment is a universal phenomenon Women across the globe struggle in ways similar or diverse, in subtle and blatant ways every time they set foot outside the four walls. It is not limited to Asia, Africa and South America. Women in the US, Canada, Australia and Europe are by no means immune and report similarly high rates of harassment. The very pervasiveness of street harassment makes it extremely important to study. This chapter has twofold purpose – to attribute to the understanding of the problem of gender based street harassment on one hand and on the other to outline the prevalence of street harassment and the protection provided to woman against street harassment in various countries. While other forms of sexual harassment have been considered a problem large enough to garner the attention of the academic, legislative, and judicial community but most of the laws addressing sexual harassment focuses solely on sexual harassment at workplace or within the domestic sphere. Sexual harassment in public space such as streets and public transportation remains largely neglected. Many countries do not recognise street harassment serious enough to legislate on it. Very few countries definition of sexual harassment has constituents of street harassment and considers it an offence.

Keywords: Street Harassment, Gender Discrimination, Neglected, Offence

Street harassment is a universal phenomenon, a common activity on streets, public transports, parks, shopping malls, stores in all the countries of the world. Women across the globe struggle in ways similar or diverse, in subtle and blatant ways every time they set foot outside the four walls. Street harassment is a problem that knows no bounds, it cuts across age, colour, religion, clothing, class and time frames. It is not limited to Asia, Africa and South America. Women in the US, Canada, Australia and Europe are by no means immune and report similarly high rates of harassment. This harassment is nothing but frightening and threatening messages of power and subjection. The very pervasiveness of street harassment and its direct and indirect negative impact on women's life makes it extremely important to study. In many countries street harassment is illegal being treated as a form of Sexual harassment, but in almost all countries it is considered unacceptable behaviour.

Colloquially used euphemism 'Eve teasing' analogous to the term street harassment is usually portrayed as a compliment, a joke or only a trivial annoyance in our society. The seriousness of the issue is downplayed by the 'playful' connotations associated with the term 'eve-teasing'. The term is suggestive of the idea of original sin, where a 'temptress' seduces a man into doing something he doesn't want to do. To emphasise the seriousness of the issue it would be better to stick to the term street harassment. Street Harassment is a form of gender based sexual harassment, an under recognised problem with severe psychological and physical consequences. This chapter has twofold purpose - to attribute to the understanding of the problem of gender based street harassment on one hand and on the other to outline the prevalence of street harassment and the protection provided to woman against street harassment in various countries.

Street harassment refers to verbal and non verbal behaviour – such as hooting, whistling, groping, stalking, following, blocking paths, yelling comments, making obscene gestures and can go up to severe crimes like sexual molestation–perpetrated by some stranger which makes public places unfriendly, frightening and dangerous for females, thus resulting in the violation of one's right to 'gender equality' and 'life and liberty' C.B. Bowman's article in Harvard Law Review (1993) defines stranger harassment is the *"[sexual] harassment of women in public places by men who are strangers"* The remarks are frequently sexual in nature and comment evaluatively on a woman's physical appearance or on her presence in public.

Street Harassment and Sexual Harassment

However both the terms street harassment and sexual harassment are often used interchangeably, the terms overlaps considerably with the main difference lying in the intensity of the acts. Street harassment though treated as milder issue but it may prove to be the first rung on the ladder of sex crime. Sexual harassment tends to take place in closed spaces and the identity of the culprit is usually known whereas street harassment is generally experienced on the streets and the teaser is an unknown male. Sexual harassment is an established crime and can be easily proved while street harassment is almost thought of as a recreational activity by most of the people and it is a difficult crime to prove.

Causes of Street Harassment

The question still lurks in our mind why do men succumb to such low and cheap acts in public spaces. Aren't they worried about their respect and dignity in society? Social scientists suggest street harassment is a result of the frustration that majority of the youth suffer because of unemployment, illiteracy, indifferent parents etc. They display their depression ultimately resulting in aggression on street; others feel that it is the direct outcome of a sexually repressive society, in which women by tradition have no voice whatsoever and do not possess equal rights, still others consider it as the moral degradation of society, while still others attribute it to the objectification of women in advertisements and commercial movies which treat woman as an object to be looked and touched, provoke such acts.

Feminists argue it as the old age reflection of male chauvinism. The reasons for keeping women away from public spaces may be rooted in the patriarchal demands for closely monitoring and controlling the sexuality and thus the mobility of women. Sen (1984) discusses the different ways in which patriarchal setups control and channelise young women's sexuality. One of these ways is to dominate and control public spaces and for men to claim that public spaces are male-only dominions. When women do enter these spaces, they are tolerated only within very strict limits of movement, action, and dress and "transgressions" are often met with harsh retribution in the form of sexual and physical assaults. Anwary (2003) for instance discusses how the increase in acid violence against women in Bangladesh since the late 1980s may partly be a result of a reassertion of patriarchy in the face of perceived threats of female employment and independence.

A psychological reflection of the issue reveals that it is rooted in sexual need of a man. It is more a distorted and perverse sexual behaviour which finds expression in such contemptible acts. Another prominent reason includes weak and poorly implemented laws and lack of awareness about the laws which lead the perpetrators to grope women in public spaces. Moreover there is a lot more to blame when considering why the young people of our country have been aggravated to this level.

Impact on Women

Robin West, a law professor at Georgetown University depicts street harassment as a *'disempowering injury'* as fear of rape and that the trivialisation of it causes women not to talk about it, reinforcing its invisibility and effects. They suffer unpunished and uncompensated sexual assaults continually. Street harassment has a traumatising affect on women whether it is in the form of verbal comment or physical assault. It limits woman's ability to be in public spaces and to move around as often or as comfortably as men do, often cause them to choose less convenient routes and alters their routine. Many a times compel them to take serious steps like quitting their jobs, move neighbourhood or lock themselves at home. Fredrickson and Robert's research suggests that stranger harassment has negative implications for woman's well-being. Women who experience greater amounts of stranger harassment are likely to self-objectify, they start blaming themselves for it. MacMillan et al.'s (2000) research indicates that stranger harassment may be a more pervasive problem than non-stranger harassment and it has a more consistent and significant impact on women's fears than non-stranger harassment.

Street harassment affects negatively both in direct and indirect ways. One of the most adverse consequences of eve-teasing is the rise in drop-out rate of girls from school. Many cases have been witnessed where victims unable to bear the repeated insult or out of fear are forced to the level of committing suicide. It not damages her self esteem and dignity in public spaces but also disturbs her peace of mind. Consequently curtailing her freedom of movement in public spaces and in status too, thereby affecting her human and social development.

Why doesn't Woman Come up?

Moreover, street harassment is so pervasive that it is a part of the social fabric of public life. Women usually brush the issue aside instead of reporting it, believing that no one will think anything of significance has happened. It is perceived to be an innocuous part of daily life. Street harassment is construed as trivial issue unless it rises to the level of assault.

The moment a woman comes up with the issue of street harassment, she is barraged with questions like what were you wearing? Where were you going? Were you alone? and similar questions as if trying to prove her wrong, consequently many cases go unreported for fear of things escalating into something worse. In cases when the culprit is some strong entity women back off for fear of retaliation ,which may take the form of threats, beatings, being run over by vehicles or even sexual assault, throwing acid on the woman they target. Moreover Street harassment is not effectively legislated it is a much difficult crime to prove as compared to sexual harassment taking benefit of which the culprits are easily roaming the streets. It is impossible to sue a stranger who disappears instantly in the crowd. The lack of legal recourse provides an environment more conducive to harassment and discourages women to come up.

Problem and Protection in India

With urbanisation and the rapid population growth in India, women inevitably become more prominent on the streets. Women from all social backgrounds are joining the work force or educational institutions in large numbers as opportunities for female participation increases. This trend is certainly a triumph of the modern women in India. But with the increase in women's participation, sheltering these women is extremely necessary owing to the growing crime rates against women. In the last few years India has garnered the reputation of being extremely unsafe for women. A recent report submitted by the Delhi police to the Supreme Court of India revealed that complaints about harassment in public spaces registered a fivefold increase from 154 in 2012 to 793 in 2013(Mahapatra 2013). The findings of a survey conducted by (Jagori 2011), a nongovernmental organisation working on women's safety indicated that most incidents of violence took place in broad daylight in public spaces. Roads and public transport emerged to be most unsafe.

In India street harassment results in violating fundamental rights of a woman mentioned in the constitution under article 14- Right to Equality, Article 15 Right against discrimination, Article 19(1)Right to practice any profession or to carry out any occupation, trade or business, implying right to free and safe environment free from such violation and Article 21- Right to life and to live with dignity, but there is no law in the Indian Penal code that exists specifically for Street harassment. Complaints of street harassment are usually registered under the following sections of the Sexual Harassment of Women at Workplace (Prevention, Prohibition and Redressal) Act(2010). Section 294 (A) which punishes person found guilty of passing comments, remarks, making obscene gestures and singing vulgar songs with imprisonment for three months. Section 292 punishes a man showing porn to girl or woman with a fine of Rs. 2000 and imprisoned for two years for first offenders and case of repeated offence could be sentenced to a fine of Rs.5000 and with. five years of imprisonment. Section 354 for criminal force or assault intended to outrage modesty and Section 509 which deals with word, gesture or act intended to outrage modesty. Direct addressing the issue of street harassment finds expression in "Delhi Prohibition of Eve teasing Bill 1984" and the National Commission for Woman(New Legislation 1988) No.9 Eve teasing Legislation to curb this menace, for which a long time has passed.

Prevalence and Protection in Bangladesh

Street harassment is a common phenomenon in Bangladesh. Every other day, women come across some sort of street harassment incidents that leave a deep psychological scar on them. This is a pathetic state of affairs faced by women of different age. Every single daily newspaper must have the news almost every day. Though the term 'Eve teasing' is commonly used in Bangladesh, its legal definition is not established. All laws concerning street harassment are dealt under sexual harassment laws, the ingredients of the offence of street harassment are easily distinguishable in these laws. The High Court Division on the petition of Bangladesh National Women Lawyers Association (BNWLA) issued their Judgment on 14.5.2009 in its eleven-point directive – remarked that the term eve teasing downplays the seriousness of such crimes–suggested a detailed definition of sexual harassment that includes all other existing definitions of non-contact sexually connoting offences. The court also ruled that stalking, either physically or electronically, must be considered sexual harassment.

Under the Constitution of Bangladesh (1972), women`s rights are protected under the broad and universal principles of equality and participation. Article 10 of the Constitution ensures participation of women in all spheres of national life. Article 19 (1) provides equality of opportunity to all citizens. Article 27 specifies that all citizens are equal before the law and are entitled to equal protection of the law. Moreover, Article 28 (1) provides that the State shall not discriminate against any citizen on grounds only of religion, race, caste, sex, or place of birth. Article 28 (2) more directly and categorically says that women shall have equal rights with men in all spheres of the State and of public life. In Bangladesh all the metropolitan police acts/ordinances penalises the offence of teasing women. Section 76 of the Dhaka Metropolitan Police Ordinance (1976) declares eve-teasing punishable with a maximum one year of imprisonment, or with a maximum two thousand Taka fine, or with both. The ordinance defines women teasing as, *"wilful and indecent exposure of one`s person in any street or public place within sight of, and in such manner as may be seen by, any woman, whether from within any house or building or not, or wilful pressing or obstructing any woman in a street or public place or insulting or annoying any woman by using indecent language or making indecent sounds, gestures, or remarks in any street or public place".*

Though these ordinances have no jurisdiction outside their respective metropolitan areas-making the offence exclusively a local and urban phenomenon–but "The Protection of Women and Children Act-2000" penalising the offence of teasing women has nationwide jurisdiction which comes down heavily on the oppressors of the women. Section 10(1) of the act of sexual torture punishes the offender with rigorous imprisonment of minimum Three and maximum Ten years and also an indefinite amount of fine. Section 10 (2), was abrogated in 2003 and a new provision has been added under section 9(Ka) of the present law which states–if a woman is forced to commit suicide as a direct consequence of somebody's wilful dishonour/sexual harassment/ assault, then the offender will be liable to a maximum of ten years and a minimum of five years of imprisonment. The amendment actually denied the remedy of sexual harassment of non-contact nature. Besides this, to combat this problem the government of

Bangladesh has authorised "Mobile courts" to prosecute the crime of stalking and harassing a woman, convicting the person with one year in jail or pay a fine of about Tk. 5000 or both. The idea behind the move is for a speedy trial in cases of sexual harassment and stalking. On June 13, 2010 the Education ministry of Bangladesh announced June 13 as `Eve Teasing Protection Day' which is an appreciable step in this direction.

Prevalence and Protection in Pakistan

Street harassment is familiar problem faced by the Pakistan women on daily basis, its state being pathetic compared to other societies. Citizens acknowledge that it is not possible for a woman in Pakistan to get down from her house to get a piece of bread without a couple of male eyes following her around. Each woman has stories of being disgraced and humiliated at public places like buses or markets to tell. It is so common a practice and had been going on from so long that now it is not even being considered as an issue. It's the very same for those who veil or adorn the Hijab and for those who don't. Girls report that it's the preying eyes of men rather than religion forcing more and more women to wear the Hijab at the same time agreeing that wearing a piece of cloth does nothing to change the men's attitude nor has it provided any protection to women. Harassment of women emerges in this painful manner because of the conservative mind-set existing in the society, where boys and girls are forced to stay segregated, such repressions come on the surface in negative ways.

Criminal Law (Amendment) Act 2010, Section 509 (1)points out whoever–"intending to insult the modesty of any woman, utters any word, makes any sound or gesture, or exhibit any object, intending that such words or sound to be heard, or that such gesture or object shall be seen by such woman " shall be punished with imprisonment extending up to Three years or a fine of Rs 500 shall be levied or both. Further explaining it, the act mentions that such behaviour might occur in public place, including, but not limited to, markets, public transport, streets or parks, or it might occur in private places including, but not limited to work places, private gatherings, or homes. The act protects the citizens of Pakistan from street harassment. Section 509(2) deals with insulting women's modesty at workplace, which is also punishable under 'Protection against Harassment of women at the Workplace Act, 2010.

Prevalence and Protection in China

China is often seen as a relatively safe place for women, but according to a survey from China-based research firm 'Canton Public Opinion Research Center' (2013) incidents of sexual harassment are on the rise (Boomerang News). Speaking about the street harassment, out of 1,500 women above the age of 16 surveyed, 35 per cent of victims reported that they suffered sexual harassment in verbal form, in person, or through text messages or phone calls. Research from the University of Chicago (2006) suggests that with the massive transformation of Chinese's economy in the last two decades, Chinese women are increasingly in places-schools, work and public transportation, where there is more opportunity for them to be exposed to sexual harassment.

Laws against sexual harassment of women exist in China but law specifically related to street harassment is lacking. In 2005, China added new provisions to the *Law on Women's Right Protection* to include sexual harassment which was fully implemented in 2007. In 2006 "The Shanghai Supplement" to the Women Protection law became the first law in China's history to clearly define sexual harassment. It stipulates that words, pictures and electronic information insinuating sex or bodily contact that "injures" a woman is sexual harassment. Despite implementation, which enables women to take perpetrators to court, the burden of proof is on the victim.

Prevalence and Protection in Japan

It's true that Japan has low crime compared to the U.S., but low crime doesn't mean no crime. Japan has a reputation for females being groped on trains and buses. In Japan, men who grope women in public are called *chikan.* A chikan gets off by rubbing himself on female passengers in the overcrowded Japanese subways and they take advantage typically on school girls, female teenagers and young women. Metropolitan Police Department' Stalking cases analysis report women as victim of gender stalking , accounted for about 80 per cent a similar trend over the past four years 2008-2012. In 2000, there were 2280 reported cases of stalking in Japan while even after the enforcement of act National Police Agency (NPA) reported 19,920 cases in 2013.

In May 2000, the national law "Stalker Control Act" was put into effect after the murder of Shiori Ino. The Chikan penalty depends on seriousness of the crime. Minimum is 500,000 yen to 1,000,000 yen or six months in prison. The law of criminal procedure permits the immediate arrest by a private individual. The criminal courts have traditionally been lenient in cases of groping and have only recently made efforts to combat the social problem with tougher sentences. Over the last decade or two, steps have been taken to change this, with stricter sentencing for those convicted of the crime and awareness campaigns to help bring the issue to light. While awareness and enforcement efforts have led to an increased number of victims filing reports, but the problem is still widely believed to be rampant if not entirely out of control.

Prevalence and Protection in United States of America

Gender violence against women is widespread in advanced, liberal democracies, as it is in other parts of the world. The national study "Unsafe and harassed in Public Spaces" released in June '2014 by a non profit organisation 'Stop Street Harassment' shows that 65 per cent of American women have experienced some form of street harassment and 41 per cent of all women were subject to physically aggressive harassment in public like being flashed or fondled. Fairchild and Rudman research (2008) on stranger harassment from American female college students found that 41 per cent experienced stranger harassment at least once a month, 31 per cent experienced it every few days or more which includes non-physical harassment such as catcalls, whistles, stares, sexist comments and "come-ons." More than a quarter experienced forceful grabbing at least once a month. The lack of legal recourse provides an environment more conducive to harassment. Unless one is physically harassed it's not a crime. However there are a number of legal options for filing a complaint in the U.S. i.e., with the 'Equal Employment Opportunity Commission' EEOC or under a 'Fair Employment Practices' (FEP) statute but both of them are for workplace sexual harassment. It does not assure that all sexual harassment will be considered severe enough to form the basis for a legal claim. There are several types of harassing behaviours present, and there is no minimum level for harassing conduct under the law. It is reported that many more experienced sexual harassment than have a solid legal case against the accused. Because of this few cases ever make it to federal court.

In the USA, there are no federal laws prohibiting gender discrimination. Civil Rights Act of 1964 Title seven landmarks Supreme court cases dealing with sexual harassment in work places but its scope is limited with no place for street harassment. Executive Order 13087, signed by President

Bill Clinton outlaws discrimination based on sexual orientation against federal government employees, remarking that the small business owner should abide by the state's law against sexual orientation discrimination, regardless of there not being a federal law. Twenty states and the District of Columbia have laws against this form of discrimination in the workplace, giving no scope to street harassment.

Prevalence and Protection in Australia

Sexual assault as a weapon of gender discrimination is easily visible on Australian streets and public spaces. According to the Australian Human Rights Commission (AHRC, 2012) national sexual harassment survey, one-third of women surveyed have experienced sexual harassment since the age of 15. Further, one-quarter of women had experienced sexual harassment in the workplace in the past five years. With other forms of sexual violence, these statistics are likely to underestimate the true extent of women's experiences of sexual harassment. It is estimated that as many as 85 per cent of victims do not report their experiences to police, or otherwise disclose to friends, family or service workers (ABS, 1996). Almost 17,800 victims of sexual assault reported to the police in the year 2000 alone out of which 85 per cent of recorded victims are women. The Australian Bureau of Statistics (ABS) study conducted during 2002 and 2003 reported that close to 60 per cent women had experienced at least one sexual or violent crime.

A range of informal and formal avenues are active for reporting or disclosing experiences of sexual harassment and street harassment in Australia. Sexual harassment is currently addressed under the Commonwealth Sex Discrimination Act 1984. The legislation covers sexual harassment in the workplace, educational settings, in the provision of goods and services (AHRC, 2012). Some forms of sexual harassment are also covered under various state and territory sexual offences legislation. The Australian Human Rights Commission is the peak body that deals with sexual harassment complaints in Australia. Established under The National Plan to Reduce Violence against Women and their Children 2010-2022, 1800RESPECT provides best practice, professional counselling, information, advice and referral services for individuals and their family and friends who have experienced, or are at risk of sexual assault.

Prevalence and Protection in United Kingdom

Street harassment is as common activity on the roads and transports in London. Many incidents of women being followed, scared at, secretly filmed on phones are reported on the website of Hollaback, London. Tilly Grove a Stop Street Harassment (NGO) correspondent's survey reports 90 per cent women faced street harassment several times but not reported what happened to them to the police. The British Transport Police (BTP) recognises sexual harassment on public transport is a major concern for travellers, and vastly under-reported. 'Project Guardian' is an initiative in this seeks to deter offenders by deploying up to 180 officers to stations at a time, using undercover officers, creating a high police profile at vulnerable times and places, using CCTV footage, and publishing details of all successful prosecutions. The Discrimination Act of 1975 was amended in 1986 to establish sexual harassment as a form of discrimination. The London Anti-Street Harassment campaign (or LASH campaign) is a campaign against the sexual harassment of women on the streets of London. The campaign aims to reduce street harassment by calling for a public debate about the issue. It calls for the education of the perpetrators and encourages women to stand up for themselves.

Conclusion

Gender discrimination has a age old history and street harassment is just one of its expression pervasive in almost all the countries of the world with Scandinavian countries as an exception. There women have the most gender equity throughout the world. Women also have the right to live freely and lead life as their male counterparts in this world. Independence is their birth right. Street harassment must be stopped. Women deserve equal respect. Our lack of consciousness has lead to a loss of many lives. But we don't want any more lives to say good bye to this world. Street harassment must be eliminated if women are to have equal opportunities in society. To seriously change society's passive acceptance of street harassment, the legal system must act, while other forms of sexual harassment have been considered a problem large enough to garner the attention of the academic, legislative, and judicial communities but most laws addressing sexual harassment focus solely on sexual harassment in the workplace or within the domestic sphere. Sexual harassment in public spaces such as streets and public transportation remains largely neglected. Many countries do not recognise street harassment serious enough to legislate on it. Very few countries definition of sexual harassment has constituents of street harassment and considers it an offence. A major loophole in the law in almost all the countries is that the burden is on the prosecution to prove that the accused had uttered the words or made the sound or gesture and that such word, sound or gesture was intended by the accused to be heard or seen by some woman. This appears to be a chronic problem in harassment cases–the victim is often made out to be culpable. Normally, it is difficult to establish this and, seldom, woman files complaints and often the wrong doers are left unpunished even if complaint is filed since there is no effective mechanism to monitor and follow up such acts.

Countries like Japan, India have tried to mitigate the harassment by introducing separate coaches in trains, Brazil has the option of riding female only, pink striped subway cars during rush hours, Dubai in 2001 opened woman only bank but such measures doesn't discourage chauvinist remarks–it merely limits the opportunities to make them. To truly make an impact, it is necessary that laws be issued targeting the offenders themselves. Men who harass women on the street are not apprehended, they are not punished, the victims are not compensated, and no damages are paid. The entire transaction is entirely invisible to the state. It is appreciable to note that on the informal level there are currently a number of, consciousness raising and activist websites that provide the opportunity for women to disclose experiences of sexual harassment and street harassment. They encourage women to share their experiences of sexual harassment and street harassment. There are a number of NGOs in India and worldwide, working for the cause of women empowerment, they teach women how to fight back against the harassment in domestic spheres, at workplace or on the street recognising it, not trivialising it, reacting to it. But still we have to go a long way to completely rectify the situation. People should start acknowledging street harassment as a problem, and not to accept it as a convention. The family and society of the victims should have the courage and resolve to support them at the same time the government must take things seriously.

References

- Bowman, C. G. (1993). Street Harassment and the Informal Ghettoisation of Women, *Harvard Law Review,* no.106
- Sen, G. (1984). Subordination and sexual control: A comparative view of the control of women. Review of Radical Political *Economics* no.16
- Anwary, A.(2003).Acid Violence and Medical care in Bangladesh: Women's Activism as Care work, *Gender and Society,* no.17
- Fredrickson, B. L., Roberts, T. A. (1997). Objectification Theory: Toward Understanding Women's lived Experiences and Mental Health Risks, *Psychology of Women Quarterly,* no.21

- MacMillan, R. Et.al. (2000). Experiencing the streets: Harassment and perceptions of safety among women. *Journal of Research in Crime and Delinquency,* no.37
- Mahapatra, D. (2013). Crimes against women up in 2013. The Times of India. October 3, 2013.
- Safe Cities free of Violence against Women and girls Initiative: A daft Strategic Framework for woman's safety in Delhi, 2010. Published by Jagori (2011)
- The Sexual Harassment of Women at Workplace (Prevention, Prohibition and Redressal) Act, 2013 published in The Gazette of India. Press Information Bureau.
- Government of National Capital Territory of Delhi. (2006). Delhi Human Development Report: Partnerships for progress.
- National Crime Records Bureau Ministry of Home Affairs. Crime in India 2012: Statistics. Retrieved from http://ncrb.nic.in/CD-CII2012/Statistics2012.pdf
- Fairchild, K., Rudman, L. A. (2008). Everyday stranger harassment and women's objectification. Social Justice Research no.21,
- Gardner, C. B. (1995). Passing by: Gender and public harassment. Berkeley: University of California Press.
- Australian Human Rights Commission. (2012). Working without fear: Results of the sexual harassment national telephone survey 2012. Sydney: AHRC.

26

Eve Teasing, Tears of Girls: A Study of Patiala

Palwinder Kaur

Abstract

Eve teasing is a euphemism used in India for sexual harassment or molestation of women by men. It is an action of perversion like touching, rubbing, groping, teasing, staring, pinching, slapping, display of private parts and even pornographic material. Today, it is projected that women stand tall in every sphere of life yet not secure enough physically, mentally and emotionally from their counterparts. It has also been defined as crime committed against women everyday but the criminals are not punished and continue violating a women's privacy assuming they have a right to do so. It is an offence every women faces in her life and not just once and ignores the offence and accept it as a price she has to pay for being a women. When the force is immediate, of short duration, or infrequent, society's attitude towards this particular violence against women has been dismal. According to constitution of India, women are legal and prominent citizens of the country and have equal rights when compared to men Day in and day out there are headlines of victimisation of women in one way or the other, be it dowry or dowry death, molestation or rape, physical torture or physical abuse, eve teasing and such endless list of violence against women. According to constitution of India, women are legal and prominent citizens of the country and have equal rights when compared to men. Due Eve-teasing is not a victimless crime as it appears on paper. It has resulted in deaths, and when it goes unchecked could lead to public humiliation of women even in broad daylight. In the backdrop of this scenario, an attempt has been made to study Eve teasing among the girl's of Patiala.

Keywords: Eve teasing, Impact, Women, Molestation, Mobility, Crime, Law.

Introduction

Violence against women is experienced by women of all ages and social classes, all races, religions and nationalities, all over the world. It is overwhelmingly perpetrated by men (Krug et al., 2002). It is the most pervasive violation of human rights in the world today Eve teasing stands for a kind of sexual harassment of a young woman. At present it has become a big problem. Most of the girls cannot walk on the streets without being teased by an opposite sex. Many girls committed suicide as a result of eve teasing. Many female students stopped their studies and even going outdoors. It is a horrible scenario.

Definition of Eve Teasing

According to Encarta, the 'eve-teasing' is the harassment of young woman (Microsoft Encarta 2007). According to Wikipedia, 'eve teasing' is a euphemism used in India, Pakistan, Bangladesh and Nepal for public sexual harassment, street harassment or molestation of women by men (Wikipedia, 2012).

However, in our country, Eve-teasing was a means to disturb young women as light matter up to a certain period of time. But now it has taken a tremendous shape of sexual harassment for a female counterpart by its male counterpart. Using filthy languages, movement of body in various ways and whistling are some of the ways to disturb young girls. Some people believe that practical sex is also eve-teasing this may be either wilful or by force. Now-a-days many people believe that there is no difference between eve-teasing and sexual act. The word eve teasing is usually used when a female is harassed on the streets or pavements. On the contrary, the word sexual harassment is used when it takes place at offices, houses or any other barricaded places.

Meaning of Eve Teasing

Eve-teasing to-day has become pernicious, horrid and disgusting practice. The Indian Journal of Criminology and Criminalistics (January-June 1999 Edition) has categorised eve-teasing into five heads viz: (1) Verbal eve-teasing; (2) Physical eve-teasing (3) Psychological harassment; (4) Sexual harassment and (5) Harassment through some objects. Menace of eve-teasing of woman is on the increase. Eve-teasing in public places has been a perennial problem. Recently, incidents of eve-teasing leading to serious injuries to, and even death of a woman have been reported. Such act of eve-teasing, apart from dehumanizsing act, is an unlawful intrusion on the right of privacy and sanctity of a female. It is a serious blow to her supreme honour and offends her self-esteem and dignity. It humiliates the victim and leaves a traumatic experience behind her. Eve-teasing is a euphemism, a conduct which attracts penal action. Eve-teasing is a menace to society as a whole and has to be eradicated. But there is no specific legislation in the country except the state of Tamil Nadu which has enacted Tamil Nadu Prohibition of Eve-Teasing ordnance, 1998 which later became an Act, namely, the Tamil Nadu Prohibition of Eve-Teasing.

Who are the eve Teasers?

Eve teasers are any person on the street, in front of schools and colleges, in the bus, train, lift, shopping mall anywhere teases girls in any form of vocabulary, gesture, or directly physical assault. Among the eve teasers from rich to poor, being illiterate to educated, being young to middle age men are included. Eve teasing in various forms:

- **Eve Teasing with Girl Students:** Most of the eve teasing occurs near girl's school. Adolescent's boys wait there sometimes for particular targeted girl sometimes generally. Normally the boys follow the girls from their house when they started for school. Sometimes they pass bad comments; sometimes they throw a letter with bad proposal, sometimes the teaser force and threat the girls to make a relationship with them, sometimes they propose the girl for marry. If any girl refuses, they are threat to be raped or kidnapped. As a result the girl has to leave the school and forced to do early marriage just to rescue her from the in secured situation sacrificing her total potential life.
- **Teasing by Mobile Phone:** With the advancement of technology everyone is enjoying the fruits of modernity. From one side it is an

advancement using mobile for communication on the other side, misuse of this mobile practice, girls lives are becoming hell. The teaser sends an SMS in an ornamental, romantic and rhetorical language; as a result the adolescent girls are easily trapped with the false appreciation of the teasers. The girls sometimes take it as a love with the boy and become the victim. The boy capitalises the innocence of the girl by using mobile camera or video recorder, some intimate moments or dialogue. Sometimes use of technology becomes curse to some people.

- **Sexual Abuse through Internet:** In the face book or in chatting young boys and girls are coming closer to each other. Sometimes the boys exploit the girls with some photograph by insert with modern technology, blackmail them, sometimes the boys encourage the girls to watch some restricted side as a result they fall victim of the sexual extreme world. It is a most dangerous form of violence through technology.

Constitutional and Legal Provisions

The principle of gender equality is enshrined in the Indian Constitution in its Preamble, Fundamental Rights, Fundamental Duties and Directive Principles. The Constitution not only grants equality to women, but also empowers the State to adopt measures of positive discrimination in favour of women for neutralising the cumulative socio-economic, education and political disadvantages faced by them. Within the framework of a democratic polity, our laws, development policies, plans and programmes have aimed at women's advancement in different spheres. India has also ratified various international conventions and human rights instruments committing to secure equal rights of women. Key among them is the ratification of the Convention on Elimination of All Forms of Discrimination Against Women (CEDAW) in 1993.

Law Related to Eve Teasing

Under Indian Penal Code the term eve teasing is not used. There are three sections under which action can be taken against eve teasers. Section 294 punishes any obscene act or recital of any obscene songs or ballad or words in a public place with a punishment of three months or fine or both. Section 509 (Indian Penal Code) punishes anyone who, to intrude upon the privacy of a woman or with an intent to outrage her modesty utters any word, makes any sound or gesture or exhibits an object with an imprisonment for one year or fine or both. It is a cognisable as well as a bail able offence. A question can be raised as to what constitutes an obscene act. Another section is 354 (IPC) according to which anyone who uses forces or assaults a woman to outrage her modesty will be punished with two years of imprisonment or fine or both.

Causes of Eve Teasing

It is a social issue and one of the issues among other forms of violence. Eve teasing is not a recent phenomenon, it was there and it is and it will be but the pattern, definition and intervention are changing. With the advancement of technology the mechanism to tease the girls are changing. Eve teasing mainly occurs due to attitude towards girls, family culture and education and loss of morality among others there are eight major causes of eve teasing found out by various social research organisation and prominent persons. These are: family and social causes, unemployment facimisism, open sky culture, political atmosphere, administrative, carelessness, social cultural activities, demonstration effect, Lacking of respect to each other. However the following points may be taken into account as causes of eve-teasing:

1. ***Natural Attraction to Each Other:*** One of the great causes of eve teasing comes from the natural tendency of man and woman to attract each other when they openly see each other at the stage of puberty. Sometimes male who cannot control himself indulges with eve teasing.
2. ***Lack of Religious Education:*** When people are not religiously educated they will not understand respect of women by man and vice versa.
3. ***Unmindful about Religions:*** There are a lot of persons who remain unmindful and blind to religious boundary. Religion teaches a person good behaviour, morality, ethics, social and personal dealings, code of conduct, manner etc. When a man is careless about his religion naturally he falls under some bad dealings like eve teasing.
4. ***Unfair Dress:*** Unfair dresses are great causes for eve teasing now days.
5. ***Open sky Culture:*** Open sky culture, satellite communication, internet etc are to great stand responsible for eve teasing. People see free sex, free mixing of men and women via various television programmes; internet etc. and they try to do same thing which causes eve teasing.

6. ***Absence of Family Education*** Parents now a days remain careless about the movement of the son and daughter. Students are going entertainment spots, markets, streets etc. for getting fun instead of going to their educational institution and this carelessness encourages eve teasing.
7. ***Political Patronise:*** Some time political parties do not take legal action against eve teaser for their political motives and sometimes political parties use their activists to harass their rival parties and thus eve teasing increases.
8. ***Cultural Aggression:*** Sometimes alien cultural aggression may induce eve teasing. Some countries try to dominant another country by cultural aggression and the culture of those countries is not viable in our country that is why eve teasing increases.
9. ***Absence of Law:*** Absence of Law is a great factor of encouraging eve teasing. There are some laws to prevent eve teasing but these are not enough and the implementation of these laws is difficult due to procedural complexity, political influence etc.
10. ***Alcoholism and drug Addiction:*** Uninterrupted alcoholism and drug addiction is a great cause of eve teasing. When a man devours intoxicating materials he loses his conscience and that time he can do any bad things like eve teasing.
11. ***Unemployment:*** Unemployed people are evil doers and engaged in eve teasing. When a man has no work to do he becomes a devil and only for spending his time do eve teasing.
12. ***Lack of Social Bondage:*** Lack of social bondage is a big cause of eve teasing. Now a days, people are busy with their own purposes and not looking with their brother, sister, relatives, neighbours. Fellow feedings are lessening day by day that is why eve teasing is increasing day by day.
13. ***Computer, Mobile etc:*** Computers and mobiles have become mobile cinema house with free call, free talk time, free SMS. Without showing his identity a man can make friendship with opposite sex, and this kind of friendship causes a lot of eve teasing.
14. ***Obscene Cinema, Drama and Song:*** Obscene cinema and drama sometimes encourage eve teasing. If a boy finds in cinema or drama an eve teaser a hero then he is encouraged to involve with eve teasing.
15. ***Environment:*** A great factor of encouragement of eve teasing is negative environment in the society. Quarrel between parents,

neighbours, relatives makes a negative environment in the society and this causes impact on the mind of the children and they involves with negative works like eve teasing (Najneen Akhter, 2010).

Impact of eve Teasing

- ***Drop out from the Educational Institution:*** As a result many young girls are depriving from their basic rights to education. And ultimately they are becoming burden to family and society because without economic independence no one could be empowered. They ultimately become parasite in nature.
- ***Reduce the Mobility:*** Due to threat of eve teasing young girls are getting confined within the four walls, devoid of enjoying education, entertainment, outside work. By reducing physical mobility, they are losing their mental mobility also, they are staying within a limited and narrower mental state which ultimately destroy their mental clarity and independent thinking for any development.
- ***Early Marriage:*** Early marriage destroys the dream and total life of the girls. Due to early pregnancy and too many responsibilities in household work their physical and mental health becomes very week. Neither can she take care of herself, nor to her children and family. Due to early pregnancy mothers and child mortality is higher in Bangladesh.
- ***Psychological Problem:*** Many girls become psychologically abnormal out of fear and social security. Sometimes they do not get support from family due to mistrust. All these causes and frustration leads many girls towards committing suicide.

Eve Teasing in Patiala City

Patiala is situated in the state of Punjab. Patiala is increasingly becoming more and more unsafe for women. Eve-teasing cases, even during broad daylight, are going on unchecked.

Prone Eve Teasing Areas in Patiala City

1. ***Bhupindra Road*** : This commercial hub area is known as 'Geri Route' among youngsters and is one of the most vulnerable places for women. As showrooms of branded clothes, mobile phones, eateries and Thapar University are located here, it is

visited by women from the entire city and the presence of male youngsters in groups at every nook and cranny, especially in the evening, creates fear among girls. Special women cops have been deployed in the area to infuse a sense of security among women, but a large number of snatching incidents in the area remains a matter of worry among the police too.

2. ***SST Nagar*** **:** This residential area comprises houses, Government Polytechnic for Girls and Shivalik Public School. The area is located at the periphery of the city and is a deserted one. Due to minimal policing in the area it is prone to eve-teasing, harassment and chain snatching cases. Women complained that even during broad daylight, incidents of eve-teasing usually occur frequently outside the college and during early morning and late evening hours chain snatching cases are common here.
3. ***Bus Stand Area*****:** Despite a police post situated right outside the bus stand, it is a vulnerable spot for women as a large number of eve-teasing and harassment cases have been reported from here. Culprits are often seen passing vulgar comments on girls and forcing conversation with them. During late evening hours, the presence of men in large numbers, including male police personnel, makes the area a nightmare for women. Most women said that they were in most cases harassed and teased by elder men while travelling.
4. ***YPS Chowk*** **:** The most reputed and biggest government Women Colleges and schools of the city are situated in this area. A large number of incidents of eve-teasing, especially at the time of closure of schools and the college, have forced the city police to deploy several policemen in this area. Nabbing eve-teasers and awarding on-the-spot 'punishment' to them by the cops has become a routine in the area, still youngsters can be spotted in the area on their 'new bikes' to impress eves.
5. ***NIS Chowk*** **:** The oldest government college and national sports coaching institute is located in this area. Colloquially, it is known as "Loafers Point" as several young men can be seen here, especially during college hours. Heavy traffic on the road has made it more vulnerable for girls as several incidents of eve-teasing have been reported from the area. Though female policemen have been deployed on the road to keep watch on male youngsters, however on daily basis many cases of eve-teasing are reported from here.

Objective of the Study

The present study is an attempt to study the nature and dimensions of eve teasing among the girls of Punjabi University, Patiala.

Research Methodology

The present study has been conducted by eliciting the views and perception of girls. Both primary and secondary data was collected. For the purpose of primary data, (convenient both ways) sample of 45 respondents were taken, of different age groups and of varied disciplines. For secondary data various books, journals, articles, and websites were browsed. Interview Schedule was prepared for the respondents to draw views of the respondents about the menace of eve-teasing. The collected data was analysed and the findings.

Analysis of Statements: From Statement one to six

The Table below Presents the Respondent's Responses in Yes Or No

Table 1.1

S.No.	Statement	Yes	No
1.	Eve-teasing is a common phenomenon in the society.	45(100%)	0
2.	Eve-teasing is irritating	45(100%)	0
3.	You are fed up with the eve-teasing on the campus	45(100%)	0
4.	Have you ever been eve-teased?	43(95.55%)	2(4.44%)
5.	You avoid going to the market at odd hours to prevent eve-teasing	45 (100%)	0
6.	University/college should be free of eve-teasing	45(100%)	0

Discussion

The sample of 45 respondents was exposed to an Interview Schedule. In the first six questions, the girls were to respond in Yes or No. The analysis of the data presented in the Table 1.1 clearly reflected that eve-teasing was a common phenomenon in the society and it was irritating as well (100 percent). Further, very high proportion of the respondents was fed up with the eve teasing. The girl respondents were admitted that they avoided going to the market at odd hours to avoid eve teasing. All girls wished that university/college should be free of eve teasing.

Analysis of Statements: From Statement seven to eleven

Statement 7: Eve Teasing is Commonly Committed :

(a) While going to the university/college
(b) In the evening
(c) While going to the market
(d) Any time of the day

Table 1.2.1

Total Number of Respondent	A	B	C	D
45	18	8	2	17
	40%	3.6%	4.44%	37.77 %

Table 1.2.1 clearly reflect that 40 per cent of the respondents agreed eve teasing was committed while going to the university or college. However, next higher proportion 37.77 per cent of the respondents indicated that it can happen any time of the day (only a chance be there). The 4.44 percent of the respondents agreed that eve teasing commonly took place while going to the market and 3.6 per cent of the respondents agreed that eve teasing was mostly indulged in the evening.

Statement 8: Which areas of the University are Highly Teasing Prone?

(a) The market areas
(b) Front of your college /university
(c) Near your home
(d) Near cinema hall/Omax Mall

Table 1.2.2

Total Number of Respondent	A	B	C	D
45	13	17	4	11
	28.88%	37.77%	8.88%	24.44%

Table 1.2.2 asserts that as per the respondents front of the university/ college was highly teasing prone i.e., option number second with 37.77 percent of the respondents agreed to it and 28.88 per cent of the respondents marked that market is another area of eve teasing. Then 24.44 per cent of the respondents stated that they were teased near or around cinema hall/Omax Mall. However, 8.88 per cent of the respondents expressed that it happened near home only.

Statement 9: The Eve Teasers Generally Indulge in

(a) Hooting
(b) Using vulgar language
(c) Using indecent gestures
(d) Physical teasing

Total Number of Respondent	A	B	C	D
45	9	22	12	2
	20%	48.88%	26.66%	4.44%

Table 1.2.3

Table 1.2.3 elucidates that highest number 48.88 per cent responded that eve teasers use vulgar language. and 26.66 per cent expressed that eve teasers used indecent gestures whereas another commonly indulged eve teasing has been hooting 20 per cent. However, only 4.44 per cent of the respondents agreed to option number four i.e., physical teasing.

Statement 10: You Shoot Back to the Teasers with

(a) Verbal volley
(b) Report the matter to the university authorities
(c) Report the matter to the police
(d) None of the above

Total Number of Respondent	A	B	C	D
45	9	22	12	2
	20%	48.88%	26.66%	4.44%

Table 1.2.4

Table 1.2.4 exuberates that highest proportion of the respondents 48.88 per cent responded that they reported the matter of eve teasing to the university authorities, followed by option number three i.e., 26.66 per cent of the respondents stated that they report the matter to the police, then 20 percent of them responded that they shoot back to the teasers with verbal volley and 4.44 per cent of the respondents stated that they did not like to do anything to the teasers and just passed by without paying any heed to them.

Statement 11: Eve Teasing is Generally Committed by :

(a) Some selected students

(b) All the students of the university /college
(c) By outsiders
(d) By the male residents (Hostel).

Total Number of Respondent	A	B	C	D
45	24	3	14	3
	53.33%	6.66%	31.11%	6.66%

Table 1.2.5 highlights that 53.33 per cent of the respondents stated that eve teasing was mostly by university/college students indulged in the menace of eve teasing and 31.11 per cent of the respondents viewed that eve teasing was by the outsiders in campus whereas 6.66 per cent of the respondents stated that eve teasing was generally done by the male residents of the hostels of university and same percentage of respondent agreed that all the students indulged in the menace of eve teasing.

Findings

1. Majority of the respondents agreed that eve teasing is a common phenomenon.
2. Highest proportion of the respondents agreed that eve teasing was irritating.
3. Maximum proportion of the respondents was fed up with the eve teasing in the campus.
4. The study also highlighted that the respondents agreed that they did avoid going to the market during odd hours.
5. Majority of the respondents stated that university/college should be free of eve teasing.
6. Findings revealed that Eve-teasing was commonly committed while going to the university/college.
7. Further findings also stressed that front areas of the university/ colleges was highly prone to eve teasing.
8. Findings stated that majority of the respondents expressed that the eve-teasers indulged more in using vulgar language.
9. Findings unveiled that highest proportion of the respondents reported the matter of eve teasing to the university authorities.
10. Lastly, the findings exposed that the some selected students were generally involved in eve teasing.

Recommendations to Combat Eve Teasing

- Education policy should ensure equality and equity between girls and boys.

- Curriculum has a strong role to take initiatives to portray girls and boys equal.
- In the textbook, moral education should be included immediately and should have a chapter on the violence against women by giving emphasis to establish eve teasing as 'a social curse.
- Healthy family atmosphere and progressive family education and the trust between the members of the family are necessary.
- Teachers in the class should be aware of treating both boys and girls equally. They should talk about morality about violence to make them understand the gravity of violence on total humankind.
- Law should be implemented strictly.
- Local police and school security should play a strong role.
- From government level, an award could be announced for the person who could resist eve teaser.
- Electronic media and printing media should aware about the consequence and negative impact of eve teasing.
- Journalists should get training on gender issues, so that they could handle the issues very carefully. Some news in the newspaper due to the week presentation of the newspaper makes the girl vulnerable.

Conclusion

Eve Teasing is a cancer of the society. It is a mindset in which the men show their supremacy. A woman, weak, helpless and crying out provides the eve teasers with a perverse pleasure which is both sickening and tragic. Though it is true that strong laws and punishment are an effective deterrent but that is not enough. Our purpose is not just to punish eve teasers but to prevent such crimes. Besides, all of us have to stop being mute witnesses to such crimes. We must stand up and speak and act against this menace. The punishment given to the eve teasers should be strong enough so that it sets an example for others. And, above all, women need to be aware of and fight for their rights. As someone has rightly said, rights that are not asserted cease to exist.

References

- Krug, E., Dahlberg, L., Mercy, J., Zwi, A., and Lozano, R. (2002). World report on violence and health. Geneva: WHO.
- Najnin Akhtar (2010). Eve teasing - 01. *The Daily Janakantha*, Dhaka: May 29, 2010. P 01.

- Microsoft Encarta (2007). Microsoft Corporation. See word: eve-teasing.
- Oxford Advanced Learners Dictionary (8th Ed, online version). Oxford: Oxford University Press. Retrieved October 10, 2012 from http://oald8.oxfordlearnersdictionaries.com/ dictionary/tease.
- Wikipidia, The Free Encyclopedia. "Eve teasing" Retrieved October 10 from http://en. wikipedia.org/wiki/Eve_teasing.
- India, Ministry of Statistics and programme Implementation, Women and Men in India 2012, (14), 13.

Websites

- http://www.mightylaws.in/799/menace-eve-teasing-problem-solution)
- http://e-pao.net/epSubPageExtractor.asp?src=features.Spotlight_On_Women.
- Supreme_court_on_eve-teasing_of_woman_And_Its_guidelines

27

Name Calling: Misanthropic Crude form of Eve Teasing (Analysis of Punjabi Song on Time line)

Puneet Kaur Dhillon and Ritika Goenka

Abstract

Women all over the world have been subjected to different types of discriminations and crimes. Present century claims to have been toiling for women empowerment and equal status for women in society but the ever prevailing trend of crime against women round the world overshadows the idea of women empowerment. Talking about India, the Delhi gang rape case where a young physiotherapist from Delhi was raped and beaten to death by a bunch of hoodlums in a local bus emerges out as a shameful example in supporting the fact. One of the most common crimes against women have been a part and parcel of every society is eve teasing. Problem attached to eve teasing of calling it a light comment ironically makes it more serious and eternal crime. The recent case of Sonipat sisters where the brave sisters taught a lesson to a bunch of eve teasers by beating them with their belts supports the presence of eve teasing incidents in India. Eve teasing is a common practice where men of all age groups try their hands by passing bad comments, touching or intending to touch, whistle and even screaming at women in public or in private. Many factors like law, societal set up and cultural backgrounds of a society play important factors in eve teasing. Another very important factor which contributes disgracing women by teasing them is the crude and vulgar lyrics of songs. The same trend line is followed by the lyrics of Punjabi songs which observe a deteriorating inclination towards calling women by bad names, symbolising them as objects of sexual desire and comparing them with trifle of the society and households. These types of songs have been accepted in the society and are promoted by different media. But as a negative impact these songs have added on to the practice of eve teasing by adding to the vocabulary of the eve teasers, promoting such psyche among the eve teasers and even encouraging them as they consider their comments to be acceptable with the acceptance of such songs in the society. The study aims at studying and carefully analysing the lyrics of Punjabi songs which use crude lyrics against women and are used as a tool of eve teasing by the anti social elements.

Introduction

Women, the fairer sex has been discussed, attributed and remarked by the opposite sex and even the same sex. Biological difference among men and women could be counted as one of the reasons for the typical style of societal responsibilities and division of labour among men and women. Women being biologically designed and created in such a manner that she is the one who can accomplish the tasks of bearing a child, nursing a child and also unleashing the fantasising beauty by upholding the tenderness and delicacy of her existence. The patriarchal style of the contemporary society has its roots in the same biological difference between the two sexes. Poets, painters, lyricists, filmmakers and writers have tried to re carve this marvellously patient creation of almighty in their own unique fashions. Some of these intellectual people claim the rights of women and some merely exploit them to decorate their literary or artistic piece of works. Attribution of women by different scholars has emerged out women as a nigger in the same world she belongs to where she has to stand out and fight for her rights, dignity and equality. The name calling has given rise to a society which demands to identify the origin of women and dissecting her by out rightly ignoring her talent. Women have right to be free, to fight for freedom but that right is the duty of the society. Women who make half of the human race would care thousand times for respect, relations, duties and even the institution of marriage than a minister for its ministry. Women's mind is never young, her brain is always more mature than her body. A notion that all men are born free and women as slaves, is reflected in the lyrics of the songs of past as well as present. The disgrace reflected in the songs and lyrics tend to portray that women may bear humans, nurture them and love them but are treated as things and objects. A male intellect clouded by a jagged sexual impulse has begun calling the undersised, narrow-shouldered, broad -hipped and short- legged sex as the fairer sex. The primary focus of Punjabi songs depicting the hot sexual temperament of Punjabi men is always on the stamping high heels, bulging curves and pouted lips of a woman by completely ignoring the power of a woman which can drag a man to her merely by a single strand of hair. Song is a mirror that travels over a highway which at times may reflect to the listeners' eyes the blue of the sky and at times may cast to the face of the listener slinging mud of road. Magnificent beauty and magnetism of a woman's body as always remained as a source of inspiration for the entire Punjabi lyricist where the woman is praised of her long tresses, fair complexion, tall height and deep eyes. In the song "Balle Ni Punjab Diye sher Bachiye(Bravo, O Valiant daughter of the land of Punjab), famous Punjabi singer Asha Singh Mastana sings laurels of the fearless and heroic daughter of the land. He praises the daughter of the land in the way she maintains the households and uphold her dignity. Again the living Punjabi legend Gurdas Maan sings the whole saga of the life of a woman in the heart rendering song "Kudiye Kismat Buriye Tenu Ki Satkar Deyan (What reverence should I pay to the ill fated girl child). He portrays and depicts the undefined status of a girl or a woman in Punjab where she is considered to be her husband's property at her parent's home and then at husband's place she is considered to be a stranger. She finds herself as a recluse both at her father's house as well as that of her husband. He also narrates the famous Punjabi legend of two lovers Mirza and Saheba where Sahiba elopes with her lover Mirza but breaks away Mirza's arrows when the couple is encountered on the way by her brothers. Sahiba's dilemma of saving her brother's life or saving her beloved forces her to act as an infidel beloved. But the saga has been sung, written and acted in Punjab only by calling Saheba as an infidel beloved without any mention of the state of mind of a sister.

But the ever prevailing trend of name calling women with negative, objectified and sexual attributions have fulfilled the purpose of slinging mud on the faces of the listeners. Lyrics of Punjabi songs which come surrounded by a neighborhood of crude and vulgar words give rise to another form of eve teasing and even promote the same mindset. As clearly could be observed in one of the very prominent Punjabi singers Kuldeep Manak " Ni Heere Ni Heere" in which he calls the woman by the names of "Malliye Ranne, Patiye Leere" (Dirty woman and a Torn Rag). This name calling of a woman for whatsoever sin she may have committed brings a shameful ignominy to not only the singers and writers but to the whole community and the heterogeneous audience it is meant for. The practice also provides an impetus to the psyche of the eve teasers who discover a novel bad comment with the arrival of any of such songs. The word not only brings disgrace to the whole human race but is also immediately updated in the dictionary of the roadside eve teasers for the future reference in the act of eve teasing. Eve teasing may be called nothing but a sort of smoke emitted from dirty tobacco pipes of those who diffuse them proving nothing but the bad taste of the smoker. If songs be called the sublimation of the feeling of a man then a woman fails to define her feelings in a language which is primarily constructed by man.

Hypothesis

1. Punjabi songs are bringing disgrace to the existence of woman by Name Calling.
2. Name calling of woman in songs promotes eve teaser psyche.
3. Bad names used in Punjabi songs for woman are easily accepted and practiced by eve teasers.

Punjabi Folk Songs and their History

Punjab is a land of vibrant culture blended in different colours. It derives its name Punjab from "Panj Aab" (five rivers) namely Ravi, Sutlej, Beas, Chenab and Jhelum. Punjab embraces a culture where respect, dignity and pride are attributed to all the relationships in the society. Various folk songs, folk dances, folk music and folk stories play as the soul of this culture. Punjabi folk has been celebrated as it is since ages, without any known author or composer. Women have been an integral part of this society. Women are supposed to be revered and considered as "Raunak Vehre Di" (part and parcel of a home). The same is depicted in the lyrics of Punjabi folk songs which has always remained an inseparable part of the culture. Punjabi folk music represents the traditional lifestyle and culture of Punjabis. Major themes of folk songs are marriage, birth, death, love, beauty, separation, socio-economic status, lifestyle of villagers, food, nature, bravery, folklores, folk tales, folk romances, heroes of Punjab and festivals. Punjabi folk songs are referred to as “Lok Geet” in Punjab. These are sung by men while farming their lands and grazing their cattle. Women sing these songs in the absence of men when they get sufficient space in order to vent out their feelings and emotions. These songs are sung by them while they are fetching water from wells, cooking, spinning the wheel and doing other household chores. Punjabi folk songs represent some of the common and most adorable relationships in Punjabi Families like Brother- Sister, Mother-Daughter, Mother-Son, Father- Daughter, Maternal Uncle and Nieces, Parental Aunt - Nephew, Brother in Law- Sister in Law etc. Punjabi songs have been an effective tool in Punjab while expressing historical events, heroic deeds and tragedies of Punjabis. Punjabi "Lok Geet" includes the following formats:

1. **Tappa/ Tappe** : A couplet which shows a chunk of specific feelings, colours, notions, moods or circumstances.
2. **Boli** : These generally rhyming words in an elaborated form which are sung at different celebrations and festivals. Bolis are collectively called Boliyan and take the form of Gidha when performed with folk dance.
3. **Keerne** : These are mourning songs which are used at the times of death in a family or any other disasters.
4. **Sithnian** : These are songs which include light hearted teasing lyrics usually sung at the times of weddings.
5. **Sohellere** : These are auspicious songs sung by women at the time of the birth of a baby boy which express praise for the new born and the mother.
6. **Suhag** : These are heart touching songs sung at the time of the wedding of a girl expressing the feelings of the girl and her family at the time of parting from each other.
7. **Ghorian** : These are auspicious songs sung at the time of the wedding of a boy by his near and dear ones, which depict the praise of the boy.
8. **Puggata** : These are sung by kids while they play and decide about their teams and terms of the game.

Status of Women in Folk Songs

Folk Songs have always played a very significant role on expressing Punjabi society but women have always remained a male dominated element of this society which is even depicted in many of Punjabi folk forms. Punjabi Society has always remained a male dominating society where only men are supposed to speak and raise voice. Women are not usually allowed to make a choice even for their own self. This difference in the status of men and women is clearly observed in many folk songs. There are examples of Punjabi folks where women are considered as inferior to men and are made to sacrifice their own self for the sake of their Father, Brother, Husband or Son. For example.

"Kariye Kariye Kariye

(A general Rhyming triplet usually used in the beginning of many folk forms)

Russe Mahiye Da Ki Kariye

(O! What should I do to please my annoyed Husband)

Andar Ware Ta Magre Wariye

(I should follow him wherever he goes- *A self Promise by ignoring self respect)*

Chunni Lah Pairan wich Dhariye

(Or I should shower my Duppatta in his feet- Duppata is otherwise a piece of cloth carried by Punjabi women and is considered as a symbol of her pride and dignity.)

Ik Wari Bolo Ji

(Commit it to self)

Apa Fer Kade Na lariye".

(That I will never fight or get annoyed with my husband who is above

everything even my existence)

Punjabi folk forms depict a difference between social status of men and women but folk has not been a tool of considering women as an object of sexual fulfillment. Lyrics of folk songs do not deteriorate identity of women by comparing them with any type of sexual object, drug abuse or any bad comments on their biological structure etc.

Looking Back to 80's

The period of 80's faced very shameful lyrics which could be considered to be born out of an unhealthy mind. Songs are a series of sentences those rhyme and are meant to relax the mind of the listener. Songs as literature and any other form of art are a mirror of the society which they belong to. Punjabi singers like Amar Singh Chamkeela with his duet partner Amarjot Kaur, Bagga Safri and Jagmohan Kaur present a hint of humiliating women by name calling and referring them as mere objects of sexual pleasure in the lyrics of their songs.

Amar Singh Chamkeela and Amarjot Kaur

The famous Punjabi duet has always been talk of the town in the region of Punjab less for their contribution to Punjabi singing but more for the vulgarity and obscenity in their songs. Multitalented personality who was singer, musician, lyricist as well as a composer was born in the village "Dugri", Punjab on July 21st 1961. He was killed along with his duet partner and wife Amarjot Kaur on March 8th 1988. The murder has been alleged on Khalistan militants but the controversy is not clear yet. This has also been assumed that one of the reasons for the murder of the duo was the vulgar content of their songs which popularised extramarital relationships, drinking, drug abuse and hot sexual disposition of Punjabis.

In his famous song "Chak lo Drivero Purje Nu" (Comeon drivers lets Kidnap the striking woman), he calls woman by the name of "Purja". "Purja" generally refers to some part of a machine or any other thing which could be used for a purpose. Reference of woman as a "Purja" or a part to be used for a purpose completely derogates her identity and portrays her as a symbol or an object for fulfilling sexual desires. This humiliation of woman is commonly practiced in the region of Punjab where the roadside eve teasers debase woman by calling them as "purja".

Again in his song "Atte Wangu Gunn Ti Begane Putt Ne" (A stranger boy used the woman in bed as if he is kneading the flour), he brings out a shameful contrast between a woman and the household objects. These types of associations diminish the character of a woman and also bring a reprehensible mark on the entire human race. It also encourages the patriarchal system of our male dominating society by merely symbolising women as objects which could be assessed at the time when necessary.

Bagga Safri

Another famous Punjabi legend of 80's who gave a collage of melodious songs to the Punjabi audience. He sung praises of Punjab by rejoicing the beauty of the land, heroes of the land and their heroic deeds. But the lyrics of his songs at times become objectionable when he intermits some disparaging comments against women. In thesong "Solah Saal Di Kawari" (Lass in her sixteens), lyrics of the song obscenely depicts a yarn narrating the pros and cons of a young woman's body and her youth in a very vulgar manner. Such songs not only provokes young minds to get disturbed but also agitate all the age groups which further target the female species of humans.

In another famous song "Chunni Thale Do Ambran", (there are two sweet mangoes under the dupatta), he talks about the bulging breast of a young woman. Duppatta otherwise in Punjab is a piece of cloth which is generally shrugged by women of all age in order to cover themselves and is also considered as a symbol of her dignity. But lyrics of such songs promote the eve teaser psyche and women have to face filthy comments on duppatta.

Moving on to 90's:

Era of 90's observed some pacifying effect on the songs and lyrics. Famous singers of this era included legendry singers like Gurdas Maan, Hans Raj Hans, Surjit Binderakhiya and Malkit Singh. This era laid stress on relationships and dignity of a woman as a mother, sister and beloved.

Gurdas Maan

Gurdas Maan is a voice which is not only popular in Punjab but also overseas. He has performed as a background singer in various Bollywood films including superhits like "Veer Zara". In one of his very famous songs "Ki Khatya Mai Teri Heer Banke" (I did not find any happiness being your beloved) he sings the agony of a beloved by questioning her lover that why were they destined to part away from each other. Here the relationship between two lovers has been marked with respect with the beautiful lyrics of the song.

Hans Raj Hans- He is also entitled as "Raj Gayak" (Voice of the region) by awarding him with various awards by critics as well as the Government of Punjab. But lyrics of one of his songs "Au Dekho Sadakan Te Ag Turi Jandi hai" (Look! fire is walking on roads), compares women with fire. This has also been a common practice in Punjab by calling women by the name of "Ag" (fire) by roadside eve teasers.

Harbhajan Maan

Dimple cheeked famous Punjabi singer also sings the beauty and glory of a young woman in his song "Gallan Goriyan De Wich Toye" (dimple cheeks). The lyrics of the song attempt to sing the praise and beauty of a young woman in a very elegant manner.

Surjit Bindarakhiya

Punjabi voice which took a leave from this world at a very young age also discussed women as a mother and daughter in his song "Ma Mai Mur

Ni Peke Aona Peke Hunde Mawa Nal" (Dear mother, I will never come back to my maternal house as my mother is dead and my house is not the same without my mother).

The same trend was followed by many renowned singers of this era including Pammi Bai and Kulwinder Dhillon. Though some of the examples could be spotted in some songs like "Kudi Zeherili Hai" (girl is poisonous), by Sarabjeet Cheema, solve the same purpose where women have been referred to as "Zehar" (poison). These songs tend to bring disgrace to women and promote incidents of eve teasing with a novel outlook.

The Status quo

Present decade has seen much technical advancement in Punjabi music. A wide spectrum of Punjabi singers emerged in the era. With the advent of computer age many amateurs have been able to write, sing and perform publicly. But the quality of the songs and the vulgarity of the content has shoot out very swiftly. Attempt to success overnight has lured many lyricists and singers to write and sing unhealthy vocabulary, knowingly or unknowingly disgracing women. Name calling of women as "patola" (a rag doll), Band Botal, (a bottle of wine), Kabootri (dove) etc. has deteriorated the lyrics of Punjabi songs. It has also provided the eve teasers with new updates of vocabulary where these people tease women by using the words depicted in such songs.

Daljit Singh

One of the upcoming singers in Punjab has given many popular hits in the region but lyrics of certain songs are totally in clash with the respect of women. In his song "Proper Patola" (single track 2012), (typical bomb), he compares women with an item or a bomb where the word "patola" has become a widely used term in Punjab by roadside Romeos who choose to call women by the name of "Patola". This type of comments and name calling is commonly observed in Punjab region.

Sherry Maan

Another famous Punjabi singer who provided the Punjabi music industry with a couple of hits brings out a shameful comparison between women and busses in his song "Kurian te Bussan Yaro Aondia hi rehndia"(girls and busses are very common). The reprehensible comparison between women and busses make women to be called by a very cheap name by totally ignoring her self respect.

Sippi Gill

A young singer who has compared women with a "Dove", in his song "Biath Ke Je Chatri Ton Ud Gi Kabootri Dus Mai Shikari Kehere Kam Da" (the master hunter who would not let the dove (girl) fly before he hunts her). A common practice of calling women by the name of "Kabbotri" has also been commonly observed and experienced by women all over Punjab.

Deep Mani

Another attempt to describe women as "symbol of drugs" in Punjabi song "dope-shope" in which woman is advised not to take drugs (both alcohol and synthetic drugs) which in a way promotes drug culture and also depicts women as a symbol of drugs.

Honey Singh

Young rapper cum singer from Punjab became a sensational success overnight. Beats and lyrics of Honey Singh songs rock the DJ's, bars and clubs all over the world. But a careful analysis of songs shows a usage of innumerable unethical words which degrade the dignity of woman in the society. He was accused of singing a controversial song called "Mai Hu Balatkari" (I am a rapist), which was uploaded on you tube. FIR and PIL was filed against the young singer for using vulgar words in his songs and promoting the psyche which included crime against women like eve teasing and raping. After a long controversy in which the critics also burnt effigies of Honey Singh, the Chandigarh High Court dismissed the case because of lack of proof against the singer. The present situation of the region shows that there has been no lack of such vulgar songs in the region which would bring disgrace to the whole community. In one of his songs "O Meri Rani Teri Jawani" (O young woman your adolescence is mesmerising), he discusses women in a very crude manner. Again in one of his songs where he has rapped "Chako Chako Chako Kuch Fresh Nai Milna" (none of the girls is a unused thus you should accept any girl) in album "Break Up Party", he completely disgraces women as a second hand object.

Another odd method of disgracing women as a synthetic drug is a connotative Punjabi song by singers Abby and Rabbab, "Kudi Chitte Chitte Rang Di te Munda Chitte Te Hai Marda" (boy is in love with white coloured object and the girl also has white complexion). Fair complexion of a girl is deliberately translated as white (chitta), which is otherwise "gora rang" (fair complexion) in Punjabi language because "chitta" in Punjab is usually associated with opiate drugs.

Conclusion

The use of such language and comparing women to vulgar objects is a common practice not only in the region of Punjab but in each and every corner of the world. There have been millions of cases of eve teasing and the problem is that most of these cases are not even reported rather suppressed by the victim and the family. Most common practice of teasers are whistling at women, touching or intending to touch, showing vulgar signs and marks, passing bad comments and even singing vulgar songs. Punjabi songs come richly blended with a vocabulary which disgrace women by comparing them to cheap objects and call them by disgraceful names. Thus Hypothesis 1is proved positive. The idea of singing vulgar songs is provided with an impetus when the culture is fully loaded with songs with earthy lyrics. Such practices increase the vocabulary and the courage of teasers where women are compared with sexual objects, household trifle and spare parts is commonly observed in lyrics of Punjabi songs. Hence Hypothesis two is proved positive. Words and phrases used in such songs are picked by roadside teasers who disgrace women by using such words and keep on updating their vocabulary with the arrival of any such song. Music has always been a very powerful medium of discussing, narrating and expressing in Punjabi culture and hence is its impact as potent. Thus the lyrics used in these songs become popular among youth and also leave a great impact on their thought processes. Besides adding to the vocabulary these songs also provide courage and support to these anti social elements who consider their words to be acceptable within the norms of their culture. Thus the vulgarity depicted in the songs is providing psyche of eve teasers with a fresh and novel idea with the arrival of any such song. Hence Hypothesis three is proved positive.

Suggestions

1. Lyrics of Punjabi songs should undergo screening before their release in order to prevent women from verbal disgrace.
2. Lyricists in Punjab should consider it their moral and ethical responsibility to take care of any such crude vocabulary which would harm women and their status in society.
3. Songs with vulgar lyrics should be totally banned even on internet.

4. Songs with healthy lyrics should be promoted and awards should be given to lyricists for respecting women in their lyrics.
5. Women should raise a voice whenever they experience any unhealthy comment on their existence.

Limitations of the Study

Major limitation of the study is that it takes into account only the lyrics of Punjabi songs but such bad comments for women could be observed in the lyrics all over the world. The study also confines to the lyrics of only popular songs of each decade.

References

- Batalvi, Shiv Kumar. (1963). *Gazlan Te Geet.* Ludhiana: Lahore Book Shop.
- Bradford, Margaret. (1966). *Fireside Book of Folk Songs.* New York: Simon and Schuster.
- Chatterjee, Saibal. (2007). *Echoes and Eloquences The Life and Cinema of Gulzar.* New Delhi: Gopson Papers Pvt. Ltd.
- Chawla, Naresh. (2014). *Hit Punjabi Geet.* Samana: Sangam Publication.
- Kumar, Shekhar. (2012). *Crime Against Women A social Perspective.* New Delhi: Globus Press.
- Rao, M.K. (2005). *Empowerment of Women in India.* New Delhi: Discovery Publishing House.
- Gill R.S and Singh Nahar. Folk songs of Punjab. E-Book

Web References

- http://en.wikipedia.org/wiki/Folk_music_of_Punjab
- http://www.sikhiwiki.org/index.php/Music_of_Punjab
- http://www.allaboutsikhs.com/punjab/punjab-the-folk-songs-and-music
- http://gupp.in/punjabi-music-history/

Index